Counterfeiting Exposed

Protecting Your Brand and Customers

DAVID M. HOPKINS

LEWIS T. KONTNIK

MARK T. TURNAGE

WILEY

John Wiley & Sons, Inc.

*To my wife Michele, who can spot a fake at a hundred yards
but married me just the same.*

David Hopkins

*To my colleagues at Reconnaissance who helped me,
and to Spencer and Mia who
put up with me as I worked on this project.*

Lewis Kontnik

*To Natalie, who is infinitely patient and truly genuine
in every sense of the word.*

Mark Turnage

About the Authors

David M. Hopkins is currently Director of International Business Programs in the Daniels College of Business at the University of Denver where he is a tenured Associate Professor of Management. Dr. Hopkins was the second recipient of the Piccinati Endowed Professorship for Teaching Excellence. He was also selected in 1993 for the Fulbright International Education Administrators Program in Japan and Korea. He has over 30 years of college teaching in various areas of

international business. He is a member of the Academy of International Business and other professional organizations. He is also on the Board of Directors for the World Trade Center in Denver. Dr. Hopkins has a Ph.D. and M.A. from the Maxwell School at Syracuse University, an M.B.A. from the Wharton School at the University of Pennsylvania, and a B.S.B.A. from Miami University.

Lewis T. Kontnik is a principal and cofounder of Reconnaissance International, which publishes *Authentication News*®, an internationally respected anticounterfeiting newsletter, as well as *Currency News*™, and *Holography News*®. With offices in Denver and London, Reconnaissance has organized more than a dozen conferences on anticounterfeiting in the Americas, Europe, and Asia, including the first Global Forum on Pharmaceutical AntiCounterfeiting with the participation of the

World Health Organization. Reconnaissance is also the creator and sponsor of the Global AntiCounterfeiting Awards. Mr. Kontnik has served as a consultant on anticounterfeiting issues to major brand holders, security companies, and government entities including the U.S. Food & Drug Administration. He holds an LL.D. from Northwestern University School of Law and an M.S. from the University of North Carolina. *www.Reconnaissance-Intl.com*.

Mark T. Turnage is the Group Chief Executive Officer of Applied Optical Technologies plc. Applied is one of the largest providers of anti-counterfeiting technology to governments and companies worldwide. He was previously President and COO of Optical Security Group, Inc. ("OpSec"), which specialized in brand protection and identity document authentication solutions. Prior to joining OpSec, Mr. Turnage was a consultant with McKinsey & Co. in New York and a lawyer with the Denver law firm of Davis, Graham & Stubbs. He holds a J.D. from Yale University; an M.A. from Oxford University, England; and a B.A. from the University of Colorado. *www.AOTgroup.com*.

Contents

Foreword

The global explosion in product counterfeiting over the past few decades has created one of the most intractable problems facing brand owners today. Clandestine, unquantifiable, often devastating in its impact, and increasingly embraced by the tentacles of organized crime, counterfeiting is here to stay.

Counterfeiting Exposed strips away many of the myths surrounding this international plague and shows that it is far from a "victimless" crime. The authors explore the key issues that flow from the phenomenon and look at ways in which brand owners can protect their products and tackle the problem effectively. This book is also a welcome and invaluable resource for those who wish to know more about the evolution, scope, and consequences of counterfeiting.

The trio of authors with their different backgrounds bring their own unrivalled experience and perspective to bear in analyzing and assessing the counterfeiting phenomenon and must be commended for producing a highly readable and informative book on a complex subject.

As one of the fastest growing economic crimes in the world, counterfeiting defies any "quick fix" solution but can be contained and beaten by those with a thorough understanding of its nature and some of the strategies that have worked. *Counterfeiting Exposed* will illuminate and inspire.

PETER LOWE
ICC Counterfeiting Intelligence Bureau
London, March 2003

Acknowledgments

No book, especially one in a relatively new field, is written and produced by the authors alone. This is definitely true of *Counterfeiting Exposed*. Therefore, we wish to acknowledge the following individuals and organizations for their help and support.

Special thanks go to Ian Lancaster, principal with Reconnaissance International, who silently helped by developing ideas, supplying facts, and supporting our efforts. Thanks also to the entire staff at Reconnaissance for their past investigation and reporting of case studies, analyses, and data in *Authentication News*. *Authentication News* was the first independent publication to cover the issue of counterfeiting globally. Its past issues proved to be an important research resource and it continues to supply an important stream of information to those concerned with the issue on a monthly basis.

There are a number of anticounterfeiting and trade organizations around the world. Some are described in this book, and all have offered their assistance or helped in a number of ways. Much gratitude and thanks go to Peter Lowe at the International Chamber of Commerce Counterfeiting Intelligence Bureau (CIB), who throughout the entire process has offered encouragement, guidance, information, and his usual good cheer. Also, the International AntiCounterfeiting Coalition (IACC), the Anti-Counterfeiting Group (ACG), Global Anti-Counterfeiting Group (GACG), Quality Brands Protection Committee (QBPC), and Pira International Ltd. deserve a great deal of credit for their tireless work in uncovering and fighting counterfeiting, and exposing how it works. Thanks for the help and the information they supplied.

We also want to thank numerous people who helped to "make it all happen." First, thanks to Stan Wakefield, who reached out to us when we most needed help in finding a publisher for our idea. Thanks to Tim Burgard, Wiley, who helped us turn our piles of notes into a book.

Special thanks and recognition to Julie Terry who served tirelessly and in good humor as the organizational glue to hold the whole project together. It is doubtful if this book would have been published without her. Thanks to Applied Optical Technologies plc, and Optical Security Group, Inc. before it, who provided assistance and encouragement throughout the writing of this book. Also, thanks to Amy Grimes and Jon Senft, Reconnaissance, for their contributions.

Finally, to all those we did not mention, who encouraged us to move forward with the project of "exposing counterfeiting," a heartfelt thanks.

Preface

Counterfeiting Exposed is intended as a "wake up call" regarding the rapidly increasing problem of product counterfeiting. We are well beyond the point where the only concern is whether you purchased a fake designer handbag or watch. There is much more serious counterfeiting going on, often with life and death implications. This may involve fake pharmaceuticals, auto and airplane parts, toys, fertilizers, liquor, computer software, personal care products, and many other types of products where counterfeiters attempt to usurp the value of another's creative activity.

People have died from taking fake drugs. They have died because of fake auto and airplane parts. Farmers have had their primary crops decimated by imitation fertilizers. Children have suffered serious injury from sham toys that did not meet required safety standards. Consumers have suffered harm from using contaminated shampoo and from drinking counterfeit liquor. And, yes, sometimes people have suffered mere embarrassment from buying goods that were not the authentic brands they believed they had purchased.

This book details the harm done to consumers, to those trying to protect their brands and intellectual property, and even to entire societies and economies. It analyzes the types of damage done and the degrees of control available to various parties. To do this, the authors employ a tool called the "Harm Matrix," which examines the degree of deception versus the functionality of the fakes.

This book examines many of the critical issues and dilemmas surrounding the problem of counterfeiting. For example, counterfeiting has often been seen as a "victimless" crime and, therefore, has not ignited real concern on the part of consumers or even lawmakers and enforcement officials. This book explains why there should be genuine concern from all quarters regarding this pernicious and expanding criminal activity. At a time of growing global production and trade and the Internet, the tools for counterfeiting are becoming available to everyone. These opportunities are being exploited by organized criminal organizations, who use complicit governments and companies. More recently, counterfeiting has been found to be a source of funding for terrorist groups and organized criminals.

The authors focus primarily on the owners of intellectual property (brands, trademarks, patents, and copyrights) and what they can do, individually and by acting in concert, to combat counterfeiters and protect their intellectual capital. By protecting consumers, companies also strengthen their brands. There is, in fact, a symbiotic relationship between producers, consumers, governments, and societies. For the most part, counterfeiters gain at their collective expense. Therefore, this book devotes considerable attention to what steps can be taken to mitigate the problem. These measures range from internal organization, legal action, and private investigators to the use of a variety of cutting-edge technological weapons to authenticate products.

This book draws on the unique experience and knowledge of three authorities in the field. Lewis Kontnik has followed the area as a journalist and conference organizer for more than ten years. Mark Turnage is the chief executive of one of the world's leading, publicly traded anti-counterfeiting companies. And David Hopkins is an international business scholar who brings an academic's eye to this little understood field.

Whether you are a corporate executive, public official, or consumer viewing this problem, *Counterfeiting Exposed* is a "must read."

PART ONE

An Introduction to Product Counterfeiting and the Threat to Brand Value

M ost brand owners and consumers are not aware of the extent to which the counterfeiting of products is a growing problem throughout the world. The gravity of the damage caused by the production and use of these counterfeits also is not well understood. The "Harm Matrix" introduced in the following chapters provides a basis for understanding the threat posed by counterfeit products to brand owners and consumers alike.

At its core, counterfeiting affects brand value and the equity of brand owners in their brands. This brand equity is in large part based on a promise to consumers of consistent high quality, product utility, and customer support. All of these attributes are absent with counterfeit products—in fact, counterfeit products can actively work to undermine these attributes. The effect can be devastating for brand owners.

CHAPTER 1

If You Can Make It, They Can Fake It

THE GROWTH OF COUNTERFEITING

And you thought counterfeiting was a small matter.

Most people consider counterfeiting to be a problem involving the production of fake currency—by skilled criminal gangs, drug lords, or the occasional amateur using a color copier. Sometimes, the presence of obviously counterfeit Rolexes for sale on the streets of New York will draw a wry smile from passersby, who may stop to purchase one as a gag gift for a friend. Or, news of the occasional seizure of counterfeit T-shirts will make its way into the press.

Much less publicized and well-known, however, is the growing problem of widespread counterfeiting of spare parts, pharmaceuticals, luxury goods, software, consumer goods—indeed, almost anything manufactured in today's market—and its impact on companies in today's global economy. Consider just a few examples:

- In 1989, a Convair 580 airliner disintegrated over the North Sea off Norway killing all 55 people on board. The tail had sheared off because substandard counterfeit bolts and bushings were used in the tail assembly of the plane. Six years later, in 1995, two men were killed when the helicopter they were flying in crashed in New Zealand. The culprit was again counterfeit parts that had failed.[1]
- In 1990, 89 children in Haiti died after taking fake pharmaceuticals containing antifreeze. In 1996, more than 2,500 people are

believed to have died in Niger due to a fake meningitis vaccine distributed in the country.[2]

- In 2002, two men were accused of running a pirating operation out of a store in Brooklyn. Authorities say they found more than 30,000 bootleg DVDs, along with 30,000 compact discs by well-known musical performers. The discs had a retail value of about $1 million.[3]

The phenomenon of counterfeiting is not new. Modern archeologists have discovered that ancient Babylonian and Egyptian priests forged monuments and inscriptions from earlier civilizations in order to bolster their own prestige and legitimacy. Some of these forgeries date back to as early as 1500 B.C. The counterfeiting of Spanish colonial silver coinage in South America in the late seventeenth century, by the King of Spain's own mint, caused a run on the currency and a monetary panic which reached all the way across the Pacific to Chinese merchants in Shanghai. Counterfeit substandard ammunition, sold by unscrupulous arms merchants, plagued the troops on both sides of the World War I conflict.

What has changed about counterfeiting today, though, is that the scope and scale of the problem are growing at a rate previously unknown and little recognized by those most affected. Today, no product is too cheap to counterfeit, and no brand immune from the gaze cast by counterfeiters looking to pirate a brand or in some cases hijack it altogether. Soap has been counterfeited for profit by unscrupulous counterfeiters, as have the most basic office supplies. So have the most sophisticated pharmaceuticals and electronics. The most sophisticated software sold today is often duplicated and on sale in the market within days of its launch. "We are talking about every damn product under the sun: medicine, food, batteries, car parts, clothing—you name it"[4] said Joseph Simone, the former vice chairman of the China Anti-Counterfeiting Coalition, a group which includes more than 80 multinational companies with investments in China.

The statistics tell a frightening story in just about every industry and market. It is estimated that today, between 5 to 7 percent of *all world trade* is in counterfeit goods—a total annual value exceeding $250 billion.[5]

Over $12 billion in sales is lost globally due to counterfeiting in the apparel and footwear industry—according to the International Trademark Association. Swiss watch manufacturers lose an estimated $850 million in annual sales due to counterfeit watches sold in the market. Italian leather goods manufacturers are estimated to lose approximately $1.5 billion in annual sales to counterfeit merchandise.[6]

In the spare car parts industry in the United States alone, it is estimated that over $3 billion is lost annually because of counterfeit parts. In some parts of the world—notably the Middle East—counterfeit parts account for up to 30 percent *of the entire market*.[7]

In the pharmaceutical market, it is estimated by the World Health Organization (WHO) that the lost revenues due to counterfeiting exceed $10 billion per annum—almost 30 percent of the 2001 revenues of pharmaceutical giant Pfizer. Up to 80 percent of the pharmaceuticals sold in Nigeria are thought to be counterfeit according to government officials.[8]

Annual losses to the music industry due to music piracy exceed $4 billion, according to the International Federation of Phonographic Industries (IFPI). The Business Software Alliance estimates that nearly $11 billion in software is pirated every year.[9]

CAUSES OF EXPONENTIAL CHANGE

What has caused counterfeiting to become such a large, and growing, problem in today's economy? Why has the scope and the magnitude of the issue suddenly changed? Four primary factors account for the sudden and explosive growth we have witnessed over the last several decades.

1. *Widespread availability of technology makes counterfeiting easier.* The advent of color copiers and photographic-quality computer scanners has made the production of high-quality counterfeit documents much easier. Computer graphics software makes the replication of logos much easier, while modern digital printers can produce high-quality packaging for products in seconds. Modern disc replication technology allows counterfeiters to replicate thousands of music or software videos, CDs, or DVDs in one day. And, most of these technologies are available to anyone with a few thousand dollars and little training.

   In addition, the explosion of information available via the Internet puts an enormous amount of information at the fingertips of the average citizen. Within a few minutes, anyone using a basic search engine can find literally thousands of websites for manufacturers of any basic goods, as well as for complex engineered products such as spare parts or pharmaceuticals. Many of these manufacturers operate in countries with limited, if any, enforcement of international intellectual property laws and openly advertise their willingness to produce products for any and all comers.

Technologically, it is much easier for anyone — particularly someone who deliberately and systematically sets out to counterfeit products — to acquire the means or methods to do so. The expense of doing so need not be very high. Using the Internet, it would not be difficult to locate a possible manufacturer of goods or products should you not wish to do so yourself.

2. *Increased globalization of world trade makes the markets for counterfeit products a global one — and brands themselves are global — increasing the ease of distribution and the incentive to counterfeit.* The World Trade Organization estimates that throughout the 1990s, worldwide merchandise trade grew at a faster rate than average GDP growth in every year of the decade. International trade is now a feature of modern consciousness and daily commentary in the public press.[10] The International Monetary Fund (IMF) has pointed out that "globalization is not just a recent phenomenon. Some analysts have argued that the world economy was just as globalized 100 years ago as it is today. But today commerce and financial services are far more developed and deeply integrated than they were at that time. The most striking aspect of this has been the integration of financial markets made possible by modern electronic communication."[11]

    One of the clear consequences of globalization is that it is easier to manufacture items in one geographical location and distribute them elsewhere. In fact, supporters of globalization and the opening of free markets cite this as one of the prime benefits of open markets — the ability to use the comparative advantage of one economy in deciding where and how to manufacture.

    The result of having more open borders and more trade flowing across borders is that it is also easier for counterfeit products to flow across borders. A counterfeiter in Asia or the Middle East has relatively little difficulty manufacturing large quantities of products and shipping them elsewhere. In this respect, counterfeiters are ultimately behaving as rational economic actors—even if behaving unethically or illegally—in that they also seek to maximize their return on investment and minimize their costs.

Perhaps even more important is the fact that as legitimate manufacturers increasingly produce their products in countries remote from where they are ultimately sold or distributed, their own control over their supply chains diminishes. The result is that among the web of subcontractors and licensees who manufacture products for the world's largest brands in places like China, Vietnam, Egypt, and Colombia, are found the same counterfeiters who will often ship products illegally and outside the normal course of business dealings. Sometimes, these are manufacturing establishments set up alongside legitimate operations, taking advantage of skilled local workforces. Many times, though, the same manufacturers who operate as subcontractors at one time become counterfeiters at another. The result can be chaotic for legitimate brand owners, who find products in the market that are not manufactured at their direction or with their approval but that may be indistinguishable from their own products. This type of counterfeiting is often the most difficult to detect and control.

3. *Legal penalties for counterfeiting are low in most countries—if they exist at all.* In most countries, even many of the most highly modern industrialized countries, the penalties for counterfeiting products are quite low, providing little if any deterrent against counterfeiting. Until 1984, there was not even a U.S. federal criminal statute prohibiting product counterfeiting. Even if a counterfeiter is successfully caught and prosecuted, the outcome may only be a fine. Given that counterfeiting is often viewed as a "victimless" crime by many law enforcement organizations, it is little wonder that counterfeiters view the rewards as often outweighing the potential legal penalties.

Finally, there are countries where laws meant to protect legitimate brand owners and manufacturers may not exist at all. China's application for entry to the World Trade Organization (WTO) in the late 1990s revealed a dearth of laws aimed at combating counterfeiting, and this ultimately became a point of contention in the decision to allow China entry into the World Trade Organization.

4. *The influence and prevalence of organized crime and terrorists in counterfeiting appears to be on the rise.* There has been increasing evidence of a linkage between organized crime, terrorist activity, and counterfeiting of products.[12] In the early 1990s, a global pharmaceutical company discovered that one of its veterinary products was being counterfeited. An extensive investigation revealed that the product was being counterfeited by the IRA as a means of raising money for its activities.[13] Similarly, linkages have been established between counterfeiting and Islamic terrorist groups, including the terrorists who were involved in the first World Trade Center bombing in 1993.[14]

WHAT IS "COUNTERFEITING"?

Before proceeding further with an examination of the nature, costs, and consequences of counterfeiting, it will be helpful to define counterfeiting. What do we mean by "counterfeiting" versus "simulation"? How

© Leo Cullum, 2003.

HARVARD BUSINESS REVIEW

EXHIBIT 1.1

does "gray marketing" enter into this analysis? What are "overruns"? And how does one type of counterfeiting differ from another?

For the purposes of this book, *counterfeiting* is defined as *the knowing duplication of a product by a party who wishes to usurp the brand or trademark of another.* This would mean that the garden-variety counterfeiter producing counterfeit Tommy Hilfiger shirts is counterfeiting a mark (the Tommy Hilfiger brand) without acquiring a license to do so and without paying any royalty. The counterfeiter can thus enjoy the benefits of the equity inherent in the brand without having to pay the costs of building this equity or ensuring the product is of the same quality as the branded good.

By contrast, a *copycat* or a *simulation* is a *copy of a product in form or substance with no attempt to actually duplicate the brand name.* For example, in airports throughout America, shops sell "look-alike" Rolex and other famous watches. The brand name on the watches is not, however, Rolex (usually it will be some other unknown brand). The watch just mimics the look of a Rolex. Unless Rolex has been able to trademark a specific design or "look," those manufacturing or selling the watches may not be guilty of "counterfeiting" using our definition. However, they are attempting to profit from association with a brand and may face other legal challenges.

What happens when subcontractors, say in Asia, overproduce the product they have legitimately been ordered to produce by the brand owners, and sell the overproduction directly into the market? These are *overruns which, although often of identical quality to the legitimate product, are produced in violation of the brand owners' rights.* In most cases, the brand owners are not aware of the presence of these overruns and are unable to distinguish the legitimate product in the market from that for which they receive no economic benefit (as the subcontractor simply sells the product into the market without paying royalties or license fees). We define unauthorized overruns of branded products as counterfeits, because they fit our definition—they are a knowing duplication of a product by a party who wishes to usurp the brand or trademark of another. The only difference is that, in this case, the third party is a legitimate producer (at least part of the time).

Gray marketing or *diversion* occurs when products which are shipped into specific distribution channels are shipped out of those channels into others, often in violation of distribution or sales contracts.

Consider the case of a manufacturer of printers and printer cartridges. The same cartridges are used in printers manufactured by the company all over the world, and often the packaging is indistinguishable from country to country. However, in recognition of the fact that Latin America has a lower GNP per capita than North America, the company may sell the identical cartridges in Brazil for 60 percent of the price it sells them for in North America. A distributor for the printer company in Brazil, upon receiving a container load of printer cartridges to sell in his country, receives an offer by a diverter in North America to buy the entire container before it is even unloaded in Brazil. Although the distributor's contract with the printer company may preclude him from doing so, he decides to accept the offer. The distributor wins because he has sold an entire consignment without even unloading the container— often at a premium to what he could have received in the market had he sold it retail. The diverter wins because he is sourcing product cheaper than if he had bought it directly from the manufacturer (at North American prices). The consumer may even benefit because they can buy the finished product cheaper, too. Manufacturers, though, are penalized in that they are realizing less margin than they would have otherwise.

It is important to note that, in this case, the product purchased by the customer is in fact a *legitimate, real product,* even if it was distributed outside normal sales and distribution channels. It is not a counterfeit, but is often confused with one.

THE HARM MATRIX
AS AN EXPLANATORY TOOL

The definitions above provide a starting point for understanding the counterfeiting problem. Consider the following examples:

- If an individual buys a counterfeit watch *knowing* it to be fake— and would not have bought the real watch even had the counterfeit not been available—what kind of crime has been committed and what damage done to the legitimate producer of watches?

- If a consumer buys a fake CD or other product *believing* it to be real, who is harmed and how?

- If a consumer buys a product which was manufactured in Asia *at the same facility* which is subcontracted to manufacture legitimate product (an overrun)—but which is shipped into the market without the knowledge or approval of the brand owner, has the consumer been deceived? Has the consumer been injured?

One way to examine these issues is through a *Harm Matrix,* a useful explanatory tool for understanding the various nuances of counterfeiting and how it affects different parties—consumers, counterfeiters, distributors of product, and the brand owners (see Exhibit 1.2).

Each of the quadrants in the Harm Matrix tells a different story in the interaction between the counterfeiter and the customer, and points to the many nuances of counterfeiting in the market today. Similarly, each quadrant points to a different set of issues which have to be addressed by brand owners and by governments in addressing the issue of counterfeiting.

Consider the lower-left quadrant, where the customers *know that they are buying a counterfeit and that the quality of the counterfeit is low.* This would be the case in the "fake Rolex" example cited above, where the customer strolling down the street in New York passes a street vendor

		Low Quality	High Quality
Deception Level of deception inherent in the sale of the product	**High**	Cheap toy purchased in belief that it is genuine.	High-quality counterfeits purchased by customers believing they are buying a genuine article.
	Low	Fake product purchased with knowledge it is fake.	Overruns or very high-quality counterfeits deliberately purchased with knowledge they are fake.

Low   **High**

Quality
Quality and functionality
of the counterfeit product

EXHIBIT 1.2   **Harm Matrix: Level of Deception versus Quality**

selling counterfeit watches and, on impulse, buys one for $30. The customer knows full well that this is not a real Rolex and, in fact, may never have any intention of buying a real Rolex. But the customer purchases the watch as a gag gift.

If the watch breaks after several days of wear, as cheap counterfeits often do, the customer may not be disappointed and indeed may laugh about the poor quality of the obviously fake Rolex. But, although it is unlikely in this case that the Rolex company may have lost a sale to a potential real customer, Rolex is nonetheless damaged because there is a palpable degradation of its brand when it is so widely available in (so obviously) a counterfeit format. Brand exclusivity is due in part to its relative scarcity. The relative prevalence of the brand due to counterfeiting causes damage to Rolex. Imagine, if you will, what would happen if everyone suddenly started wearing fake Rolexes—the pleasure of wearing a real one would be diminished.

Consider, then, the example of the upper-right quadrant, where the quality of the product is high but customers are not aware that they are purchasing a counterfeit. This would be the applicable quadrant if an individual were to purchase a counterfeit spare part for an automobile, believing it to be a real part, and the counterfeit part performed well. Customers may be none the wiser that they have purchased counterfeit parts (unless they ultimately fail in their performance). But in this case, the parts company is very clearly damaged because it has not sold a part that it would otherwise have sold. The customer was seeking a real part and would have bought one if the counterfeit had not been offered in place of the real part. Also, if the part fails at a later date, the legitimate producer may find itself covering damage and repairs under a warranty—for a product it did not produce.

It is an irony of modern counterfeiting that an increasing percentage of the problems faced by legitimate producers and brand owners falls in this quadrant. Gone are the days when most counterfeits were of visibly poor quality. They have been replaced instead by high-quality counterfeits that often find their way into the market unbeknownst to either the producers or the customers.

The lower-right quadrant is also very damaging—high quality counterfeits purchased in full knowledge by the customers that they are fake. An example of this would be auto parts in the Middle East, where legitimate parts distributors often offer, in addition to genuine parts, one or more counterfeit parts at the same time. In fact, sometimes a range of counterfeit parts of varying quality is offered. The customer may choose to buy a high quality counterfeit part simply because it is cheaper than the authentic one.

In this case, like the upper-right quadrant, the producer of the genuine part is damaged by virtue of a lost sale. In all likelihood, the customer would have purchased a genuine part had the counterfeit not been available.

Finally, the upper-left quadrant describes an uninformed buyer who purchases a substandard counterfeit in the belief that it is real. An example of this might be a consumer buying a counterfeit name brand apparel product at a "bargain" price, only to discover that it disintegrates in the laundry. While safety may not be an issue in the purchase of a watch, it can be fatal in the case of a purchase of a spare part for an automobile or an airplane.

The Harm Matrix frames the context in which a purchase of counterfeit product occurs, and particularly describes the level of deception inherent in getting a customer to purchase a counterfeit product. This Harm Matrix will be used throughout the book in describing markets in which counterfeits are sold, and their effect on brand owners and legitimate producers.

CHAPTER 2

Creating and Protecting Brands

BRANDS: VALUABLE AND VOLATILE ASSETS

No one has ever branded domesticity the way Martha Stewart has. The "domestic diva" extended her success with *Martha Stewart Living* magazine into several media realms, TV, publishing, and the web, that became part of Martha Stewart Living Omnimedia, and a mega-outlet for her popular tips and ideas. However, 2002 has represented a bad harvest for Martha. An unflattering biography, the bankruptcy of K-Mart (which carried her branded goods), and then an investigation for insider dealing and obstruction of justice in the ImClone case, has caused the share price for Omnimedia to drop like unleavened bread. In early October 2002, the stock was down over 70 percent year-to-date, and down over 82 percent from its price of over $35 in 1999. The future of the brand is bleak at best, because Martha Stewart *is* the brand. As noted by *The Economist,* "With a tainted Ms. Stewart on board, it is hard to see how Omnimedia can recover. But without her, it is not clear that the company has any future at all."[1]

Today, brands are a natural part of daily life in the United States. This is also increasingly true for consumers in developed and developing countries throughout the world. They are valuable assets to companies; you will be surprised how valuable. They must be developed, promoted, managed, and protected. Their value, while difficult and costly to grow, can be diminished rather quickly. This loss in value can result from unfortunate circumstances that are difficult to predict, let alone control. Loss in value can also result from negligence and mismanagement, or from intentional infringement such as counterfeiting. Before exploring the threat of counterfeiting, it will be valuable to better understand this phenomenon of "branding" that has become so commonplace in today's global economy.

THE IMPORTANCE OF BRANDS

What do brands represent? Why are they important to both the producer and consumer? How does one increase the value of a brand, and similarly how can that brand's value be diminished?

What Is a Brand?

According to Thorsten Nilson, the term "brand" comes from a Scandinavian word for burning (branna). "Brand" is the Swedish word for fire. Thus, branding originated from the act of putting your identifiable mark on something you have produced. Originally, this often meant burning the mark on the product, much like the cowboys of the early West began branding their cattle for identification purposes.[2]

A brand is a symbol of quality and service that the consumer attaches to the product. A good brand increases the customer's confidence and expectation as to what will be experienced by using a particular product. In a sense, the brand represents an implied contract between the producer and the consumer as to the attributes that can reasonably be expected when purchasing the product—design, durability, taste, attractiveness, after-sales service, functionality, reliability, and so on. A brand is often bolstered by a combination of names, logos, slogans, marks, and other symbols. (See Exhibit 2.1.) Sometimes colors are strongly associated with a brand; recent TV ads for Target rely solely on the colors red and white with never a mention of the name. McDonald's is a very strong brand represented by the "golden arches" logo, pictures of Ronald McDonald (the clown), and by slogans such as "McDonald's, They Do It All For You" or "Did Somebody Say McDonald's?" Whether you are in a McDonald's in Moscow, Manila, Milan, Mombasa, Melbourne, Madrid, Mexico City, or Minneapolis, you have some common expectations of what you will experience: clean facilities, courteous and friendly service, similar tasting food, a familiar, though not identical, menu. It is not an easy task to make sure that these expectations are met for every customer in every restaurant

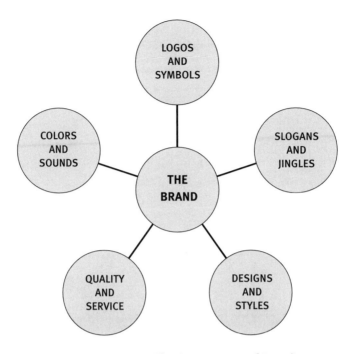

EXHIBIT 2.1   The Components of Brands

in every country, every time. But, to the extent that McDonald's can approach this ideal goal, the value of the brand will continue to increase. If they fail, the brand will lose value.

Almost all businesses involve a combination of product and service. Certainly this is true for McDonald's which probably falls toward the middle of the product/service spectrum. A bank or real estate company is no doubt more focused on the service end, whereas the companies we are focused on in this book are more heavily involved at the product end of the spectrum (e.g., Nike). After all, it is usually the product that is counterfeited, not the service. Whether product-focused or service-focused, to build and maintain brand value requires keeping the promise made to the consumer.

A strong corporate brand is a valuable communications tool and a prime method of differentiating a company and its products in the marketplace. The power of a strong corporate brand is an extremely valuable asset. According to Raymond Perrier, head of the New York office at

Interbrand, a consulting firm that is generally recognized as the leader in the area of brand valuation: "It is clear that global brands are still the main creators of wealth and will continue to drive wealth creation in the foreseeable future. Technological advances, such as the growth of the Internet, will continue to accelerate this globalization trend. As demonstrated by this year's Top Ten list, which remains nearly intact from last year, brands are arguably the most stable business asset a company can have."[3]

As with personal or corporate reputations, brands generally grow in value through hard work over a significant period of time. However, the demise of a brand can happen swiftly. Note Ford, whose brand value dropped nearly a third in a single year according to the Interbrand rankings presented in Exhibit 2.3 later in this chapter and lost nearly $16 billion in value between 2000 and 2002. This drastic decline was primarily the result of the highly publicized debacle involving Ford SUVs and Firestone tires. Seven hundred injuries and 174 deaths were attributed to Firestone tires losing their treads at high speeds. Both companies initially reacted to these incidents by blaming each other for the defective tires instead of taking responsibility. Ford later backed off this stance and offered their SUV customers replacement tires, but a large amount of damage was already done. The mishandling of the situation left both companies and brands badly damaged and with a lot of work to do to gain back consumer confidence in their products. This shows how even the most powerful brands are vulnerable to swift declines in value if they are mismanaged.

How Brands Are Developed

Brand development is contingent upon two kinds of purchases, the initial purchase and the repeat purchase.[4] For the initial purchase, *communication* is the key. The customer must somehow be made to know about your product. This communication may come through public relations, advertising, direct mail brochures, or through the positioning and appeal of the packaging (colors, ingredients, design). Communication by relevant third parties (friends, testing organizations) may also play an influential role in the initial purchase. For repeat purchases, communication plays more of a supporting role. The most important factor in winning repeat business is the *experience* the consumer had from the initial purchase. One should strive to "oversatisfy" the consumer in that first experience to maximize the chance that the customer will come back.

The development of a successful brand must meet four requirements.[5] First, the brand must convey distinctive values and deliver on these values. What does the brand promise to deliver—taste, safety, style, prestige, performance, satisfaction? These may even be arranged in some hierarchy which is rearranged for different emphases in different markets, as shown in Exhibit 2.2. Then, of course, the brand must deliver on those promises. This is critical to winning the repeat purchase. All the fancy packaging and advertising in the world will do little to convince the consumer to purchase again if the basic promise is not kept.

Second, the brand must differentiate a specific product from others in the class or industry. This can be easier to accomplish in some industries than others. It is easier to differentiate a product in the food and beverage industry where unique tastes or products help to make the differentiation than in the PC market where technology seems common to all.

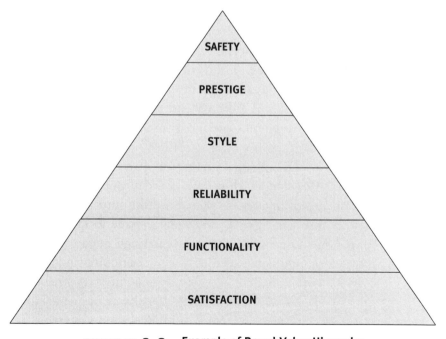

EXHIBIT 2.2 **Example of Brand-Value Hierarchy**

However, companies such as Apple and Dell have been relatively successful in differentiating their products. Apple has created a distinctive look and the promise of ease-of-use, while Dell focuses on customization, price, and service.

Third, the brand must be appealing to the customer. While this is similar to the first requirement of conveying and delivering specific experiences, it is focused on ensuring that the promised experience is desirable to the customer. You could deliver on a promise of *performance* in an automobile brand only to discover that most consumers are looking for *style* or *safety.* BMW masterfully covered itself in this area by appealing to several customer needs at the same time with its catchy slogan, "BMW—the ultimate driving machine."

Fourth, successful brand development means that your brand must have a clear identity. In the clothing industry, this can be accomplished by attaching recognizable symbols, part of the brand, to seemingly undifferentiated articles of clothing. Many of today's hottest brands are less obtuse and write the brand name itself on the garment (e.g., Guess, DKNY, Calvin Klein, Fila, Nike, Lucky, Polo, Victoria's Secret, B.U.M., Old Navy, and, of course, Tommy Hilfiger), making it very easy for the customer to recognize an article of clothing by brand.

Sometimes, companies can increase the value of a brand by associating, rather than differentiating, with other well-known brands in the same industry. This, in part, is what Samsonite hopes to do with Point A. These new retail stores will sell high-end competing brands such as Andiamo, Hugo Bosca, Kenneth Cole and Zero Halliburton, in addition to their own brands as they have done in their existing retail outlets.[6]

In *No Logo,* Naomi Klein suggests that there was a sea change, as recently as the mid-1980s, in which many successful corporations became more focused on producing brands than on producing products. The focus shifted from manufacturing to marketing as more and more of the production function was contracted out and/or shifted offshore. Tommy Hilfiger is perhaps the ultimate example. Klein observes:

> *Tommy Hilfiger, meanwhile, is less in the business of manufacturing clothes than he is in the business of signing his name. The company is run entirely through licensing agreements, with Hilfiger commissioning all of its products from a group of other companies: Jockey International makes Hilfiger underwear, Pepe*

Jeans London makes Hilfiger jeans, Oxford Industries make Tommy shirts, the Stride Rite Corporation makes its footwear. What does Tommy Hilfiger manufacture? Nothing at all.[7]

When this is the case, it may be more difficult for the consumer to understand the source of brand value. After all, anyone can subcontract the manufacturing; basically, that is what counterfeiters do. And, if the quality of their product is comparable to that of the genuine branded article, consumers must ask themselves what value is really added by the brand. This is not an argument for counterfeiting, but rather an attempt to comprehend brand value. When the brand is associated with superior quality, design, performance, and reliability, then it is easy to see why a premium brand price is justified. But, when the counterfeit article provides much the same thing, then the "no logo" argument espoused by Klein has some credibility. Thus, it is important for the brand holder to continually assess the superior attributes that their brand offers (see Exhibit 2.2) and to deliver on those promises.

Klein's book is one of the most recent (and certainly one of the more popular) to chastise brands for influencing consumers to converge into some homogenous and illusory lifestyle. However, as an article in *The Economist*[8] points out, brands have also created a reciprocal influence from consumers to corporations. An Interbrand spokesperson is quoted as saying "Brands are the ultimate accountable institution. If people fall out of love with your brand, you go out of business." Pressures from consumer groups have forced some of the most popular brands to act in more socially responsible ways (e.g., Nike's production in developing countries). Recognizing this, some companies have actually tried to develop their brands by reflecting the kinds of social values that consumers hold dear. This has become known as "cause-related marketing," and it has been noted that "A company's commitment to causes that appeal to both consumers and employees can increase the numbers of the former and the quality of the latter."[9] Good examples of brand development using this approach have included Ben & Jerry's (philanthropy), Patagonia (environmental issues), and Avon (breast cancer). In fact, one consultancy firm found that "81 percent of U.S. consumers are more likely to switch brands to support a cause (when price and quality are equal)."[10]

○ FOCUS 2.1 ○

POLO AND RALPH LAUREN

Born Ralph Lipschitz in 1939, he changed his name to Ralph Lauren well before he opened his first store, selling a line of wide men's neckties he designed himself. He parlayed a $50,000 loan into a multibillion dollar fashion empire by pairing style with a brand name that conjured up an image that people desired—a lot of people. *New York Magazine* labeled Ralph "the first image-maker." Lauren himself said, "My symbol was always a polo player because I liked sports, and polo has a stylishness to it. . . . My clothes are all about mood and style I like. . . . It's all about creating a dream I'd want for myself."[11]

He successfully migrated the Polo brand into clothes (men's, women's, and children's), paint, carpeting, fragrances, and thousands of products in 60 different lines. He has even considered putting the Polo name on a chain of ritzy resorts. Few others have been so successful in branding and selling an image. The name and the image is that of the lifestyle of the landed gentry. Apparently, the name Polo was chosen "because of the power, style, and intrigue that the brand has always been associated with."[12] Polo is a "destination brand" because consumers seek it out; thus stores carrying Polo can then sell other nonbranded goods after Polo brings them in the front door. In 1997, Lauren took the company public. The stock had a rather rocky start, but is slowly recovering and was by mid-2002 about back to its high IPO price. The Polo Ralph Lauren Corporation achieved a record actual net income of $172.5 million for the fiscal year ending March 30, 2002. They have also leveraged the popular Polo brand and the Ralph Lauren name in creating several new brands—"RALPH," "Lauren," "Polo Jeans Co," "Chaps," "Polo Sport," "Club Monaco," and "RLX." The latter is a high performance line of athletic apparel which was the official outfitter of the Seattle-based OneWorld Challenge America's Cup Team. This is a great example of how Polo Ralph Lauren strategically picks its sponsorships in order to promote the brand by remaining true to the image that the brand conveys.[13]

The Importance of Valuing Brands

There are a number of situations calling for the valuation of intellectual property and other intangible assets; brands would fall in this category.[14]

When companies are sold, their assets must be evaluated in order to reach agreement on a reasonable purchase price agreeable to both parties. This includes both tangible and intangible assets. The appraised values of the assets may then serve as the basis for depreciation or amortization of the assets by the acquiring firm. Paying more for a firm than it appears to be worth from looking at its balance sheet and income statements is an age-old problem. Intangibles such as "goodwill" or "going concern" have often been used to justify a premium price. Today, the popular term is "intellectual capital" (including intellectual property and human capital) which is more easily valued and therefore is currently used to justify much of the price premium one is willing to pay.[15]

The use of intangible assets can also be licensed to another party. In order to establish licensing fees or royalties, it is necessary to attach a value to the property being licensed. An example of licensing intangible assets would be a brewery licensing the right to produce its brand to an overseas producer.

Related to the above, assets (even intangible ones) are often transferred between different units or subsidiaries of the same firm. There is a transaction value associated with this transfer, referred to as a transfer price. Sovereign governments often have a vested interest in seeing that these transfer prices are set at "arm's length." This means that the internal price must be equivalent to the price that the same item would sell for to an unrelated third party. Otherwise, these international transactions may have the intended or unintended result of reducing taxes due a particular country. Therefore, royalty rates must be determined for intangible property and must be generally equivalent between related and unrelated parties.

Intellectual property can sometimes serve as collateral for loans, and there needs to be a value given to the amount that the pledged property is worth. While this may be less common for brands than for other forms of intellectual property (e.g., patents and copyrights), a valuable brand no doubt enhances a firm's ability to borrow funds.

Furthermore, strategic decisions often require specific valuations of corporate assets. One may want to understand the return on investment in brand development. One cannot know the return on investment, unless there is a way to determine the value of the brand. Does the brand warrant increased resources? What is the brand contributing to corporate financial return on investment (ROI) or marketing (share growth) goals? Without a base of valuation for the property, these will be difficult questions to answer. Similarly, strategies to grow the brand can only be assessed by continuous valuation of the brand.

Litigation involving intangible property also requires valuation. If someone infringes on a brand (or one of its components—trademark, saying, logo, name), knowing the value of the brand is crucial to determining the damages that need to be recovered. This type of litigation is directly relevant to brand counterfeiting. Later chapters explore the various ways in which the brand holder may be damaged by such fraud.

Finally, investors need to be able to evaluate the total worth of the company, including both tangible and intangible assets. If intangibles such as brand value cannot be adequately determined, then it becomes difficult to support and evaluate expenses aimed at supporting these intangible assets, such as advertising or protection from counterfeiting. Also, new accounting rules for the treatment of intangibles went into effect January 1, 2002. The Financial Accounting Standards Board (FASB) has issued new rules for accounting for intangibles in mergers that make it so these assets will no longer have to be amortized over some period, as if they are going to wear out like machinery does. However, the new rules recognize that intangibles can be damaged and that such damage must be accounted for, which in turn requires that a value be assigned to the intangibles. A periodical commentary on this subject notes that a logical next step would be to require the accounting for intangibles be on the balance sheet in all cases, not just when they are sold or acquired.[16] This is the case in countries like Britain and Australia.

How Brands Are Valued

Intangible assets (which includes brands) are more valuable than the tangible assets (like bricks and mortar and equipment) for many of today's corporations. Brands are one of the more commonly valued forms of intangible assets, but they are not as easy to value as are more tangible assets. Following is a brief description of the three main methods for valuing intellectual property.

- *Market Approach Valuation Methods.* This group of methods would look first to the market for intellectual property in determining its value. This would include previous sales and licensing transactions made at "arm's length." Thus, prices associated with internal transfers would not be included. If the specific intellectual property had not been previously sold or licensed, then sales or licenses of "comparable" assets would be considered. Comparability would be judged, if possible, within similar industries, timeframes, and uses. This approach is not unlike that used by a real estate appraiser; appraisers would look at previous sales of your house, your purchase price, and sales of comparable properties. However, the neighborhood may have changed over time, and the comparable houses are never exact duplicates. Therefore, the evaluator must take into account the differences, as well as the similarities, and make some judgments in the final evaluation. Nevertheless, willing buyers and willing sellers of similar assets remain perhaps the best indicator of fair market value.

- *Cost Approach Valuation Methods.* These approaches usually look at reproduction or replacement costs for determining the proper value of an intangible asset. The assumptions underlying the cost approaches are, first, that purchasers would not pay more for an asset than the cost of creating a comparable one themselves. The cost of assets will certainly be affected by the supply and demand for specific types of assets existing at any particular time in the marketplace. Likewise, the current cost may be higher or lower than the original cost due to a variety of other external circumstances. Some cost approaches include "cost avoidance" as a component in the valuation process. That is, what costs would the asset owner avoid by owning said asset (e.g., the high initial costs of brand development and recognition)?

- *Income Approach Valuation Methods.* As the name suggests, these approaches focus on a variety of economic income measures. These would include gross or net revenues and profits, cash flows, or other income measures. Historical income streams are obviously relevant, but projected income streams must adjust the historical record for circumstances that would alter the probability of realizing a higher or lower income stream in the future. Calculating capitalization rates or a present-value discount rate from those projected income streams allows one to estimate a current value for the asset in question.

Counterfeiting impacts all three brand valuation methods. By reducing the *market demand* for a particular brand because of the deception experienced by the consumer (i.e., the brand not delivering what is promised in quality or service), the market price of the asset declines. Likewise, *greater costs* are incurred in fighting the counterfeits, and *lower income* results from losing sales and market share to them as well.

What Brands Have the Most Value?

Interbrand Corporation is a brand-consultancy firm that started in Britain—not surprisingly, because in that country, brand value is included on a company's balance sheet. The Interbrand analysis of brand value focuses on the increase in sales and earnings which is attributable to the brand. It also assesses whether that contribution will continue in the future and to what extent, so that future earnings can be discounted to present value thereby helping to determine the value of the brand. Interbrand values are shown in Exhibit 2.3. The reader must keep in mind that it is the brand, not the company, that is being valued. Therefore, the Coca-Cola brand refers only to those products of the company carrying the Coke brand. Thus, Sprite and Fanta (other brands owned by Coca-Cola) are not included in the value of the Coca-Cola brand. Similarly, Interbrand only evaluates those brands that have enough publicly available information, and whose foreign sales are at least 20 percent of the total.[17]

Every year the major corporate brands are valued by Interbrand. While the list rearranges itself somewhat each year, it nevertheless seems to include the expected names year after year. For example, in their ranking of the "World's Most Valuable Brands 2000," it was clear that the technology sector created the most brand value. Most notable, then, was the addition of Nokia to the top five, due to increasing its brand value by 86 percent in a year. Furthermore, Microsoft remained the second most valuable brand in the world despite all of its problems with the Department of Justice. Nevertheless, Coca-Cola was still number one, though the value of its brand decreased by 13 percent during the year. More importantly, the value of the Coca-Cola brand was over $72 billion in 2000, which represented over half (51 percent) of Coca-Cola's total market capitalization. Indeed, Coke is the real thing! And that is not the highest; in the 2001 rankings, the brand value for Apple was 80 percent of its capitalization. The most recent Interbrand rankings (2002) are shown in Exhibit 2.3.[18]

Of the top 100 brands in the 2002 Interbrand report, about two-thirds (65 to be exact) were owned by U.S. firms. Other home countries on the list were Germany and Japan (each with six), France with five, Britain with four, Switzerland and Italy (with three each), Sweden and the Netherlands (with two each), and finally Finland, the Republic of Korea, and Bermuda (with one apiece). And there is one brand (Shell) in the top

EXHIBIT 2.3   **The World's Most Valuable Brands 2002**

2002 Rank	Brand Name	2002 Value ($ Millions)	% Change from 2001	Country of Origin
1	Coca-Cola	69,637	1	United States
2	Microsoft	64,091	−2	United States
3	IBM	51,188	−3	United States
4	GE	41,311	−3	United States
5	Intel	30,861	−11	United States
6	Nokia	29,970	−14	Finland
7	Disney	29,256	−10	United States
8	McDonald's	26,375	4	United States
9	Marlboro	24,151	10	United States
10	Mercedes	21,010	−3	Germany
11	Ford	20,403	−32	United States
12	Toyota	19,448	5	Japan
13	Citibank	18,066	−5	United States
14	Hewlett-Packard	16,776	−7	United States
15	American Express	16,287	−4	United States
16	Cisco	16,222	−6	United States
17	AT&T	16,059	−30	United States
18	Honda	15,064	3	Japan
19	Gillette	14,959	−2	United States
20	BMW	14,425	4	Germany
21	Sony	13,899	−7	Japan
22	Nescafe	12,843	−3	Switzerland
23	Oracle	11,510	−6	United States
24	Budweiser	11,349	5	United States

(continues)

EXHIBIT 2.3 **The World's Most Valuable Brands 2002** *(Continued)*

2002 Rank	Brand Name	2002 Value ($ Millions)	% Change from 2001	Country of Origin
25	Merrill Lynch	11,230	−25	United States
26	Morgan Stanley	11,205	NA	United States
27	Compaq	9,803	−21	United States
28	Pfizer	9,770	9	United States
29	JP Morgan	9,693	NA	United States
30	Kodak	9,671	−10	United States
31	Dell	9,237	12	United States
32	Nintendo	9,219	−3	Japan
33	Merck	9,138	−6	United States
34	Samsung	8,310	30	Korea
35	Nike	7,724	2	United States
36	Gap	7,406	−15	United States
37	Heinz	7,347	4	United States
38	Volkswagen	7,209	−2	Germany
39	Goldman Sachs	7,194	−9	United States
40	Kellogg's	7,191	3	United States
41	Louis Vuitton	7,054	0	France
42	Sap	6,775	7	Germany
43	Canon	6,721	2	Japan
44	Ikea	6,545	9	Sweden
45	Pepsi	6,394	3	United States
46	Harley-Davidson	6,266	13	United States
47	MTV	6,078	−8	United States
48	Pizza Hut	6,046	1	United States
49	KFC	5,346	2	United States
50	Apple	5,316	−3	United States
51	Xerox	5,308	−12	United States
52	Gucci	5,304	−1	Italy
53	Accenture	5,182	NA	United States
54	L'Oreal	5,079	NA	France
55	Kleenex	5,039	−1	United States
56	Sun Microsystems	4,773	−7	United States
57	Wrigley's	4,747	5	United States
58	Reuters	4,611	−12	Britain
59	Colgate	4,602	1	United States
60	Philips	4,561	−7	Netherlands
61	Nestle	4,430	NA	Switzerland
62	Avon	4,399	1	United States

EXHIBIT 2.3   **The World's Most Valuable Brands 2002** *(Continued)*

2002 Rank	Brand Name	2002 Value ($ Millions)	% Change from 2001	Country of Origin
63	AOL	4,326	−4	United States
64	Chanel	4,272	0	France
65	Kraft	4,079	1	United States
66	Danone	4,054	NA	France
67	YAHOO!	3,855	−12	United States
68	Addidas	3,690	1	Germany
69	Rolex	3,686	0	Switzerland
70	Time	3,682	−1	United States
71	Ericsson	3,589	−49	Sweden
72	Tiffany	3,482	0	United States
73	Levi's	3,454	−8	United States
74	Motorola	3,416	−9	United States
75	Duracell	3,409	−18	United States
76	BP	3,390	4	Britain
77	Hertz	3,362	−7	United States
78	Bacardi	3,341	4	Bermuda
79	Caterpillar	3,218	NA	United States
80	Amazon.com	3,175	1	United States
81	Panasonic	3,141	−10	Japan
82	Boeing	2,973	−27	United States
83	Shell	2,810	−1	Britain/Netherlands
84	Smirnoff	2,723	5	Britain
85	Johnson & Johnson	2,509	NA	United States
86	Prada	2,489	NA	Italy
87	Moet & Chandon	2,445	−1	France
88	Heineken	2,396	6	Netherlands
89	Mobil	2,358	−2	United States
90	Burger King	2,163	−11	United States
91	Nivea	2,059	16	Germany
92	Wall Street Journal	1,961	−10	United States
93	Starbucks	1,961	12	United States
94	Barbie	1,937	−5	United States
95	Polo Ralph Lauren	1,928	1	United States
96	FedEx	1,919	2	United States
97	Johnnie Walker	1,654	0	Britain
98	Jack Daniels	1,580	0	United States
99	3M	1,579	NA	United States
100	Armani	1,509	1	Italy

100 that has dual citizenship, British and Dutch. While American brands dominated overall, non-American firms predominated in some industries. For example, Ford was the only American automobile producer to make the top 100. All of Germany's top three brands were automobile companies—Mercedes, BMW, and Volkswagen. Likewise, Japan's top two brands were automobile companies—Toyota and Honda, followed by several in the consumer electronics and optics area—Sony, Nintendo, Canon, and Panasonic. France's well-respected reputation in style and glamour is reflected in its top brands—Louis Vuitton, L'Oreal, and Chanel. It is interesting how some national reputations are reflected in their brands; or more probably, those famous brands generated those reputations in the first place.

In general, it was a tough year on brands. At least 49 declined in value from the 2001 figures. Six others remained unchanged, and several others were indeterminate, since there was no comparable 2001 data collected. Leading the losers, and losing at least a fifth of the brand value in a year, were Ericsson (down 49 percent), followed by Ford (−32 percent), AT&T (−30 percent), Boeing (−27 percent), Merrill Lynch (−25 percent), and Compaq (−21 percent). The loss of nearly half of its brand value in a year by Ericsson is indeed dramatic, but seems to be due, in large part, to increased competition and the rise of competing brands such as Samsung and Nokia. This is even more obvious as you examine the big winners in 2002. At the top was Samsung who increased its brand value by 30 percent. The only other double-digit winners were Nivea (+16 percent), Dell and Starbucks (both at +12 percent), Harley-Davidson (+13 percent), and Marlboro (+10 percent)—that horse has legs! Even more amazing is that Starbucks and Samsung were last year's big story also—Starbucks (32 percent gain) and Samsung (up 22 percent) in 2001.

Indicating that there is some stability in brand values, the top ten brands remained unchanged from 2000 to 2001, though they did rearrange themselves a bit. Likewise, in 2002, the list of top brands remained largely intact; the biggest exceptions were AT&T which dropped out of the top 10, moving from number 10 down to number 17, and Ford which went from number 7 to number 11. They were replaced by Marlboro moving up from number 11 to number 9 and Mercedes moving up to number 10 from number 12 last year. However, the 2002 top eight were also in the top 10 for the past two years. Some brand names derive value from actually managing a portfolio of more specific brands. For example, some of the more well-known brand names in the P&G nest include Crest (toothpaste), Tide (detergent), and Pampers (diapers).

It is really quite astounding how valuable these global brands are. We already noted that the Coca-Cola brand was valued at more than $72,500,000,000 in 2000 (that's 72.5 billion, not million). Even the Benetton brand (ranked last on the Interbrand Top 75 list that year) was valued at more than a billion dollars. The importance of these figures becomes more evident when they are compared to the total market capitalization for the company. In addition to Coke (which was mentioned above), the other brands in the top 75 (2000 rankings) that represented more than half of the company's market capitalization, included: Ford (75 percent), McDonald's (63 percent), BMW (64 percent), Kodak (64 percent), Heinz (76 percent), Xerox (70 percent), Nike (71 percent), Volkswagen (66 percent), Kellogg's (61 percent), Gucci (53 percent), Wrigley's (59 percent), Addidas (151 percent), and Hertz (110 percent).

◑ FOCUS 2.2 ◐

ARE BRANDS WORTH THE PREMIUM PRICE?

There is probably an easy answer to this—of course, as long as the purchaser is willing to pay a premium price. And the facts suggest that in many cases they are indeed willing to do just that. After all, it is not reality that matters, but rather the consumer's perception of reality that counts. And that is not intended to suggest that reality itself does not justify the higher price. As we have stated before, if the consumer feels that the brand delivers on its promises, whether that be quality, style, performance, reliability, status, value, service, or whatever, then they will probably be willing to pay the premium price.

However, maybe the more relevant question is how much of a premium price are they willing to pay? If the brand demands a 10 percent premium, and delivers on its promises, then the answer is probably *"Yes,"* consumers will pay. If, on the other hand, the brand demands a multiple of 100 over comparable products, then the answer may well be *"No."* Of course, when you get price differences this great, the

(continues)

comparable product is often the counterfeit or pirated good. Indeed, the "brand premium," the difference between the price of the branded good and its generic counterpart, is a rough measure of the profit margin available to the counterfeiters. Then the question becomes, "How functional is the counterfeit?" This is, of course, the basis of our Harm Matrix which we utilize throughout the book. In the case of pirated software, the efficacy of the pirated product is probably quite good (until after-sale service and updates become important). When this is the case, consumers may be less willing to pay the much higher price for the authorized and official product when they can get the pirated product at a fraction of the cost and it works fine. However, when personal health and safety are concerned (e.g., parts, pharmaceuticals, fertilizers, and toys), consumers may be more willing to pay a significant brand premium.

Sometimes brand premium is based on more irrational (or maybe we should say unrelated) factors. Is the preference for Martha Stewart's goods based on design, functionality, reliability, or the fact that Martha has built a personal reputation which is then transferred to her products? When that reputation was recently tarnished, her brand suffered and the premium which customers are now willing to pay for her goods may have declined. Yet the products have not changed a bit. But "live by the sword, die by the sword." If the brand has been built around personal reputation and that reputation is diminished, then so is the brand. So the answer to our question ("Are brands worth the premium price?") is (of course) "It depends."

The Components of Brand Value

The overall assessment of "brand power" reflected in Exhibit 2.3 is an aggregation of at least four more specific components of brand strength.[19]

- *Brand Weight (Dominance)*. Brand weight is a measure of the brand's dominance within its category or market. Those with the greatest weight are likely to be market leaders with significant market shares. However, weight can also be enhanced through innovation, as is the case for Apple in the personal computer market. A 1997 publication *(The World's Greatest Brands)* by Interbrand listed the top ten brands as to weight. At that time, they were McDonald's (first in the food category), Coca-Cola (first in the nonalcoholic beverages category), Kodak (first in the technology category), Gillette (first in the personal care category), Microsoft (third in the technology category), Tampax (third in the personal care category), Levi's (first in the fashion and luxury goods category), Kellogg's (second in the food category), Mercedes-Benz (first in the automobile and oil category), and Disney (first in the leisure and travel category).

- *Brand Length (Stretch).* Brand length refers to the ability to migrate the brand successfully into new markets (not an easy task). Yet this is a valuable attribute in brand development and growth. At the time, Interbrand identified the following top ten brands in the length category: Disney, Johnson & Johnson, Harrods, Virgin, Sony, McDonald's, Samsung, Camel, Sega, and Harley-Davidson. Disney is certainly understandable in its high ranking for length; they have gone from cartoons and movies to amusement parks to clothing to toys to TV shows to records, tapes, and discs. I am sure you could think of others. Virgin was another that was most deserving of recognition for their crossover from airlines to music to financial services to soft drinks and even to bridal gowns. Polo is not on this particular Interbrand list, though as Focus 2.1 suggests, Ralph Lauren has certainly stretched the brand into numerous, seemingly unrelated, fields.

- *Brand Breadth (Scope).* Brand breadth refers to the scope of the brand in terms of consumers (age groups, gender groups, economic groups) and geographic spread (international, cultural). Brands that are high in breadth are likely to have a lower risk profile. For example, "changes in taste, legislation, and financial instability" in some markets is not likely to affect all markets because of its broad appeal. In 1997, the top ten in this component of brand power according to Interbrand were: Coca-Cola, McDonald's, Kodak, Sony, IBM, Visa, CNN, Pepsi-Cola, Microsoft, and Gillette. Coke's high ranking is reflective of the reference (not always complimentary) to the "coca-colonization of the world." Likewise, McDonald's operates in the vast majority of countries in the world, regardless of the religious, linguistic, or political preferences predominating in each. They even operate in India where the predominant Hindu religion considers the cow sacred and, therefore, beef is not eaten.

Similarly, there is a story that the Sony Walkman was created and popularized in Japan's group-oriented society so that people could listen to music without bothering others, whereas its popularity in the United States' individualistic culture was attributed to the fact that a person could listen to music without *being* bothered by other people. Now that's breadth. Likewise, CNN has built its reputation for objectivity based on its broad cultural acceptance.

- *Brand Depth (Loyalty).* Finally, brand depth reflects the commitment of loyal consumers to the brand. Depth is based on the development of strong relationships to the brand's consumer base. There is a set of shared values between the brand and its consumer constituency. These consumers become an effective communication tool that helps to win new converts to the brand. The earlier Interbrand publication listed the top ten brands for depth as: Apple, Disney, Body Shop, Harley-Davidson, BBC, Mercedes-Benz, Nike, McDonald's, Marlboro, and Camel. Though many of these would still find themselves at the top of the loyalty list today (e.g., Apple, Harley-Davidson, and the BBC), you might expect to find some other names on the current list, maybe Honda, Coors, and Krispy Kreme (though the latter may not have much breadth). However, Harley-Davidson is a perfect example of a brand that has cultivated deep relationships with its proponents through such devices as its HOGs (Harley Owners Groups).

Which Brands Do You Value?

Put your consumer hat on for a minute and take a look at Exhibit 2.4. How would you describe your attitude about the brands listed there? The value of the brand is determined, in large part, by the consumer's perception of that brand. True, there may be several brands listed for which you have no discernible positive or negative attitude because you do not use that kind of product. If you don't drink alcohol (or at least not whiskey), then "Johnnie Walker" may have little importance to you one way or the other. Unless, of course, you strongly oppose drinking and therefore have a negative attitude about that brand because of what it represents. The same could be true for cigarettes, drugs, lingerie, or logo items in general.

EXHIBIT 2.4   **Brand Attitude Survey**

Brand Name	Favorable	Neutral	Unfavorable	Why?
Fisher-Price				
Microsoft				
Firestone				
Heineken				
Boeing				
Louis Vuitton				
Marlboro				
Viagra				
Perrier				
American Express				
KFC				
United Airlines				
CNN				
Johnnie Walker				
Disney				
Polo				
Wall Street Journal				
Hilton				
Ivory				
Sony				
BMW				
Xerox				
NAPA				
IBM				
Merck				
Victoria's Secret				
NBC				
Petrus				
General Electric				
Kodak				

There may be some brands unknown to you, and others (e.g., NAPA) may conjure up fine wine to some and auto parts to another. However, if you do find that you have a particularly favorable or unfavorable attitude toward some of these brands, then ask yourself *Why?* Is it because, in your experience, the brand has continued to deliver on the promises that you associate with it. Or, has the brand somehow broken that implied contract we mentioned earlier? Are you influenced by recent news accounts involving some of the brands (Firestone, Microsoft, or United Airlines)? This will also help you to understand how easily brand value can be damaged. You may have had years of good experience with a brand. But, one big mistake, one broken promise, or one incident of poor service may be enough for you to abandon that brand forever.

THE VULNERABILITY OF BRANDS

Reputation is the cornerstone of brand value, and, like personal reputation, it usually is built with considerable effort over a lengthy period of time. However, it can be destroyed overnight. Take another look at the damage to Martha Stewart's reputation, discussed in Focus 2.2. Despite the years she spent building up her reputation, an unflattering book and subsequent bad publicity regarding possible insider trading has done significant damage. The remainder of this section discusses the different ways that brands are vulnerable and includes examples of where and why brands have been damaged.

Brand Mismanagement

Many believe that brand mismanagement was the reason for Ford's precipitous decline. Only time will clarify where the fault rests, but the fact remains that the Interbrand valuation of the Ford brand fell to $30.1 billion from $36.4 billion in one year. A $6 billion loss in one year is not insignificant, even when we are talking intangible assets. The apparent cause was the tire fiasco involving Firestone, the resulting lawsuits, and several apparent quality problems, some resulting in recalls. Remember that the brand represents a contract with consumers, suppliers, and investors. Part of that contract involves expectations of quality and how problems are solved when that quality comes into question. Making decisions based on short-term profitability that damage the value of a brand will prove costly in the long run.

Changing the Brand

Coca-Cola remains the highest ranked brand in the 2002 Interbrand rankings presented in Exhibit 2.3. Many attribute the strength of the Coca-Cola brand to the intense competition with rival Pepsi. It was that competition with Pepsi that several years ago prompted Coca-Cola to come out with a sweeter tasting new Coke. This attempt to alter the brand was originally considered by some to be a colossal failure, as many loyal Coke customers did not take to the new product. When Coca-Cola reversed itself and returned to the classic taste, some say the overall effect actually strengthened the brand. Customers were made more loyal to the brand once they had it taken away from them.

In 1993, when Philip Morris cut the prices for its flagship Marlboro brand, it signaled to the market that PM was raising the white flag in its fight with discount brands. In what became known as "Marlboro Friday," several big consumer-goods companies suffered falling stock prices as the market reacted to this brand change by Philip Morris. Of course, changes can also help build the brand. This was the case when Samsung terminated distribution through Wal-Mart stores in an attempt to move its brand image upmarket by shedding the discount image afforded by Wal-Mart.

Counterfeiting

With brand values as high as we have seen from the Interbrand rankings, it is no secret why they are obvious targets for counterfeiters. Successful brand goods usually demand a higher price in the marketplace because the consumer has come to realize that a particular brand represents better quality, unique features, style and/or excellent service. By imitating the brand, the counterfeiter bypasses all of the expenses incurred in developing, producing, marketing, and servicing the brand. Yet they can receive a relatively high return for their counterfeit product, if they can deceive the consumer into thinking they are buying the real thing.

In 1999, *Authentication News* reported on two case studies that demonstrated how quickly a brand can be taken over by counterfeiters. In

Deception

Level of deception inherent in the sale of the product

		Low	High
	High	Significant brand threat—Lost sales and market share, reputation, warranty, and liability.	Significant brand threat—Lost sales and market share, and potential theft of brand.
	Low	Low brand threat—Share, reputation, warranty liability, product proliferation, lost exclusivity.	Moderate brand threat—Lost sales and market share, brand premium unjustified.

Quality

Quality and functionality of the counterfeit product

EXHIBIT 2.5   **Harm Matrix Applied to Brand Threat**

one case, the product went from nearly 100 percent authentic to about 12 percent authentic within a year. Nevertheless, the brand remained relatively strong with about a 30 percent share of the market, but over 80 percent of the brand was counterfeit product. (See Focus 7.1 in Chapter 7) In a second case, counterfeiters moved in when the price of the authentic product was increased. Market share plummeted from 80 percent to 25 percent over a three-year period.

The Harm Matrix introduced in Chapter 1 is a useful tool for explaining where the real threat to brand value lies. The primary factor is consumer deception (see Exhibit 2.5).

In the upper-left cell, a purchaser buys a product of low quality, believing it to be genuine. When it does not function according to expectations,

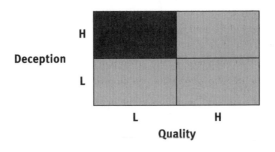

then the purchaser will conclude that the brand has not delivered on its promise. Purchasers who try to get it replaced may well face warranty problems from the legitimate brand holder, thus further diminishing their view of the brand and the service associated with it. If a purchaser is in any way injured by the counterfeit product, then the brand holder may still face liability damages, and almost certainly will face legal costs in attempting to isolate themselves from responsibility. Thus, the threat to the brand comes from several sources. This could be the case with fake auto parts, computer software, or designer apparel.

In the upper-right cell, the brand may also face significant damage, but for different reasons. Because the fake product performs (or delivers benefits) as expected, there will be fewer liability or warranty claims, thus

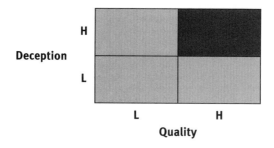

moderating the damage to the brand's reputation and the costs of protecting the same. However, the brand could be hijacked by providing similar benefits at a substantially reduced price. Some counterfeits are becoming quite good in terms of both looks and functionality. Some fake luxury handbags are a good example.

In the lower-right cell of the Harm Matrix, the threat to the brand is more moderate. Now the purchaser is not being deceived into thinking that they have purchased a genuine article. However, since the known

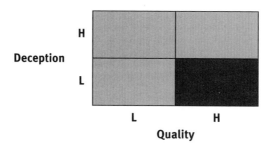

counterfeit delivers basically the same value and functionality as the authentic product, the purchaser may understandably wonder why one would pay the premium price that the brand demands. The fake will certainly be able to undercut the price of the brand for numerous reasons discussed throughout this book. This may be the example of high-quality counterfeit auto parts that perform like their famous branded counterparts. It is also the "no logo" argument that brand premiums are overstated.

Finally, the lower-left cell probably has the lowest threat to the established brand. The purchaser knows they are not buying a genuine article

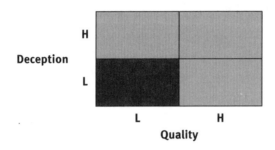

and probably does not expect their article to perform at all like the original. The threat to the brand comes from the fact that counterfeits saturate the market, thus depriving the legitimate brand of whatever exclusive reputation it might have. This is the example of buying the fake Rolex for $50. Why pay $8,000 when it seems that everyone is wearing what appears to be a Rolex (never mind that the many fake ones may not work)? A recent New York Times article confirms, "Designers, department store executives, and luxury goods manufacturers say the reasons for the decline in logos range from a backlash against conspicuous consumption to . . . the erosion of brand names through cheap knockoffs."[20]

The next chapter discusses the many areas where branded goods or services are prevalent. In discussing the threat of counterfeiting, we focus primarily on the luxury good markets.

PART TWO

Product Counterfeiting as a Problem in Specific Industries

A ny consumer strolling down a sidewalk in New York City will quickly become aware of the availability of counterfeit luxury goods, although most consumers don't realize the extent of the problem. Similarly, the average consumer may have some knowledge about counterfeits in the areas of digital media (CDs, DVDs, etc.), where the problem is usually referred to as "pirating."

But there are other areas where the proliferation of counterfeit goods is less well known and, often, extremely damaging—if not fatal. These include pharmaceuticals, automobile and airplane parts, pesticides, children's toys, liquor, and personal care products. Brand owners in all these industries are becoming increasingly aware of the threat that counterfeiting poses to their brands, although many are reluctant to acknowledge the problem publicly. Consumers are often still unaware of the counterfeiting threat in these industries.

CHAPTER 3

Branded and Luxury Goods

LEGITIMACY OF NAME BRANDS

Hey! Nice Rolex watch, Louis Vuitton handbag, Oakley glasses, Saint Emilion wine, Nike shoes, Polo shirt, Chanel perfume — or are they? And more important, do you care? Should you care? While it is often the brand name of luxury goods that is most coveted by counterfeiters, any product or service that has developed value in its brand name may be at risk of having that brand diluted by counterfeiters. How about that John Paul Mitchell shampoo you are using, those Marlboros you are smoking, or the National Football League (NFL) Super Bowl T-shirt you just bought. Are they legit?

THE HARM MATRIX: BRANDED GOODS

The Harm Matrix in Exhibit 3.1 builds on the discussion of brands in Chapter 2. Remember, the matrix combines the *deception* to the purchaser

Deception	**High**	NFL logo clothing	Unauthorized overruns
Level of deception inherent in the sale of the product	**Low**	Very inexpensive Rolex watches	Kate Spade handbags
		Low	**High**

Quality

Quality and functionality
of the counterfeit product

EXHIBIT 3.1 **Harm Matrix for Branded Goods**

as to whether the product is authentic, with the *quality* of the fake relative to the real thing.

Probably the least problematic cell is the lower-left. When the quality is obviously low, and the price is also unusually low for a brand that has

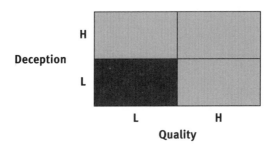

a reputation for both high quality and a price tag to match, the consumer can be quite certain they are not buying the real thing. When someone offers to sell you a Rolex that normally sells for $8,000 for $50, rest assured that you are not getting a great deal. Closer inspection may even reveal that it is a "Rollex" and not a Rolex. But, if you think it makes a great gag gift, and therefore buy 10 for your closest friends, is there really much damage done? You got what you thought you were getting at a price that was acceptable. It is also doubtful that Rolex will lose any current or potential customers because of this fraud. Likewise, their brand name is not likely to suffer much harm when your cheap fake "takes no licking and does stop ticking" after 24 hours. However, the brand may be diluted because of the proliferation of fakes, as mentioned previously.

The other cells in the matrix usually present a problem for someone. Take a look at the upper-left cell where the consumer is unaware they are buying a fake, and the quality is quite low. With the NFL logo T-shirt,

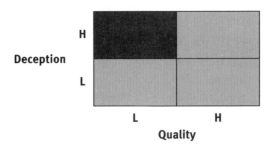

consumers may not know, nor care, that the shirt they bought was not approved by the league. But when it falls apart after a few washings, consumers may have regrets that they manifest toward the NFL. This is a much bigger problem if they buy a knockoff Streamlite Flashlight. When it quits working after a few weeks and they try to return it through normal channels for repair or replacement, there is likely to be a higher level of resentment if they are told by the company or distributor that they do not have a real Streamlite. Here customers have been deceived, and the legitimate producer is likely to be the target of their anger, even though the legitimate producer was not at fault. Finally, what about fake baby shampoo? A private investigator for Personal Care Products Inc. once found some fake baby shampoo. He said, "Look at the gunk in there. It had a bacterial count higher than human feces."[1]

In contrast, in the lower-right cell of the matrix, where the consumer knowingly buys a fake but the quality is good and it bears a strikingly good resemblance to the real thing, the consumer is neither deceived nor

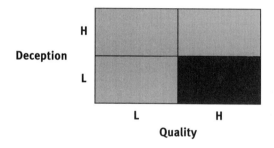

harmed significantly. If the fake is quite good, then customers might be able to have their cake (the snob appeal of a well-known brand) and eat it too (pay a much lower price). It has even been noted that some consumers "openly brag about finding a good fake."[2] But while customers may not suffer much harm in this scenario, the producers certainly do. They are likely to be both losing market share and suffering from a diminished brand name that will negatively impact future sales.

Finally, in the upper-right cell, the consumer is again deceived but ends up buying a high-quality imitation. In fact, in the case of unauthorized overruns, they may be buying the identical item. If consumers buy a pair of Reeboks that are produced by the same company that is licensed to

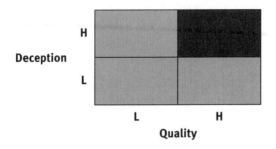

produce Reeboks, then the purchasers will not suffer much harm simply because the shoes came out the back door of the plant and they got them at half the normal price. However, sometimes what comes out the back door are the quality rejects, in which case consumers are being deceived and shortchanged. Even when a woman buys a high-quality knockoff of a luxury handbag, the real damage may be the embarrassment caused when her friends realize it is not the real McCoy, though she thought it was. Getting it repaired, replaced, or refunded will again present a problem. In the example of unauthorized overruns, it is the authorized distributor, and perhaps the local taxing authorities, that are the biggest losers. The winners are the licensed producers and their employees who are not reporting this production and the resulting sales. With good replicas, the right holders, distributors, and consumers are all likely to suffer some hurt.

THE DIVERSITY OF BRANDED GOODS AFFECTED BY COUNTERFEITING

Luxury Goods

Although there are many products that might be considered luxury goods, the most prominent luxury goods being counterfeited include wearing apparel, flat goods, sunglasses, watches, perfumes, and pens. Some of the best-known brands are at the very high price points in each category, but there are also well-known brands at more moderate pricing levels. Likewise, some popular brands have migrated successfully to several different luxury categories. In wearing apparel, one thinks of such well-known brands as Polo, Tommy Hilfiger, Armani, Guess, Nautica, Versace, Escada, Burberry, Calvin Klein, Carolina Herrera, Prada, Benetton and Donna Karan. Flat goods refer to things like handbags, wallets, and luggage. Famous brands in this group might include Louis Vuitton, Gucci, Samsonite, Tumi, Coach, and Kate Spade. Branded sunglasses would include Oakley, Bolle, Vuarnet, and Ray-Ban. Rolex is undoubtedly the highest profile brand in the watch category, but others would include Tag Heur, Swiss Army, Omega, and Seiko. In perfumes and makeup, names like Chanel, Estee Lauder, Lancôme, Bvlgari, L'Oreal, and Maybelline would stand out. Finally, Mont Blanc, Cross, or Sheaffer would be well-known brands of luxury pens. But these are only examples; there are many more in every category.

◗ FOCUS 3.1 ◗

THE COMPETITIVE FASHION INDUSTRY

The fashion industry is competitive in a big way. The competition rages both in style and design of the products and in the board rooms where deals are devised. The biggest conglomerate in this consolidating field is LVMH (which stands for Moet Hennessy Louis Vuitton in reverse). The group controls such other well-known brands as Givenchy, Christian Dior, Tag Heuer, Ebel, and Dom Perignon, plus recent acquisitions like Fendi, Bliss, and Pucci. But it failed to acquire Gucci in 1999 after Gucci's IPO in 1995. Gucci successfully fought off a takeover bid by LVMH by acquiring some premier fashion brands of its own (e.g., Sergio Rossi and Yves Saint Laurent).[3] Later in 1999, conglomerate Pinault-Printemps-Redoute (PPR) bought a controlling interest in Gucci.[4] However, despite acquiring Gucci's roughly 2 billion Euros of cash, PPR had more than three times as much debt.[5]

Gucci is a good example of a company that has successfully migrated to several product lines in luxury accessories and apparel, in part by the brand acquisitions mentioned above. Thus, they are now involved in designing, producing, and distributing many kinds of leather goods, shoes, watches, home accessories, jewelry, ties and scarves, eyewear, fragrances, skin-care products, and ready-to-wear clothing. They distribute their wares through directly owned and operated stores, franchise stores, department stores, and specialty stores. The fashion industry has experienced consolidation by the acquisition of several high fashion brand names by larger conglomerates (e.g., LVMH and PPR), and by expanding some prominent brand names (e.g., Gucci) into a variety of fashion fields.

(continues)

FOCUS 3.1 *(Continued)*

Sometimes the competition in design comes close to the line. In fact, Gucci has experience on both sides of the issue. When Gucci had financial problems in the mid-1990s, there was some speculation that it had received financial assistance from a man (Delfo Zorzi) who himself was alleged to have been involved with fashion counterfeiting.[6] Also, in 2001, a Paris court found that Gucci had illegally copied two shoe designs of Berluti, a luxury shoemaker owned by LVMH,[7] though imitating successful designs of others is apparently not uncommon in the fashion industry. In fact, this may have been a spite suit brought as reprisal for LVMH having lost the takeover battle for Gucci. And don't forget it was a French court finding in favor of a French company.

However, Gucci has won some too. Gucci America's suit against Internet service provider (ISP) Mindspring for trademark infringement was upheld by the courts. The Communications Decency Act normally makes ISPs immune from defamation and other torts caused by their clients' websites, since the ISP is only providing the site, much like someone renting a building to a tenant. However, the court said that this immunity did not apply to trademark infringement. While the ISP may not have to monitor its various websites for content, it will have to take action to remove the site once notified of an infringement.[8]

The fashion industry has also been impacted by economic and political events beyond its control. Since 1996, the majority of Gucci's stock has been publicly traded and new management talent substantially turned around a rather stagnant performance. Sales in 1995 were up 90 percent from 1994, and earnings rose from $6 million to $42 million in the first nine months of that year. But luxury goods producers like Gucci have had a tough time since the 9/11 terrorist attacks and the general downturn in the economy. The increase in counterfeiting activity also has taken its toll. Fashions change quickly, and it used to be that the trendsetters had some leeway between the time they introduced new fashions and the illegal copies arrived. Today, not only are the counterfeits much better but they arrive within days of the introduction of the authentic goods.

Why Do People Knowingly Buy Fake Luxury Goods? Some examples of brand-name counterfeiting in the luxury goods area might be helpful. A *Los Angeles Times* article[9] reported on the counterfeiting of

Kate Spade handbags. While the real bags were retailing for $165 to $500, some women were able to pick them up for $45 each. According to the article, while it used to be tacky to be caught with fake designer merchandise, now it is intentional. It is a badge of honor for beating the system and demonstrating resourcefulness by searching out "good fakes" that were obtained at a substantial savings. Bragging rights go to those who find the best deals, though some still try to pass the fakes off as legit. The attitude of one purchaser was, "This is L.A. It's form above substance." Another said, "If you have a fake Kate Spade, it really doesn't matter as long as you have a label on it."

Another young shopper was quoted as saying, "With a luxury bag, you're bored of it after one season."[10] Why pay the high prices for designer goods (a real Hermes Birkin bag sells for around $5,000) when you can satisfy your desire with a good counterfeit? And the counterfeits are getting better and better. As they become more authentic looking, finding a good "trophy" fake has become something like a shopping merit badge, even for those who can afford to pay full price.

◑ FOCUS 3.2 ◑

WOULD YOU BUY A COUNTERFEIT PRODUCT?

This is an important question because it may help us understand why people do buy counterfeit goods, even when they know they are fakes. In 1997, the Anti-Counterfeiting Group (ACG), headquartered in England, commissioned a survey of public attitudes toward counterfeiting. It was conducted by Market Opinion and Research International (MORI) and is commonly referred to as the MORI study.[11] The ACG felt that before they could successfully educate the public as to the harm caused by counterfeiting, they must first understand how the public regarded this problem.

The survey revealed some very interesting findings. First, almost one-sixth of the nearly 1000 respondents said they were unaware that counterfeit products were being sold in five of the most common categories. These included categories of brand-name merchandise such as perfume, watches, clothing, and footwear. This lack of knowledge was slightly greater for women than for men, and for older respondents compared with younger ones.

(continues)

FOCUS 3.2 *(Continued)*

Forty percent of the respondents said they would knowingly purchase a counterfeit product. Interestingly, 30 percent of those who said they would knowingly purchase fakes also said they were against any kind of counterfeiting. When asked in what product categories they would knowingly buy counterfeits, the three heavily branded categories mentioned above were at the top of the list: clothing/footwear (76 percent), watches (43 percent), and perfume/fragrances (38 percent). Once again, men were more likely than women to knowingly purchase a fake product, as were younger consumers. However, the really startling finding in this study was that wealthy consumers were more likely than poorer consumers to purchase counterfeits, even though they knew they were fakes. In fact, 52 percent of those in the highest income group said they would buy fakes, while only 26 percent of those in the lowest income group would.

The MORI survey also found that younger people were rather unconcerned about the problem of counterfeiting. Only 43 percent of those under 24 were actually against it, and about 30 percent didn't have an opinion. It was also clear that most people (61 percent) were unaware of any link between counterfeiting activity and other illegal activities of organized crime (e.g., drug dealing). Even if people unknowingly purchased a fake item, it was clear that many would not do anything about it. Nearly 30 percent said they would do nothing, while another 18 percent said they wouldn't know what to do or didn't know what they would do. Only about one-fifth said they would contact the police.[12]

Los Angeles has apparently become a major center for this type of counterfeiting in the States. In part, this is the result of several garment manufacturers' relocating overseas, leaving many garment workers looking for work. However, it may also be linked to the economic downturn in Asia, and the need for overseas plants to stay busy. Often, the fake products are imported into the United States without the labels. The fake labels, which are often intentionally misspelled (Kade Spate), are then attached in this country. This makes it more difficult for U.S. Customs to spot the forgeries entering the country.

While some distributors may honestly believe they are dealing with legitimate overruns from the gray market, others go out of their way to avoid detection by using phony names and post office boxes. Companies can choose to fight back using tipsters, investigators, and attorneys. Some have even provided training to police and customs agents so they might be able to spot the fakes more easily. More high-tech weapons are available from a number of companies that offer web-searching capabilities and services that allow brand owners to search the web and identify sites offering infringing or unauthorized products.

Why Have Fake Luxury Goods Become More Prevalent?   There are many reasons why brand counterfeiting has increased rapidly in recent years, and they are discussed throughout this book. Certainly, the rapid development of the electronic marketplace is partly to blame. The title of a 1999 *Wall Street Journal* article says it all: "Sleaze E-Commerce: The Internet Has Become Designer Labels' Worst Enemy." The Counterfeiting Intelligence Bureau (CIB) of the International Chamber of Commerce (ICC) estimated that there may have been as much as $25 billion worth of on-line counterfeit sales in 1999. While it may be difficult to find the street vendors selling fake wares, it is many times more difficult to track cyber vendors who can be located almost anywhere. Plus, once their site is located, they can simply change web addresses and start again.[13]

Few, if any, of the major designers sell their goods on the Internet; neither do they license anyone else to sell on-line. That's why Chanel believes that a "significant portion" of Chanel products being sold at auction on eBay is probably counterfeit. On-line sales of counterfeits are made easier because buyers can't feel or closely examine the merchandise. Of course, as we said before, some buyers won't care if they are getting the real thing if the fake is good enough to fool others. And sometimes, the counterfeited items are good enough to confuse even the legitimate producer. Some websites make no secret that they are selling replicas; however, even replicas infringe on the rights of legitimate trademark holders and therefore may violate trademark laws.

Some of the luxury good manufacturers have dealt with this problem by posting on their website some tips for spotting fakes.[14] For example:

- *www.cartier.com* The watch should have the Cartier signature engraved on the back, along with a serial number in a different typeface.

- *www.chanel.com* There are no authorized dealers on-line.
- *www.coach.com* The quality of the leather is often inferior.
- *www.gucci.com* Every nail should display the Gucci name, and all Gucci bags are made in Italy, so if it says "Made in India" it is a fake.
- *www.vuitton.com* Some counterfeits may use an "LX" logo, which they hope will be confused with the recognizable "LV" symbol used on real Louis Vuitton products.
- *www.tommypr.com* Tommy Hilfiger doesn't make watches, so any being advertised on-line are obviously fakes.

It is not clear how effective these hints are in reducing on-line counterfeiting. Some customers may not take the time to check, and some may not care.

When Is a Fake a Fake? Italian police traced some bogus handbags to a small factory in Tuscany that was legally licensed to make them for JP Tod's. Giuseppe Corasaniti, a former prosecutor in Rome, speculated that "This is the future of counterfeiting—the 'true fake'." Likewise, an employee at Ferragamo revealed that "We've found instances in our workshops where they've made 1,000 pairs of shoes for us and maybe about 100 have gone somewhere else."[15] These are still counterfeits by our definition, even though they are the authentic product produced by an authorized producer. But they are unauthorized overruns that enter the distribution system through unauthorized and clandestine channels. The damage to the right holder can be just as devastating. It undercuts the authorized distributors and may still damage the brand by making the official price suspect. The taxing authorities also lose.

Liquor and Tobacco Products

Producers of liquor and cigarettes have invested huge sums into building their brands. Allegiance to a particular brand is important in an industry selling products that many consumers might otherwise consider to be commodities. Brand names from these two industries that were among the Interbrand 2002 Top 100 most valuable labels included: Marlboro (number 9), Budweiser (number 24), Bacardi (number 78), Smirnoff (number 84), Moet & Chandon (number 87), Heineken (number 88), Johnnie

Walker (number 97), and Jack Daniels (number 98). However, there are several further down the list with very valuable brand names. Guinness, for example, fell out of the top 100 after being number 73 two years earlier.

In their pamphlet "The Menace of Counterfeiting," the Anti-Counterfeiting Group (ACG) shows a picture of two bottles of Ballantine's Finest Scotch Whiskey. The counterfeit is difficult to spot (even to the finely trained eye). The caption says that the fake bottle was found in the Czech Republic and notes that "Everything is counterfeit: the bottle, the closure, the label, and, of course, the contents."[16]

The Rioja region of Spain has developed a deservedly good reputation for their wine, due in part to the tempranillo grape which is a varietal native to that region. In 1999, a Briton was arrested for shipping 30,000 bottles of cheap table wine labeled as Rioja wine. In the same year, counterfeiters in Barcelona were arrested for using fake labels to falsely sell more than $1,000,000 worth of wine as Rioja. It has become more popular to try and counterfeit Rioja wine as it has increased in price. In October 2000, the Rioja winemakers began adding a small metallicized strip to the labels of some of their wines. The strip, which is difficult to simulate, assures the appellation and authenticity of the wine. While it was apparently the first such antifraud device used for wine in the world, there has now been interest in the device from winemakers outside of Spain.[17]

Cuba has always been known for the cream of the crop when it comes to cigars. In 1962 President John F. Kennedy imposed an embargo on Cuban goods and ever since Cuban cigars have taken on an even greater mystique, at least for American connoisseurs. It is the old "supply and demand" thing—that which you can't have, you want even more than before. So, prices go up. A box of 25 Cohibas or Romeo y Julietas will probably sell for $40 to $300 in Cuba, but in the United States that same box can easily bring $250 to $1,000 on the black market.[18] And when brands begin to demand those kinds of premiums, then the counterfeiters will not be far behind. In fact, the hard part is probably counterfeiting the boxes and labels. Most people would not otherwise know a White Owl from a Monte Christo.

Counterfeits are threatening Cuba's most prestigious industry. They are made right in Cuba from poor quality tobacco or even floor sweepings from famous cigar factories, packaged in stolen rings and boxes, and distributed through street vendors. The state has a monopoly on the purchase of tobacco. Being caught with black market tobacco can bring heavy fines (equivalent to seven months' pay). Likewise, tourists leaving Cuba with more than 50 cigars must have an official receipt ("factura") which indicates their name, country, passport number, when and where purchased, and even the name of the sales person. Without the official document they won't be leaving with their cigars.[19]

Other Food and Beverage Products

Branding has entered the food and beverage industries in a big way, in part to distinguish particular producers in products that are often considered commodities. It is somewhat amazing what products are being branded. An article in the *Denver Post*[20] describes the increase in, would you believe, "designer beef?" While chicken parts (Perdue) as well as turkeys (Butterball), began being branded several years ago, beef had still been treated more like a commodity. It is estimated that only about 4 to 8 percent of beef is currently sold under brands such as Certified Angus Beef, Laura's Lean, and Oregon Country Beef. The Oregon Cattleman's Association is planning to launch a new brand called Oregon Trail Beef. As the brand increases its contribution margin, it will be more attractive to counterfeiters.

Several significant brands of coffee have existed for years—Maxwell House, Folgers, and Nescafe, to name a few. However, these brands developed primarily around whole or ground coffee beans. Starbucks has taken branding in the coffee business to a whole new level by selling prepared coffee in their retail stores. As we mentioned in the previous chapter, Starbucks had the greatest percentage increase in brand value from 2000 to 2001 of all the brands measured by Interbrand. Because Starbucks is selling coffee directly to consumers, it is difficult to counterfeit. That was not the case with Kona coffee from Hawaii, which some very serious coffee drinkers consider to be the champagne of coffees. The Kona coffee that a Berkley man was passing on to wholesalers came from Costa Rica, not the "big island," so he did two and a half years in the "big house."[21]

Popcorn is another food item where branding has taken hold. Is there really a difference in popcorn? Orville Redenbacher thinks so, and he has convinced many consumers that he is right.

Personal Care Products

The whole personal care set of products have been a major target for counterfeiters. Often, they need only to replicate the packaging or labels. In 1997, John Paul Mitchell was tipped off that there was a problem with their shampoo. A man approached the bottle printer that makes the labels for Mitchell products and attempted to get bottles with the Mitchell logo printed on them. The printer then tipped off the company, and the private investigator they hired eventually tracked down the counterfeiter and much of the fake product. However, he had previously sold an estimated million dollars worth of fake Mitchell products, for which he was sentenced to 16 months in prison. He also had to pay just over $40,000 in compensatory costs, but that means he took in about $60,000 for each month in prison—not a bad salary for most people.[22]

◖ FOCUS 3.3 ◗

PROCTER AND GAMBLE

Procter and Gamble (P&G) is a company that oversees a portfolio of at least 300 individual brands. They include names such as Tide, Pampers, Olay, Crest, Pantene, Vicks, Pringles, and numerous other household and personal care items. P&G has operations in 70 countries and sells its products in twice that many. With 5 billion consumers, 110,000 employees, and net sales of more than $40 billion, it is a giant in its industry (or perhaps we should say industries).

P&G has been hard hit by counterfeiters across the globe. They have estimated losses due to product counterfeiting at $500,000,000 annually, $300 million in China alone. According to Walter Clements, Associate Director of their Global Security Services, "losses due to customer dissatisfaction, loss of customer loyalty, and loss of sales due to public health issues are beyond calculation." However, P&G hasn't stuck its head in the sand and pretended there is no problem. They spend over $5 million each year to fight global counterfeiting.[23] They have organized internally to address the problem. (For more on this as a strategy see Chapter 9.) A Corporate Steering Team includes the CEO, while anticounterfeiting efforts are directed by a Vice President. The effort is further supported by a corporate "core team" of specialists drawn from various

(continues)

FOCUS 3.3 (Continued)

functional areas of the organization (legal, sales, security, etc.). In addition, there are four regionally based anticounterfeiting teams.

P&G's strategy for combating counterfeiting is multifaceted. They utilize investigators to focus on the large manufacturers and wholesalers that are repeat offenders. Through their Government Relations Office, they elicit government support. They help to train foreign police personnel to better support efforts within their own countries. Marking technologies for products and packaging are utilized, as are publicity campaigns to alert the public to problems and indicate "certified shops" where they can be sure they are getting the authentic products. These tactics have resulted in many successes in many countries; counterfeit products, packages, and labels have been seized, as have machinery and equipment for producing fakes. Many of the counterfeiters themselves have been arrested, prosecuted, and convicted.

For example, in 2000 they seized 800 cases of counterfeit (and contaminated) Vicks Vaporub in Puerto Rico. The containers had been made in California and the labels in Miami.[24] Similarly, counterfeit and contaminated Head and Shoulders shampoo was found in New Jersey; it had been produced in Canada. Fake Head and Shoulders product, bottles, and labels were also discovered in a London raid. Equally disturbing was the fact that two other investigations were finding links between counterfeit P&G products and terrorist groups. However, P&G's anticounterfeiting efforts produced several other successes in 2000 involving raids and seizures in Russia, Mexico, Poland, Colombia, Ukraine, Peru, Estonia, and Venezuela.

Individual Brands

Many famous people have created their own brands. Take Michael Jordan; he is perhaps the most successful brand among all-time sports figures, and perhaps one of the most successful individual brands ever. Those fortunate enough to do much international traveling would, no doubt, like to have a dollar for every time they have seen some young kid in a Chicago Bull's shirt or hat with Michael's name on it. In some of the most unlikely places—from Cuba to Croatia, Sri Lanka to Sweden, Italy to Indonesia, or the Ukraine to the United Kingdom—Michael is still a known brand. Talk about appealing to a variety of cultures; this is what we identified as "brand length" in Chapter 2.

Sports memorabilia, which is really an extension of the individual, is being faked. This usually involves autographs or autographed memorabilia. You may not think of this as infringement on a brand, but it really is. A sports hero's name is his or her brand. Names are fairly easily faked, and again Internet sales have made this a growing and lucrative business. There was a funny story reported about San Diego Padre's slugger Tony Gwynn. When he arrived for a special appearance at an official Padre's gift shop, he realized that the items in the front window with his autograph were all fakes. Hardly seems worth the risk until you realize that a baseball with Mark McGuire's signature on it could fetch $200 at one time. Barry Bonds no doubt brings an even higher price today. Dealers in autographed goods often buy them from third-party distributors. They may even come with Certificates of Authentication, which have also been faked. This more elongated supply chain makes it almost impossible to know which autographs are authentic, unless the star signed it for you in person.[25]

Of course, many other sports figures could be considered brands (e.g., Tiger Woods), though many are rather fleeting, and it may be tougher to sustain and "grow" these brands as the sports hero's fame begins to fade. However, there are other examples of individual brands outside of the sports arenas. Look at Martha Stewart (in home decorations), Madonna (in entertainment), Ralph Lauren (in fashion), or Oprah Winfrey (in a variety of fields). Britney Spears achieved the top spot in the annual Forbes Celebrity 100 List for 2002. But, can she continue to selectively build her own brand, or like the Spice Girls, will she end up overmarketing herself?[26]

Athletic Teams

Aside from individual sports heroes, entire sport teams have created very successful brands. And, they have been able to parlay that brand name into sales of all sorts of clothing, equipment, and other souvenir items. Most professional teams have brand recognition and loyalty in their own local area or region. However, some teams have been able to develop a broader following, due to their success over some longer period of time.

Good examples would probably include the New York Yankees (United States—baseball), Manchester United (England—soccer), or The All Blacks (New Zealand—rugby). And don't think these brands are not subject to counterfeiting. In operation "Dream Team," Irish Customs seized more than $60,000 worth of counterfeit football jerseys being sent from Thailand; they used the names of famous teams like Manchester United, Inter Milan, and Liverpool.[27]

Services

Even service companies must be concerned about their brand. INVESCO Funds sells mutual funds, among other products and services. Part of their trademark, and therefore their brand, is the marketing slogan "You should know what INVESCO knows." Then another company in the industry published an advertisement with the slogan "You should know what [Co. X's] clients know." INVESCO considered this a clear attempt to capitalize on the value they had created in their brand. According to INVESCO, the INVESCO brand is positioned in the marketplace with a specific set of attributes that represent who they are, what they do, and how they do it. It is their position that if others "borrow" INVESCO's brand equity, they can only confuse the public with mixed messages, and eventually harm their brand investment. The American Express Company had a similar problem with a company that chose the name American Express Limousine Service, Ltd.

Industrial Products

While branding certainly got its start in the consumer goods arena, it has now transferred to some industrial products as well. *Business Week* (August 6, 2001) has a great story about the new head of Boeing's marketing and public relations department, when she took over in 1999. After referring to the brand, she was apparently chastised by another executive who cautioned her that "we aren't a consumer-goods company, and we don't have a brand."[28] Of course, that was then. Now they have developed a brand strategy so that they might try and migrate the brand beyond commercial airplanes. The IBM brand is another that has transferred quite successfully between consumer and industrial products. For purchasers of industrial products, like purchasers of consumer products, the brand represents quality and service for which one is often willing to pay a premium price.

Colleges and Universities

In academia, the benefit of "naming" certain units is not unrelated to branding. For some of the more prestigious universities (e.g., Harvard, Yale, Princeton, or Stanford) the university's name is the brand. Even so, for those schools or others, there is often an attempt to create a brand by tying the name of a particular college to a well-known person that embodies the values of the unit and thus creates a brand. Examples might include the Woodrow Wilson School of Public Affairs at Princeton, or the Kennedy School at Harvard. Many of the top business schools in the country are named (read branded) schools—Tuck (Dartmouth), Darden (Virginia), Weatherhead (Case Western Reserve), Kellogg (Northwestern), Sloan (MIT), Cox (SMU), Babcock (Wake Forest), Fuqua (Duke), Stern (NYU), Wharton (Pennsylvania), and many more. At the University of Denver, The Daniels College of Business was named several years ago after Bill Daniels, a pioneer of cable, as it was felt that his values of integrity, professionalism, and social responsibility were values that the college wanted to characterize their programs. Thus, the Daniels brand.

Pharmaceuticals

As pharmaceutical companies have become freer to market directly to consumers, they have begun relying more on brands to carry their message. Thus, Viagra or Lexium or Lipitor or Prozac or Claritan. Of course, the producers of aspirin have for years tried to differentiate an otherwise fairly similar compound by branding their products (e.g., Bayer). Counterfeiting of these products has become very big business that will be discussed in detail in Chapter 4.

WHO PAYS FOR BRAND-NAME COUNTERFEITING?

One of the reasons for the rather indifferent attitude toward brand-name counterfeiting on the part of the public is either that they are unaware of the costs or the fact that there is not a huge downside to the average consumer. If you are a woman who buys a Gucci purse, only to find out later it is a fake, why should you care? If it is a good fake then you get the "snob benefit" of owning a "Gucci" without having paid the going rate for it. If something goes wrong with it, the worst that can happen is that an official distributor will refuse to make it right. Another downside is having your friends realize it is a fake, when you didn't. In this case the "snob benefit" is replaced by the "schmuck factor" and someone loses a little face. Of course, as mentioned earlier, if you have intentionally found a good fake at a good price, that may earn you the "shopper's badge of honor" in some circles. Thus, most consumers are not too concerned about the counterfeiting of luxury goods.

If not the consumer, then who should worry? The owner of the brand should worry. The implied contract that the brand represents between the right holder and the consumer can be irreparably damaged. When the Louis Vuitton bag falls apart, the Chanel perfume indeed has a distinctive smell (though not a good one), or the Seiko watch begins losing time, and the official manufacturer won't honor the warranty (because they say it isn't their product), there are some serious customer relations costs incurred. A Reuters story on Gillette quoted Ed DeGraan, the acting CEO at the time, as saying that losses from counterfeit products "literally run into the tens of millions of dollars" and that they also threaten the company's promise "to sell the same product with the same quality anywhere in the world."[29] Officially licensed producers and distributors will also be hurt because a significant portion of their sales, revenues, and market share will be drained off by the counterfeiters. Of course, these latter two could be part of the problem. They could be running unauthorized production out the back door, or bringing known counterfeits in the front door.

The other losers with counterfeited luxury goods will be the government taxing authorities—local, state, or national. Collection of both sales taxes and excise taxes will be less than they should be because of the counterfeiting activity. Income taxes may be affected as well, if the illegal producers are paying their employees in cash under the table so as not to leave a road map to their operation.

In addition, society in general is impacted by the known links between counterfeiters and organized crime. A recent *Forbes* article stated, "The Russian mob has become a force in video piracy, and Chinese triads have become heavily involved in counterfeit software. The former leader of the Vietnamese gang Born to Kill boasted of making $13 million off counterfeit watches before he was jailed for murder."[30] More on the losers (and winners) from counterfeiting will be discussed in Chapter 7.

THE GROWTH OF BRAND-NAME COUNTERFEITING

The problem has accelerated as brands have become more global, and thus more valuable. It was noted earlier that most of the more valuable brands are American-owned. We have noted that many consumers are willing to pay a premium price for reputable brands, either because of the implied quality or because others will know that they can afford to buy "the best," (or at least the best-known). As brands (particularly American brands) have become more globally accepted, you can add to these reasons the fact that many consumers abroad want a piece of America, as represented by those well-known brands. To smoke a Marlboro may let smokers, if even for a brief moment, perceive themselves as part of the romantic American West, as portrayed in the advertising. Smoking the local brand isn't quite the same. Similar benefits accrue from drinking a Coors, wearing a Chicago Bulls T-shirt or Nike basketball shoes, driving a Ford, or showing off your kid's Barbie doll.

Of course, the same value attaches to well-known foreign brands for American consumers. It is the old "grass is greener over there" syndrome. We fantasize the best about some foreign things. Though foreign villages may seem dilapidated and void of modern conveniences, to Americans they are "quaint." To someone stuck in Cairo traffic for hours, a Mercedes may seem to come up short when compared to riding a horse through the American West. Thus, while others want a part of the United States, American consumers have similar desires for an Irish Guinness, a German BMW, or a Swiss watch.

SOURCES OF COUNTERFEIT BRANDED GOODS

The increases in technology have made it increasingly easy and cheap to produce extremely good look-alikes, particularly when it comes to logos, labels, and packages. With branded goods that is often good enough, since it may be impossible to examine the actual product for authenticity. How would you know if it were really Bordeaux wine in that bottle, or Lancôme makeup in the case, or Chanel perfume in that bottle, or Gillette blades in the dispenser? With garments, shoes, or handbags it may be somewhat easier to examine the goods, but chances are, if it looks like a Gucci, and feels like a Gucci, then it must be a Gucci. Of course, as mentioned earlier, Internet sales may have removed this advantage as well.

Many counterfeit branded goods come from East Asia, particularly China, Korea, Taiwan, and Thailand. Since there are already licensed producers in those countries, the technology and know-how have already been transferred. Once they know how to do it, it may not take long for them to realize that their newfound expertise will have a much greater payoff in the production of counterfeits than in producing authentic goods. Then they find a contact (often a relative), to serve as the importer and outlet for these goods in the United States or other more developed markets. For example, several years ago a shopkeeper in Boulder, Colorado, was selling Chanel and Louis Vuitton purses and luggage at very low prices. This attracted attention from U.S. Customs. Their investigation found that these European brand-name goods had not been imported from Paris, but rather from Korea. After checking, they also found that this store was not an authorized dealer for either brand. After obtaining search warrants, receipts were discovered that indicated the phony goods had been shipped to the store's owner by relatives in Korea. Conviction on these charges could have resulted in a five-year prison term and a fine of up to $250,000.[31]

However, as noted in a *Forbes* article, "Paying fines is just part of the counterfeiter's cost of doing business. On the rare occasions when a case makes it to criminal court, the counterfeiter seldom ends up in prison and rarely forfeits assets."[32] Furthermore, counterfeiters can minimize their costs further by leasing their cars and production equipment, using offshore accounts and legitimate businesses, and buying houses in a relative's name. That is why counterfeiting is considered by many as a nearly risk-free crime.

China

Despite efforts by the Chinese government, the People's Republic of China (PRC) remains one of the largest sources of counterfeit goods. In part, this is due to its sheer size, in addition to the influx of new technologies, as the Chinese economy has increasingly become more open to foreign investment. Even the Chinese government realizes that it has a serious problem. The conclusion, in the first officially sponsored study by the State Council, was that the country was "drowning in counterfeits." The report was initially released only to local media; the intentional delay to outside news sources resulted from the World Trade Organization (WTO) negotiations. It claimed that $16 billion worth of counterfeit goods were produced in 1998 alone.[33] China is the center of counterfeiting for export. Therefore, brand holders must be concerned with more than the loss of market share in China; the impact on other markets, even the home market, can be devastating. In 1998, U.S. Customs seized about $30 million worth of counterfeit products made in China. When you realize that Customs actually inspects only about 2 percent of the goods coming into the United States, you begin to appreciate how much bigger the problem is.[34]

Yiwu is a city about five hours from Shanghai; it has been described as China's "counterfeit central." Among the counterfeit brands being sold in the markets of Yiwu and other Chinese cities were Gillette razor blades, Safeguard soap, Skippy peanut butter, Kotex feminine care products, Budweiser beer, Microsoft software, Duracell batteries, Yamaha motorcycles, Oakley sunglasses, Marlboro cigarettes, and Tide detergent. It was even discovered that they were assembling fake Audis from spare parts. And that is a very small sampling of the brands being knocked off in China. In many cases, the consumers were convinced they were buying the real thing at very good prices; a 10-pack of fake Gillette blades was selling for 65 cents, whereas a 10-pack of the authentic blades went for $9.60.[35] Serious damage to the brand results when consumers find the fakes less than satisfactory, regardless of the price. Some of the major brand owners have estimated that as much as 30 percent of their products in mainland China are fakes. That's a lot of unhappy consumers.

Why China? As multinationals rushed to enter the huge Chinese market, many legitimate Chinese enterprises became licensed producers of famous brand-name goods. The technology and know-how was transferred. When the sale of local brands began to fall, it became irresistible to many to instead use their excess production capacity to imitate the more famous global brands.

This became particularly easy with the ability to duplicate labels and packaging that was nearly identical to the authentic brands. In 1997, an investigator who posed as a garment dealer was given a quote of $17.80 per thousand fake labels for brands such as Nike and Guess.[36] That is less than two cents a label. Disney labels were closer to five cents each at the time. More upscale gold logos that can be attached to designer purses might go for as much as 30 cents apiece, but that is a pretty good deal, if it can than be stuck on a cheap replica and sold for a significantly higher price. Once you have the label, you are more than halfway home. For example, a fake Prada handbag purchased by a vendor for $60 could easily be sold for $100. After all, the real thing sells for nearly $1,000. The fake labels also make it easy to bypass problems with Customs. Generic handbags, for example, can easily be imported without question. Then the labels and logos can be affixed, once they are in this country.[37]

The technology to make high-quality fake labels and logos is relatively cheap. Computerized embroidery machines can make excellent replicas on almost any kind of fabric. A single-head embroidery machine can be purchased for as little as $3,000, and it is small enough to carry in a suitcase. Larger machines (12- or 18-head) can obviously pump out fake logos at a much higher rate. An electronic scanner is used to get an initial image of the logo, which is then transferred to the computerized embroidery machine. These so-called "cyber-fakes" are fast, cheap, and difficult to detect because of their high quality.[38]

Furthermore, global supply chains have become increasingly fragmented and indirect. It is, therefore, relatively easy to blend fake product with legitimate product in the gray market, or to find unauthorized dealers over the Internet. Finally, organized crime has been a ready source of financing for some of these operations.

The Chinese government took a tough stance against smugglers bringing legitimate products into the country. They were much more lax in their enforcement of counterfeiting within the country. After all, these bogus producers provided many jobs. And sometimes the producers of fake goods in China are state-run enterprises. China's recent entry into the World Trade Organization may provide a framework and incentive that will allow the central government in Beijing to take a tougher stance. (See Focus 13.1 in Chapter 13.) Likewise, as the government becomes aware of the taxes it is failing to collect from many counterfeiters, they have a vested interest to become more proactive.

Italy

Of course, some merchandise ends up with street vendors rather than more legitimate-looking retail shops. An October 2000 article in the *Los Angeles Times* reported on the influx of immigrants selling fake designer label products on the streets in the heart of Rome's high fashion district. This is particularly damaging in a country that is synonymous with high fashion. The street vendors are quite mobile, selling only what they can carry, and relying on their cell phones for quick resupply. While some may think of counterfeiting as "high risk, high reward," it is really "low risk, high reward." One particular African vendor intimated that when caught, he only loses the merchandise he is carrying. Furthermore, whatever the fine, "he always claims to be broke, doesn't pay, never stays long in jail and is never expelled from the country."[39]

WHAT CAN BRAND OWNERS DO TO FIGHT COUNTERFEITING?

We have already mentioned a few steps that brand owners have taken to hopefully reduce the impact of counterfeiting on their brands. For example, we noted that several luxury brand holders attempted to educate the public by putting tips on their websites for spotting fake merchandise. This assumes that consumers check the websites and that they care whether their purchases are fakes.

Some others, like Gillette, have conducted or participated in raids to confiscate fake products. This probably requires the cooperation, or at least tacit approval, of the local authorities. Gillette claims to have captured tens of millions of fakes in nearly 100 raids on Chinese producers. The fake products acquired may be helpful in supporting further legal action against those illicit producers.

Others use private investigators to locate the source of illegal production, or the distribution channels being used to bring the fakes to market. Others will take legal action. However, it is time-consuming, costly, and difficult to bring legal action in a foreign country. And even if you win, it may be particularly difficult to obtain relief by enforcing any awards granted by the courts. Even in the United States, the courts are not automatically going to find for American producers. In the late 1980s, Samsonite Corporation, a producer of hard-sided luggage, lost an important case before the International Trade Commission in Washington. Samsonite had claimed that four Taiwanese manufacturers had copied its "Silhouette" line of luggage. However, the administrative law judge found that the Taiwanese companies did not violate the Samsonite trademark because the latter's design and utility patents had expired. He further noted that the design was "incapable of becoming a trademark" since it was determined by its function.[40]

Some brand owners attempt to better educate law enforcement officers and U.S. Customs officials, so that they might be more effective in recognizing and confiscating counterfeits. In 1998, the United States Customs Service seized about $76 million worth of counterfeit products. However, for the first half of 2002, the figure was only $26 million. Nevertheless, in reality, these figures no doubt represent a very small fraction of the fake goods that are imported.

Some brand owners have found strength in numbers. In 1998, a group of 27 producers of branded consumer products formed the China Anti-Counterfeiting Coalition (CACC). This group is now called the Quality Brands Protection Committee and includes some very prominent brands, including Coca-Cola, Dell, Johnson & Johnson, Nike, and Procter & Gamble. This group has worked with the Chinese government to discuss the problem and to make recommendations for remedies. They are also concerned that serious injuries from counterfeit products were up 80 percent in a year, while permanent injury and deaths from counterfeits increased 100 percent and 73 percent respectively in the same year. Similarly, their market shares have plummeted in some cases. In their *Report on Counterfeiting in the People's Republic of China* (December 1999) the group made four recommendations:

1. To increase the central government's power over local authorities who may have reasons to be less enthusiastic in enforcing regulations against counterfeiting. This would also entail a strengthening of anticorruption laws.

2. To enact a unified and comprehensive law that would clarify the definition of counterfeiting and the jurisdictional confusion

between the administrative and judicial arms of government. It would also increase the penalties for counterfeiting and require the destruction of counterfeit products and the equipment used to produce them.

3. To designate a high-level central body to develop policy and oversee the implementation of the law and its enforcement.

4. To enhance the current enforcement system by increasing resources. In addition, they proposed that the counterfeiters pay restitution to the victims and also pay enforcement costs, plus strengthen export controls.

Brand owners may be successful in getting lawmakers to treat this crime more seriously. However, this may be difficult, given the public attitudes previously discussed, or the low priority given by law enforcement to counterfeiting relative to other crimes. But, at least 15 states have passed laws that make counterfeiting a felony, as opposed to a misdemeanor. For example, Georgia recently passed such a law that makes it possible to seize property from convicted counterfeiters, including their equipment, cars, and homes. By increasing the costs to counterfeiters, it alters the cost-benefit ratio in a way that may make it somewhat more difficult to jump back into business under nothing more than a new name. President Clinton also signed a tough federal law in July 1996. Known as the "Knock Out the Knock-Offs Act," it made counterfeiting a RICO (Racketeer-Influenced and Corrupt Organizations Act) offense and increased jail time, fines, and forfeiture of assets including production equipment. It also provided for civil penalties that were linked to the value of the authentic goods, all of which again raises the costs to counterfeiters.

There are also a number of new authentication technologies available today to help protect brands. These will be discussed in more detail in the latter chapters of the book, particularly Chapter 12. But first, the next chapter will discuss an industry where counterfeiting can have harmful, or ineffective, health consequences for consumers. In the worst cases, the consequences have been lethal. Fake pharmaceuticals can be far more damaging than fake designer labels to consumers. For brand owners, both can be very damaging.

CHAPTER 4

Pharmaceuticals

FROM SYMPTOM TO DIAGNOSIS AND CURE?

Pharmaceuticals are probably the most closely regulated and quality-assured product in modern society. The world's leading pharmaceutical companies spend on average $802 million researching and qualifying new drugs as human medicines. Of every 5,000 compounds tested, only one will ever be approved for human use. Drug companies around the world devote billions of dollars and commit thousands of scientists to ensuring that these vital products meet Good Manufacturing Practice (GMP) standards for quality. In addition, governments devote thousands of inspectors and regulators to ensuring that these companies are meeting their obligations.

The chilling reality is that intersecting with this global pharmaceutical system are criminals producing fake "medicines" that look like the real thing but are not! The fakes under discussion here are not real products produced by generic manufacturers and are not pirate medicines, produced in violation of patents. Counterfeit pharmaceuticals refer to materials of unknown origin, which may, or may not, contain any medicinal material. The U.S. Food, Drug and Cosmetic Act defines a counterfeit drug as: "A drug which, or the container or labeling of which, without authorization, bears the trademark, trade name, or other identifying mark . . . of a drug manufacturer . . . other than the person . . . who in fact manufactured, processed, packed, or distributed such drug."[1]

Criminals are creating these fakes or repackaging expired, or less potent, real products and are inserting them into existing and developing distribution chains for distribution by pharmacists and for use by doctors and patients.

CHECKING VITALS: A TERRIBLE TRIAGE

The idea of fake medicines is so far from most peoples' experience that it is useful to look at actual cases that illustrate the problem, and the great harm that it causes. The following three cases show the potential harm that can be caused by counterfeiting medicines.

Sinister Serostim

Kelly Burke, a young woman living in San Diego, California, developed AIDS when she was given HIV-contaminated blood in a transfusion. As a part of her treatment to prevent physical deterioration, doctors prescribed a powerful growth hormone, Serostim, approved by the FDA as an "AIDS-wasting" therapy. This is a relatively new product developed by Serono, one of the world's leading biotech companies. In 2000, Kelly was given a prescription for the product and told to give herself injections with the medicine. Unfortunately, some of the medicine she obtained was fake. It contained no active ingredients and actually caused her to develop a rash.

Criminals who were not connected with the legitimate manufacturer, Serono, had somehow managed to slip worthless fakes into the U.S. pharmaceutical supply. Ultimately, this is what Kelly bought from her local pharmacy. The fakes looked almost indistinguishable from the real product. Based on this and other incidents, Serono and the U.S. Food and Drug Administration (FDA) announced a recall of certain lots of Serostim on January 22, 2001, followed by additional recalls on May 17, 2001 and May 16, 2002.[2]

Where did the fakes come from? How did they get into the U.S. drug supply chain? Why didn't somebody catch the problem earlier? The answers to these questions are not entirely clear, and criminal investigations are still ongoing. However, there are weaknesses in the drug distribution chain that allowed these fakes into the system. Indeed, an unrelated case, but one also involving Serostim illustrates the point.

Serostim is sought after by bodybuilders including professional baseball players because it is so effective at building muscle mass. It has been known to command as much as $21,000 per box on the street, 12 times the retail price of $1,700 per box.[3] Obviously, there is the potential for huge profits for counterfeiters at massive costs to the legitimate manufacturer and the consumer.

Kelly, and at least one other plaintiff that received and used the fake Serostim, sued Serono, Cardinal, McKesson, Chronomed, the Pharmacy of Berkeley and others. Plaintiffs claim that the manufacturer and distributors should have taken more care to use security markings on the products and should have taken more care in securing the distribution of the product, given the black market abuse in the product.[4] Serono has since added security holograms to help authenticate Serostim. The parties settled out of court in early 2002 for an undisclosed amount.

The Serostim case is not, by any means, the only one of its kind. In the period from January 2001 to July 2002, at least eight cases of counterfeit high-value biotech and pharmaceutical products were identified by the FDA: Serostim (somatropin [rDNA origin], Serono), Neupogen (filgrastime, Amgen); Epogen (epoetin alfa, Amgen), Combivir (lamivudine plus zidovudine, GlaxoSmithKline), Zyprexa (aloanzapine, Eli Lilly), Nutropin AQ (somatropin [rDNA origin], Genentech), Procrit (epoetin alfa, Johnson & Johnson/Ortho), and Gamimune (Immune Globulin, Bayer). On July 9, 2002, the FDA Senior Associate Commissioner for Policy, Planning and Legislation, William Hubbard, told Congress that the agency had opened 55 counterfeiting cases between October 1998 and June 2002. Of those, 16 were opened in 2002 alone, with 12 arrests and seven convictions.[5]

Fake Artesunate

Malaria is a deadly tropical disease that afflicts some 300 million people around the world. Each year 1 to 1.5 million people die from the infectious plasmodium parasite carried by the anopheles gambis mosquito. Treatments are available. Of the treatments available, Artesunate is one of the most effective.

While selling at only a fraction of the cost of Serostim, Artesunate is also a target of counterfeiters. Criminals have discovered that public health authorities and the individual patient can be duped into buying look-alike products, even though they contain little or no active medication.

Research by Drs. Nicholas White and Paul Newton of Mahidol University, Thailand, found that up to 33 percent of the Artesunate being sold in Cambodia, Thailand, and Vietnam contained no active ingredients. White and Newton purchased blister packs of the product from 104 shops in 2001 and analyzed their contents. Some of the fake Artesunate contained chloroquine, which is a useless antimalarial drug in Southeast Asia. Apparently, it was added to give a bitter taste to the tablets in order to fool patients. Antimalarials are expected to be bitter (from earlier quinine and chloroquine use). In the June 19, 2001 issue of the *Lancet*,[6] White and Newton reported finding several different types of counterfeits. Some could be identified by the absence of holograms on the packaging and some by the absence of the "AS" logo on the tablets themselves. They also pointed out that fake Guilin Pharma (one brand) cost only 40 percent of the cost of the real medicine.[7]

In a companion study performed in Nigeria, also published in the same issue of the *Lancet*, Professor Taylor, from Robert Gordon University in Scotland, analyzed 581 samples that were supposed to contain one of 27 different medicines. He found that 48 percent of the samples were defective, and many contained no active ingredients at all.[8]

Bulk Gentamicin

The preceding two examples concern counterfeit dosage or finished form pharmaceuticals. In these cases, the criminal actor is aware that his "handiwork" is going to reach patients. There are also instances where the criminal counterfeiting act takes place upstream at the raw product level. The bulk active pharmaceutical ingredient (API) or excipients (the inactive materials) may be substituted or faked, putting the dosage form manufacturer in the position of using defective ingredients, but possibly not knowingly producing a fake finished form product.

The bulk Gentamicin case illustrates this type of counterfeiting. It was the first pharmaceutical counterfeiting case to catch the attention of U.S. Congressional investigators in 2000. Gentamicin is a powerful intravenous antibiotic. From 1989 until August 1994, the FDA identified 1,974 adverse reactions (including 49 deaths) associated with the use of Gentamicin. The "vast majority" of these were linked to formulations in which the bulk APIs were alleged to have been manufactured by Long March Pharmaceuticals of Sichuan, China.[9]

The fraud actually took place in the supply chain. A number of Long March's products were, in turn, identified as part of a complex international counterfeiting scheme. A criminal investigation found that international bulk drug brokers, including Flavine International, were falsifying records, substituting products, and repackaging drugs for sale to the U.S. pharmaceutical industry. In 1996, Flavine pleaded guilty and, as part of its plea agreement, described how the counterfeit API trade functioned, with layers of middlemen working to hide the actual source of the product. It also paid nearly $1 million in fines, and key management personnel were sent to prison.

Adverse reactions to Gentamicin continued to be reported, however, and in 1998 and 1999, both Fujisawa and ESI Lederle voluntarily recalled batches made from Long March bulk APIs. From May 1, 1999 to January 11, 2000, 254 adverse events were reported (including 17 deaths). Congressman Thomas J. Bliley expressed great concern that the contaminated Gentamicin and other counterfeit products could still be entering the United States either directly, or through various transshipment points (including Germany and other European centers). Bliley also criticized the FDA for not debarring Flavine from trading in pharmaceuticals.[10]

The number of deaths and degree of certainty linking deaths to specific APIs is still being debated. But, the fact that dangerous counterfeit bulk drugs can and have, entered the U.S. health care system is not in dispute. One FDA investigator wrote in 1996: "Counterfeit and unapproved bulk drugs can unknowingly be . . . turned into tablets/capsules and . . . can reach anyone including the President."[11]

There are other equally tragic accounts documented of counterfeiters selling bulk industrial products as pharmaceutical grade materials, some of which can be tainted with lethal contaminants. In 1995, a Haitian manufacturer of children's cough syrup purchased allegedly pharmaceutical-grade propylene glycol from a Chinese chemical company through a series of international distributors. The propylene glycol contained up to 60 percent diethylene glycol (antifreeze). Eighty-nine children died as a result. The same false pharmaceutical grade material was sold around the world leading to hundreds of deaths in Nigeria, Bangladesh, and India as well.[12]

HARDLY A JOKE: DECEPTION AND CONTROL

While in Los Angeles or New York, it may be camp to buy a fake Kate Spade bag on the street, knowing that it is a counterfeit. The patients described above would not share the view that "it's all in good fun."

Patients get fake pharmaceuticals through different channels and with different levels of "warning." These different routes can be analyzed in the Harm Matrix (see Exhibit 4.1).

In the case of malaria sufferers buying fake Artesunate, the patients may have an indication that the medications are fake (and even defective). They may see that the packaging is slightly different, or the pills do not have the proper embossed logo. However, in at least some cases, the patients may be desperate to "get what medicine they can." In developing countries, medicines are sometimes sold unpackaged by vendors on the streets. Buyers must rely totally on the credibility of the seller (or their good luck). In May 2000, Dr. Idrissou Abdoulaye, senior official at the Ministry of Health of Benin, told the World Health Assembly in Geneva "Every day people die because of counterfeit drugs. How many? We'll never know. But they keep buying these drugs because they're cheaper."[13]

People buying medicine they know has a high chance of being fake adds a new and troubling aspect to the lower-left cell of the Harm Matrix shown in Exhibit 4.1. Not only is there a threat to the patients receiving the ineffective medicines, there is a threat to the public health system as well. With the rate of ineffective fakes running at a third or more in some countries, counterfeits could very well contribute to the development of drug-resistant strains (through on-and-off exposure of the infectious agents

		Quality (Low)	**Quality** (High)
Deception Level of deception inherent in the sale of the product	**High**	Substantial patient and manufacturer threat— Dispensed medicines: Serostim, fake APIs.	Some threat to patients and health system— Serendipitous outsourcing.
	Low	Substantial patient and public health threat— Unpackaged medications, Internet sales of fakes, Artesunate.	Low risk to patient, some risk to health system—Conspiracy, pirate production.

Quality

Quality and functionality
of the counterfeit product

EXHIBIT 4.1   **Harm Matrix for Counterfeit Pharmaceuticals**

to the real medicine), and may facilitate the spread of disease. Likewise, a pattern of patients using what appears to be real medicine but failing to respond will undercut confidence in the use of pharmaceuticals, and in the medical system as a whole.

Internet buyers and Americans traveling to Mexico to buy their medicines also fall into the lower-left cell. These buyers are intentionally avoiding the regulatory and dispensing systems put in place by the national and local public health agencies to acquire their treatments. They may be motivated by pride, cost, or avoidance of medical restraints, but they are choosing to ignore the warnings and protections established, in large part, to protect them from misused or defective products.

The Serostim and Gentamicin examples fall in the upper-left cell. Kelly and the victims of the rogue international bulk API brokers had no indication of the risk they faced. They received their medicines through the regular course of medical treatment. The results were no less serious. Another recent example took place in the United States, where a pharmacist, Robert Courtney, compounded cancer treatment medicines for numerous doctors in Kansas City but at only one-tenth of their prescribed strength. He admitted to diluting more than 100,000 prescriptions over several years, affecting hundreds of patients. This has certainly eroded the confidence of people in the public health system regionally, if not nationally.

By virtue of the fact that the right side of the table assumes the products are of adequate quality, the patient is not generally injured, at least not directly.

Consider the top-right cell. Here, the example is essentially the Gentamicin/Long March story "gone right." That is, patients received effective antibiotics, produced by an unidentified third source, relabeled so that they appeared to come from an approved source. There could be some economic harm because a legitimate manufacturer may have lost sales. In the Long March case, it is likely that the company was at least complicit with the fraud. If so, it may have been involved in the transaction and therefore suffered no loss. Flavine and the other parties behind the relabeling scam weren't harmed because they all received what they expected. The parties at risk in this case were the dosage-form manufacturers, assuming that they did not know about the unapproved source substitutions, because they could be subject to a recall or a legal suit, if there were injuries. And, of course, the patients were at risk if something did go wrong. Again, the public health system is put at risk, as well. By losing assurance of a secure supply chain, the system for tracking medicines and for recalling dangerous drugs is compromised.

Assuming, for the moment, that the dosage-form manufacturers in the Gentamicin case knew that they were buying unproved, relabeled API, then the lower-right cell of the Matrix would become relevant. Because, at least in this hypothetical, if not in the actual Gentamicin case, we are assuming the quality of the bulk drugs was good and the patient may not be harmed. Of course, because the manufacturing supply chain is compromised, and the actual source of the effective APIs is masked, regulators would find it hard to analyze any problem, if it were to arise.

Some would argue that the left cell also covers the case of "Patent Pirate." Presently, some Indian pharmaceutical companies are disregarding the patents of some of the major drug companies and are manufacturing and supplying AIDS medicines to various African countries at 10 percent of the price that they are sold by the inventors of the treatments. This has created serious trade tensions and is arguably hurting the sale and profits of certain major pharmaceutical companies. Whatever the patent and trade conclusions, this is not a case of counterfeiting, as long as the medicines are sold without an attempt to disguise them as the trademarked product.

Revisiting the left cells raises additional important issues: (1) What level of control can patients actually have over their use of medicines? (2) Can more be done to afford the purchaser a better ability to distinguish real from fake?

In the case of the purchase of a "Rolex" from a street vendor, the buyer has both proximity (an ability to inspect) and control (ability to buy or not). The Rolex buyer has a direct interaction with the product vendor. Even the Internet drug buyer had some level of control over the transaction. In the Gentamicin and Courtney cases, however, both the patients and the physicians were deceived. All of the users were deprived of knowledge (i.e., deceived) and control.

This, in turn, raises the issue of product authentication. Could different approaches have been used to help alert the drug stores, medical professionals, and patients themselves to the fact that they were dealing with fakes? The short answer is yes. More companies are using security systems to protect their medicines and the FDA has recently launched an

Industry/Agency Joint Working Group project to identify improved methods of using technology in protecting the U.S. drug supply.[14]

MECHANISMS BEHIND THE MALADY

Medicines are manufactured and distributed globally. As high-value necessary products, they are increasingly a focus of business, humanitarian, and, unfortunately, criminal interest that is propelling the issue of pharmaceutical counterfeits forward in various contexts.

What Are These Fakes and Where Do They Originate?

In order to understand how criminal counterfeiters produce and pass their dangerous fakes on to patients, it is necessary to understand something about how medicines are made and distributed. Exhibit 4.2 summarizes the production of pharmaceuticals and possible points of counterfeiting attack. Pharmaceutical companies make or buy the various materials (generally bulk active pharmaceutical ingredients, and inactive excipients), process them into finished (or dosage) form medicines for packaging, distribution, and use by the medical system and patients. Attacks can take place at various different points along this chain. Likewise, discarded packaging materials and used packaging can afford counterfeiters just what they need to create their pernicious fakes.

While some patients may have a degree of notice about the possibility of fakes (as with Internet pharmacies or Mexican *farmacias*), most do not. And, the criminals do what they can to disguise the product and deceive the unsuspecting parts of the distribution chain.

The Colombian organization INVIMA (Instituto Nacional de Vigilancia de Medicamentos y Alimentos) has been successful in attacking several counterfeit manufacturing facilities. In May 2001, it conducted a number of raids on pharmaceutical counterfeiting facilities in Bogota and elsewhere in the country. INVIMA investigators discovered a thriving drug counterfeiting operation in Bosa, a poor neighborhood of Bogota. Workers inside a trio of tiny, dilapidated houses were producing more than 20,000 counterfeit tablets of the flu drug Dristan every day. They were also making a fake generic aspirin known as Dolex, and Ponstan 500, a popular painkiller developed by U.S. drug company Pfizer Inc.

EXHIBIT 4.2 **Pharmaceutical Production and Counterfeit Attack Flowchart**

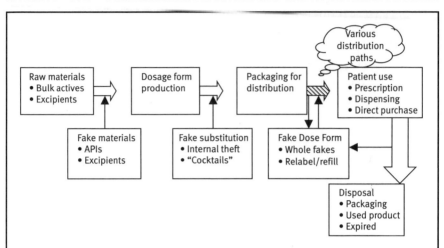

Raw materials for U.S. medicines are manufactured both by well-known major pharmaceutical companies and by smaller, less recognized FDA-regulated facilities. While many major pharmaceutical and biotech companies manufacture bulk APIs in their own plants, substantial amounts are produced by outside manufacturers and up to 80 percent of these are imported into the United States from overseas. Likewise the nonactive ingredients, excipients, may be manufactured by a range of different companies around the world. These raw materials are supplied to the dosage-form manufacturer.

The dosage-form medicines (tablets, ampoules of injectable material, etc.) once produced, are then packaged and prepared for distribution to patients. This distribution can take place through a variety of channels. It can be direct from the manufacturer through a multilevel broker distribution system. Patients can receive the medicines from medical staff through an in-house pharmacy, from a pharmacist at a retail pharmacy, or in the mail from an Internet pharmacy.

While there are have been serious cases of counterfeit APIs and excipients, and a few stories of employees at dosage-form plants stealing the real finished product and substituting fake look-alikes, the majority of counterfeiting cases involve fakes entering the retail end of the system. Counterfeiters make use of a variety of techniques to create fakes including relabeling, refilling, tampering, and recreation of look-alikes. Waste packaging and discarded empty containers also create opportunities for the criminal. Fakes can enter the distribution system through fraud or complicity by members of the distribution chain. Once in the chain, they can reach the patient.

At the patient use level, counterfeits can enter the system, via the Internet or mail-order purchases, personal purchase from less secure pharmaceutical systems (e.g., Mexican reimportation), and by buying from unregulated "street" vendors.

Taking "liberties" with its formulation, the Ponstan was being made from boric acid, floor wax and yellow highway paint. In 2000, INVIMA conducted thousands of investigations resulting in the seizure of 5 tons of tablets and capsules, and 6 million cruets of fake Voltraren (an anti-arthritic drug developed by Novartis) being produced in a clandestine lab. In these labs, counterfeiters filled vials with colored water to resemble Voltaren and probably mixed counterfeits with genuine, expired, and stolen shipments of drugs for shipment internationally.[15]

The rash of biotech and other high-value pharmaceutical counterfeits reported in the United States during the past two years illustrates further the variety of techniques used by criminals.

The cases of counterfeit Epogen and Procrit reported in the spring of 2002 involved product relabeling. Epogen and Procrit are Amgen and Ortho/Johnson & Johnson's brand names for Epoetin Alfa, a drug used to stimulate red blood cell production. In both cases, the counterfeiters obtained vials of the 2,000 U/mL injectable material, removed the original label and applied counterfeit labels. They then repackaged it as 40,000 U/mL material, increasing its retail value from $25 per vial to $750 per vial.[16]

Relabeling, as well as product substitution, seems to be the technique used to create the fake Combivir. Combivir (lamivudine plus zidovudine) is the United States' leading HIV antiviral medication. In the spring of 2002, reports of fakes began to appear. Upon analysis, the FDA concluded that in some cases, tablets of Ziagan (another antiviral) had been substituted in Combivir bottles, and in others, fake Combivir labels had been applied to Ziagan bottles. From the patients' point of view, both presented the same problem. They were not receiving the more effective and expensive drug they had bargained for. Even more troublesome is the fact that some patients can experience life-threatening hypersensitivity to Ziagan not associated with Combivir.[17]

In the case of Zyprexa and Gamimune, tampering seems to be the method of choice. The FDA and Eli Lilly reported that bottles of Zyprexa (olanzapine, the leading antipsychotic drug in the U.S.) had been emptied and refilled with white tablets marked "aspirin."[18] Likewise FDA and Bayer reported that at least some recalled counterfeit Gamimune had been tampered with and the vials showed damage to the seals and caps. Some of the injectable product appeared to have been diluted and contained extremely high levels of bacteria.[19]

Viagra is one of the world's most widely counterfeited pharmaceuticals. It is often counterfeited "from scratch" and sold in international trade. In March 2002, Thai police raided a Viagra pirate manufacturing operation, seizing more than 100,000 pills made primarily of tapioca starch. On May 17, 2002, the Manhattan District Attorney and Pfizer announced the indictment of seven individuals and five companies for making and selling counterfeits. Undercover investigators bought 25,000 fake pills for about $38,000, or a price of $1.52, whereas the genuine pills retail for approximately $10 each. Defendants in China and India made the fakes, while others in Nevada, Colorado and Hong Kong sold them over the Internet to distributors.

The counterfeiter's job has been made easier by a number of factors in recent years. Global manufacturing and easy, rapid global trade, together with digital imaging and printing, are definitely facilitating the growing problem of fake medicines. Relatively light penalties for counterfeiting, intrusion of organized crime into the field, and the difficulty of intellectual property enforcement in an international context also contribute.

Of even more specific relevance to pharmaceutical counterfeiting, however, is the apparent ability of criminals to compromise the integrity of the drug distribution system. The United States and many other countries have no absolute tractability or warning requirement for drugs. Ironically, consumers receive a notice when defects are identified with cars. The same is not generally true for fake medicines moving through the distribution chain. Neither are there requirements for the use of technological security markers to aide in spotting knockoffs, despite the fact that many of the fakes were first identified by the patients actually using (or about to use) the counterfeits.

One factor contributing to the looseness of the distribution system is that there is an active secondary market in finished-form pharmaceuticals in the United States. Congress and the U.S. Food and Drug Administration (FDA) have debated the "drug pedigree" issue, or the requirement that all drugs be traceable back to authorized distributors and the manufacturer for several years, but do not require it. Several of the foregoing examples involve "unauthorized distributors."

Unauthorized distribution is frequently called diversion or gray marketing. It is the natural outgrowth of price differentials and a central part of the counterfeit medicine story. It could become a serious threat to the integrity of the United States and other countries' drug supplies.

Diversion: A Special Link

Diversion is the sale of products outside the channels of distribution for which they were initially intended. Generally, diversion from one commercial channel to another takes place because there is a difference in pricing between the different channels, and there is an arbitrage opportunity. It can also take place when there is a legal prohibition on the sale of goods in one channel, but not another.

In many cases, diversion is perfectly legal. In the United States, the First Sales doctrine maintains that, even for trademarked goods, once a product is sold, the manufacturer has no right to control its subsequent sale or use. Similar legal protections for the free disposition of goods exist in most countries. These provisions are important in order to make commerce proceed in a free and orderly manner. There are also cases, however, where diversion is not legal and is a main vehicle criminals use in inserting fakes into the medical distribution system.

Illegal diversion operates in many areas of the pharmaceutical market. First, a number of medicines are controlled substances (e.g., narcotics, tranquilizers and other types of potentially addictive or dangerous drugs). The diversion of these medicines and dispensing outside of pharmacies and other medical facilities can be dangerous and is generally prohibited by law.

Another form of fraudulent diversion involves the use of sham institutional pharmacies. Powerful buying groups and government entities can negotiate very favorable drug pricing. This creates the opportunity for criminal abuse. Exhibit 4.3 shows how the illegal diversion of pharmaceuticals takes place with sham institutional pharmacies.

Bindley Western, a major U.S. distributor, now a part of Cardinal Health, pleaded guilty to just such a sham distribution scheme in 2001 and was ordered to pay fines of $20 million.

While counterfeits were not involved in the Bindley case, it is possible that fakes could be inserted into this sort of complex diversion chain, leading to the kind of problem that took place with Serostim. Associate Commissioner Hubbard of the FDA testified: "The current focus on drug counterfeiting and the public perception of a more dramatic increase

EXHIBIT 4.3   **Fraudulent Pharmaceutical Diversion Scheme**

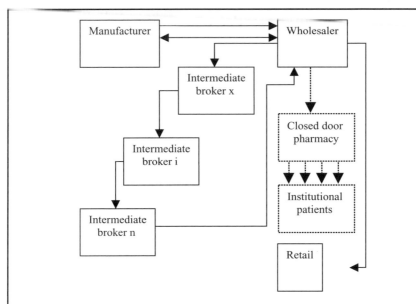

In this case, the pharmaceutical manufacturer supplies products to the wholesaler (top arrow) at wholesale average cost (WAC, e.g., $85 per unit). The wholesaler can then sell this to the retail pharmacy at $90 (for a 6 percent margin). However, there is another channel of distribution as well, to the closed door pharmacies (e.g., nursing homes and hospitals) with their own institutional patients. The sales price to the closed door pharmacy may be substantially lower than WAC, e.g., $40 per unit. In this case, the manufacturer pays the wholesaler a rebate (the double-headed arrow) to offset its loss. In one recent case, *U.S. v. Bindley Western,*[20] executives of the wholesaler sold products to a sham closed door pharmacy (broken lines). In fact, the product actually went through a series of intermediate brokers who, in turn, resold the products (often only on paper with no goods actually changing hands). Each broker marked up the goods slightly and the product was ultimately resold back to the wholesaler at $65 per unit. The wholesaler then sold the product back into the retail channel, but at an improved 25 percent margin. This opportunity for increasing company margins is a strong incentive. Industry management and FDA officials alike have pointed to this fraudulent system as a likely point where counterfeiters insert their bogus product.[21]

in counterfeit drug activity is due to the fact [in large part] . . . to the existence of an illicit wholesale drug diversion network that has grown up around tiered pricing and economic fraud."[22]

The International Dimension

Pharmaceutical diversion takes place on the international level, as well. In fact, the opportunities for international diversion are even greater. The same medications are often priced quite differently depending on the country into which they are being sold. The U.S. International Trade Commission (ITC) released a study in December 2000, on the *Pricing of Prescription Drugs* in the Group of 8 (G8) nations.[23] While indicating that price comparisons were difficult, it summarized studies that found manufacturer's prices for some pharmaceuticals were 32 percent higher in the United States than in Canada; retail prices on other drugs were 72 to 104 percent higher in Maine than in Canada and Mexico; and the average acquisition price to pharmacists for antidepressant and antipsychotic drugs was 170 to 290 percent higher in the United States than in Canada, Mexico, and European countries. Many countries formally or informally enforce price controls on pharmaceuticals.

It is illegal to import medicines into the United States not approved for use by the FDA. And, while the FDA and the U.S. Customs Service allow limited "reimportation" of FDA-approved drugs for "personal use," commercial "reimportation" is not allowed. The reality is different. Dr. Shepherd, Chair of the University of Texas School of Pharmacy, has written and testified extensively about the massive abuse of the "personal reimportation" provision by thousands of "professional reimporters" making numerous trips every day to bring controlled substances into the United States. In fact, this appears to be the primary economic justification for the hundreds of *farmacias* crowded into U.S./Mexican border towns.[24] Similar, if less extensive, reimportation takes place across the U.S./Canada border. There is also a flood of medicines entering the United States via the mails (i.e., mail, express mail and express carriers like Federal Express, UPS, etc.). The U.S. Customs Service testified before the House Commerce Oversight Committee stating that it is "impossible" to monitor the flood of shipments entering the United States every day.[25]

Diversion is not just a mechanism for importing lower-priced foreign drugs. Criminals also use it as a channel for the mixing of real with fakes and for the importation of counterfeits. Not only is diversion an important issue in the current drug counterfeiting debate, but it is likely to become much more important with the international demand for access to AIDS and other drugs.

A Coming Epidemic?

While there are current problems with the diversion of pharmaceuticals and the salting or mixing of diverted product with counterfeit and expired product, this situation could become much worse. The reason is that the world health community has embarked on a massive differential pricing program that will deliver millions, or even billions, of doses of anti-retroviral AIDS drugs to Africa and other countries with weak control systems. The results could be a wholesale diversion program leaving needy populations with poor quality treatments, undermining parts of the pharmaceutical distribution systems in developed countries, and enriching criminals and corrupt bureaucrats.

AIDS is a crushing epidemic in sub-Saharan Africa. More than 8 percent (or 23 million) adults in this region suffer from HIV/AIDS. In South Africa, Lesotho, Namibia, Zambia, Swaziland, and Zimbabwe, the rate of infection is 20 percent or more; and in Botswana it is over 35 percent. In 1999, 2.2 million residents of the region died from the disease and its complications.[26]

Based on traditional pricing, anti–AIDS drugs are totally out of reach for treating this catastrophe. A year's supply of HIV anti–retroviral drugs cost approximately $15,000 per year in the United States. Without major change, such expenditures are out of the question in sub-Saharan Africa where per capita annual medical expenditures may be as low as $10 per year. This impossible situation has led to a powerful humanitarian movement advocating the wide availability of these medicines at dramatically reduced prices (and with massive charitable contributions, as well). In 1998, 39 of the world's largest drug manufacturers, under the banner of the International Federation of Pharmaceutical Manufacturers Associations (IFPMA), went to court in South Africa to prevent the government from overriding their international patents on these drugs. The case was settled on April 23, 2001. South Africa agreed to abide by Trade Related Aspects of Intellectual Property (TRIPS), and the drug companies agreed to supply medicines at dramatically reduced prices (e.g., $600–750 for a year's dose of combination therapies).[27]

While some progress has been made, the costs are still out-of-reach by many. This fact has led to other developments: the manufacture of some of these drugs in India, Brazil, and elsewhere, without regard to international patents, and the massive international diversion of medicines. Prices can vary dramatically. A 1998 study by the Consumer Project on Technology found prices for GlaxoSmithKline's version of Amoxil was $8 in Pakistan, but was $36 in Malaysia.[28] Hence, many advocate the active use of diversion as a means for further extending treatment resources.

There are major potential problems associated with this approach. For example, in March 2002, three South African pharmacists pleaded guilty to 34 counts of counterfeiting medicines by repackaging thousands of doses of stolen and altered medications intended for the public health system. Authorities seized sophisticated blister packaging equipment that the trio were using to repackage the fakes for sale on the commercial market.

This example could be much worse in other countries where the rule of law is less developed, and where counterfeits are quite common.

◑ **FOCUS 4.1** ◐

DIVERTED AFRICAN AIDS DRUGS

On October 3, 2002, Gautam Naik, of *The Wall Street Journal,*[29] reported that: "The Netherlands' General Health Inspection Service said it was investigating a tiny Dutch company it identified as Asklepios for allegedly importing the shipments of two drugs made by GlaxoSmithKline PLC to the Netherlands and Germany." While Asklepios refused to talk to reporters, *The Washington Post*[30] reported that it has obtained an internal company memo that indicated: "The scheme involving Glaxo's products has been going on since at least July 2001 but was undetected by the giant drug maker and European regulators until this past July [2002], when customs inspectors in Belgium noticed irregularities in a shipment sent from Senegal . . . ." Apparently, air freight shipments were redirected, upon their arrival into Africa, and sent back to the small Dutch drug wholesaler. According to reports, at least 28 shipments of Combivir, Epivir, and Trizivir, or nearly 3 million doses (with a value of approximately $18 million) were diverted by this operation. There was no indication that counterfeits were involved but reports did indicate that no complaints about shortages had been received by officials.

Consider the situation where the officials of a government agency taking delivery of the drugs are more interested in personal profit than in the welfare of their population. There is ample evidence of goods intended for Africa being diverted back to the Western economies so that corrupt officials can make a "killing" by selling the diverted products. In fact, reports in October 2002 in *The Washington Post* and *The Wall Street Journal* indicate that this has actually begun taking place with important AIDS medications. And "killing" may be the right term, because the diverted goods must then be replaced with other products. The substituted material could well be placebo fakes. Of course, in this situation, inventory management may not be the top priority of the criminals, so it is likely that the ineffective substitute material could be mixed into outbound shipments as well.

In other words, laudable humanitarian access efforts could well lead to a substantial increase of counterfeits coming into the developed world.

Terrorism, Too?

The examples given above are about economic counterfeiting—criminals attempting to distribute fakes for economic gain. There is another, and potentially more serious, side to the story, too—counterfeiting as a terrorist tool.

It has been documented that Mahmud Abouhalima and other conspirators in the 1993 World Trade Center bombing financed their plot, in part, by relabeling expired baby formula and reselling it.[31] Likewise, there is good evidence that the Irish Republican Army (IRA), has used counterfeit movies, as well as fake veterinary medicines, to finance its activities.[32]

Following the September 11, 2001, terrorist attacks on the World Trade Center and Pentagon, there appeared to be a bioterrorist attack using anthrax. This led many in the United States and elsewhere to begin buying Cipro and other strong antibiotics. Because these products were in short supply, the medical establishment limited dispensing, many knowledgeable observers began to worry that terrorists could turn this to their advantage by making counterfeit medicines a terrorist delivery mechanism.

Fortunately, this did not happen, and the FDA and other agencies of the federal government are now working on plans to minimize this risk.

THE DIAGNOSIS: TOWARD A CURE?

Pharmaceutical counterfeiting is a major international criminal problem, which is putting patient populations at risk, is a threat to confidence in the public health system, may contribute to the development of drug-resistant diseases, and is likely to become more serious with global differential pricing and increasing international and electronic trade.

So, what can be done? What is being done? And, will it work? These are the natural questions to ask once the problem has been characterized.

Examining the Symptoms

The first step toward "curing" counterfeit medicines is admitting the problem exists. As with most illnesses, until the patient acknowledges that there is a problem and recognizes the symptoms, no remedy is possible.

The industry and government are admitting that counterfeiting exists and threatens patients, business and public health alike. One example of this change is the very organization that the world's leading pharmaceutical companies organized to fight counterfeiting—the Pharmaceutical Security Institute (PSI). PSI was established in 1996. But, almost as soon as it was announced, it began operating almost entirely undercover. It set up headquarters in a remote part of Italy and began focusing on the important, but incomplete, task of investigating counterfeiting cases. This was incomplete because the industry needed a spokesperson on the issue. While it was known that the PSI existed, the organization did not provide a meaningful voice on the topic.

PSI passed through a series of three executive directors in four years. The third, D'arcy Quinn, resigned in 2001. At the same time, the issue of counterfeit pharmaceuticals was heating up, especially in the United States. The Oversight Subcommittee of the U.S. House of Representatives Commerce Committee began holding hearings. On June 8, 2000, it began with public hearings focused largely on the Gentamicin case, and its perception that the FDA had not dealt with the problem or its probable causes aggressively enough.[33]

A second hearing followed on June 7, 2001, where the subcommittee took testimony from the directors of security for three of the world's leading pharmaceutical manufacturers, Dr. John Glover, Bristol-Myers

Squibb; James Christian, Novartis International; and William Trundley, GlaxoSmithKline (each Vice President of Corporate Security). Under oath, each described parts of the problem, emphasizing the extent and severity of the international issue. In brief, they emphasized that: (1) counterfeiting of prescription drugs is a growing global problem, (2) major criminal enterprises in Mexico are a significant source of counterfeits in the U.S., (3) improved graphics technology and Internet commerce are contributing to the growth of the problem, and (4) law enforcement lacks the resources necessary to effectively police counterfeit and diverted pharmaceuticals.[34] The genie escaped from the bottle!

Following this hearing, anticounterfeiting efforts in the United States, and around the world, have picked up speed. The PSI, in particular, is undergoing a transformation. In the spring of 2002, the organization relocated from Italy to the Washington, D.C. area. Tom Kubic, former FBI Financial Crimes Section Chief, was recruited to lead it, and the organization's mission was enlarged to include governmental relations, as well as investigations.

In a similar pattern, until 2001, the Pharmaceutical Research and Manufacturers Association (PhRMA) refused to comment on the issue of counterfeiting. More recently, it has used the risks of counterfeits as an argument against broadening the pharmaceutical reimportation laws.[35] It has held several Congressional briefings on the topic and has participated in press conferences on the issue.

The trend toward increasing openness on the issue is continuing. In the first part of 2002, a number of major organizations, including the Pan American Health Organization, Generic Pharmaceutical Association, the Academy of Managed Care Pharmacies, the Global Economic Crimes Summit and the International Trademark Association, have held sessions on pharmaceutical anticounterfeiting. In September 2002, the World Health Organization, participating with Reconnaissance International, organized the First Global Pharmaceutical AntiCounterfeiting Forum that drew more than 200 public health officials, pharmaceutical manufacturers, law enforcement and security system providers and nongovernmental organizations from around the world for a three-day meeting in Geneva. This was the largest, most diverse gathering ever to consider the problem. Representatives from more than 20 developing countries attended and explained how serious the problem of fake drugs had become.

Dr. Dora Nkem Akunyili, Director General of Nigeria's National Agency for Food and Drug Administration and Control, called fake drugs "more serious than AIDS and malaria, because AIDS can be prevented and malaria can be treated, but fake drugs affect everyone." A second global forum is being organized for the spring of 2004.

While increased understanding is important, meetings alone are not enough to solve the problem.

Structural Developments

Two of the main structural drivers for change are legal liability and regulations. Both of these areas are changing.

Serono and the distribution chain involved in the Serostim case were sued by AIDS patients who injected the fake material.

But wait! Serono didn't make the fakes. How can they be sued for what the unknown criminals did?

The plaintiffs' attorneys put forward two theories of liability. First, they claimed that the medicine was "unreasonably dangerous" when used as intended and, therefore, the defendants were strictly liable. Second, they asserted that Serono (and other defendants) should have foreseen the possibility that counterfeits would be introduced into the distribution chain, given the demand in the black market, and should have taken better precautions to prevent it.

At least one law review article supports their contention. Professor Arthur Best, University of Denver School of Law, concludes "The counterfeiting problem presents a combination of grave risk and low-cost methods to avert that risk. Seen in that light, courts are likely to solve the problem by imposing a duty of reasonable care on those involved in the manufacture and distribution of products that are likely to be counterfeited and that can be protected from counterfeiting with practical countermeasures."[36] In other words, Serono, or another legitimate manufacturer of pharmaceuticals, may find itself paying a judgment for injuries caused by fakes, if it has not taken adequate preventative precautions.

While pharmaceutical companies operate with the mission of protecting and benefiting their patients, this developing legal obligation adds a strong financial motivation not to ignore the risks of counterfeiting.

The FDA is creating other important motivations for drug companies to become active in preventing counterfeiting. Responding to the

Gentamicin bulk import issue in 2001, the FDA announced Import Alter 66-66. This requires importers of bulk APIs to declare the consignee and intended use of material upon arrival in the United States and allows the raw material to be held. The agency then compares this information with data on the foreign manufacturer's status and the qualifications of the intended recipient to tell, for example, whether animal veterinarian quality product may be intended for a human drug manufacturer.

Going beyond this, the FDA's Counterfeit Drug Working Group has recently begun examining the various technologies for protecting and authenticating medicines and tracking and tracing products through an international distribution system. At the September 2002 Global Forum, the Agency announced the establishment of a joint agency/industry work group to assess the various security, track, and trace technologies to determine their usefulness in pharmaceutical industry applications. This process should result in more effective cooperation on the preventative approaches, including the use of security systems.

Developing Solutions

As with most complex problems, there is no simple solution to the problem of pharmaceutical counterfeiting. The only realistic attack is to take a systems approach.

The first step is to establish a mandate and allocate responsibility for uncovering the facts. As one Glaxo official said, at the time that its block-buster product Zantac was being counterfeited in Europe, "The CEO doesn't want to discover the problem by reading about it in the *Financial Times*."[37] Support from the top is essential. Staff cannot be made to fear reprisals for uncovering the problem, if the company wants honest information. Finding out about it in the *Times* is exactly what will happen if diligent employees' jobs are threatened as the result of raising the issue.

The company must then define and analyze the problem. The problem of counterfeit Artesunate affecting millions in Asia is very different from that of fake biotech products finding their way onto shelves in America's pharmacies. It should go without saying that law enforcement, regulatory authorities, medical personnel, drug manufacturers, and the various intermediaries should work together by sharing information to help identify whether a problem exists and characterize it for attack. In practice, this is more difficult than it may seem. What if the manufacturer is colluding with a pirate bulk API supplier? Or, what if corrupt public health officials are diverting legitimate product and filling gaps in the system with fakes?

◖ **FOCUS 4.2** ◗

CASES OF OFFICIAL CORRUPTION

In the mid-1990s, a country representative of a major pharmaceutical manufacturer based in the Americas received a report of a death that surprised him. The patient, located in a rural area, had contracted meningitis and was treated with one of the company's very effective medicines. Knowing the effectiveness of the medication, he was not satisfied to "accept" the statistic and had an investigator get a full doctor's report and samples of the medicine.

When he examined the samples, he found that the printing on the package smeared when rubbed, something that the company's printing did not do. Upon analysis, the sample proved to be a fake, not containing the necessary active ingredients.

Responding to the problem, the company added a holographic packaging seal and created an instruction sheet on how doctors and pharmacists should inspect and verify the product. It approached the national health authority to launch an educational campaign. It received little cooperation, so the company conducted field training on its own. It contacted every clinic, explained how to examine the product, told them to buy only from authorized distributors and had the clinics sign a release in the case of injuries from products bought from unauthorized distributors.

The program cost on the order of $250,000, and effectively cleared up the problem, protecting sale of approximately $75 million per year. But the rep began to receive death threats. Rather than capitulate, he had investigators pursue the source of the threats. The trail ultimately led to a former minister of health. The company chose not to pursue the matter at that level and let the issue drop.[38]

Examining the issue from the legitimate manufacturer's point of view, it must draw on all available sources of information at the outset. What do its sales records show? Have sales of the product dropped off in one region, or unexpectedly "exploded" in another? Does competition explain this? What do sample-buy analyses from the region show—fakes, repackaged expired product, refilled real packaging? All these are possibilities. What are the rumors and the experience of other product lines in the region, and of other manufacturers?

With an initial set of information and a cross-cutting management structure that involves various parts of the company (security, sales, quality/regulatory, manufacturing, packaging, financial and legal), a fuller picture begins to develop. Private investigators can be used to do more field and supply/distribution chain analyses. Information can be shared judiciously with law enforcement, anticounterfeiting associations, competitors, and so on. As the picture emerges, plans can be formulated.

Initially, the plans are unlikely to focus on specific technologies. Rather, they will focus on a risk assessment attempting to isolate the various weak points within the business system that may account for identified problems. Could contract manufacturers or packing companies be using the brand-holder's equipment to make unauthorized "fourth shift" runs? Could discarded or stolen packaging material be finding its way into criminal hands as the source of the fakes? Or, are organized groups "manufacturing" their own (possibly poisonous) products.

Based on this sort of analysis and an examination of the company's manufacturing, packaging and distribution systems, the company can formulate strategies to counterattack the likely problems. The company can then assess the suitability of different security approaches and technologies. Of course, this will include an examination of how well the approach would target the likely problem, and of how easily and effectively it can be implemented within the company. How well can it migrate to new and improved approaches, assuming the counterfeiters attempt to overcome the first line of defense? Cost is obviously an issue as well.

As the company moves to implement its countermeasure systems, it should have a plan for post-implementation assessment. On a quantifiable basis, is the program working? Is it achieving predetermined targets? If not, why not? What is being learned? What else should be considered?

Counterfeiting is not generally an acute malady. The crooks have made an investment in ripping off the company's products, and probably its competitors as well. While counterfeiting is a usually an opportunistic crime, they will not just automatically give up their "business plan" as soon as the company takes its first defensive steps.

In other words, returning to the medical metaphor, counterfeiting is a chronic problem. Once the diagnosis is made and the treatment has begun, it is important to monitor the disease and adapt the continuing treatment regimen on an ongoing basis.

CHAPTER 5

Replacement Parts and Consumables

"THERE, IT'S JUST LIKE NEW"

I t's not just fake pharmaceuticals that pose a threat to life and safety. Counterfeit replacement parts and consumables can kill and injure, as well.

When a consumer buys a new car or appliance, or when a company purchases a new piece of equipment, they inspect it, test its features, and maybe even dote on it for awhile. A company is likely to use some acceptance testing procedure to ensure the quality of the new item. When having that same car, appliance, or piece of manufacturing equipment repaired or serviced, however, the owner is unlikely to inspect and may never even see the replacement parts. Yet, increasingly, American business makes its profits from the sale of parts, consumables, and services. Take, for example, the home model ink jet printer used in drafting this manuscript. The printer itself cost $49, but a set of toner modules to print the drafts cost $34.10.

Great . . . another opportunity for counterfeiters. Clever crooks can clean and repackage used parts, package cheap knockoffs to look like genuine replacements, buy unauthorized overruns, or just set up a website offering a variety of fake and real products. The profits can be good and, because the level of inspection may be low, there may be little risk of being caught.

Returning to the Harm Matrix, who is harmed (the manufacturer, distributor and/or buyer), and to what extent? Certainly, the harm depends on a number of variables, including the nature of the products involved.

In the case of bogus toner cartridges for computer printers that cause malfunctions in the printers themselves, the fakes can damage a brand reputation and interfere with an existing business relationship. However, the failure of critical parts on a plane or in a bus can, and has, led to death and injury of the customer or the customer's customer. Yet the counterfeit may go unnoticed in any accident investigation.

A key point shown by the matrix is that in the case of parts and consumables, the deception component tends to be high. The injured (physically or economically) party is less likely to have any meaningful contact with the item being counterfeited and is likely to blame the manufacturer (or operator) for the injury. Thus, many of the examples in this chapter fall into the upper two quadrants of the matrix in Exhibit 5.1.

In the case of defective fake transportation parts, passed off as real in a repair shop, the direct customer (the shop) is deceived and will certainly be damaged if there is an accident with injuries. However, the indirect users of the parts, the vehicle passengers, will pay the biggest price, through their injuries. In the case of unauthorized factory overruns, the passengers may not be put at the same risk, but authorized producers will be cheated out of their sales. In the lower two quadrants, some buyers may opt for questionable replacement parts, even if they suspect that buying the parts is not on the "up and up," because they

		Low Quality	High Quality
Deception Level of deception inherent in the sale of the product	**High**	Consumer Harm (direct and indirect)—Fake replacement brakes, fake aviation parts.	Low Consumer Risk/ Manufacturing Third-Party Harm—Over run production.
	Low	Consumer Risk— Low-cost auto replacement parts.	Low Consumer Risk/ Some Manufacturing Third-Party Harm— Collusion on "genuine" replacement parts.

Quality
Quality and functionality
of the counterfeit product

EXHIBIT 5.1 **Harm Matrix for Counterfeit Spare Parts**

think the genuine parts are too expensive. Most likely, they will "win some and lose some." Hopefully, the "losses" don't involve parts that prevent collisions or crashes. Finally, the lower-right quadrant could be illustrated by a collusive arrangement between a repair shop and contract parts producer. The parts may be top-quality, but the business arrangement is probably configured to cheat insurance companies and genuine parts producers alike.

This Is Serious: Aviation Parts

In September 1989, a Convair 580 Turboprop airliner took off from Oslo, Norway, carrying 55 passengers and crew bound for Hamburg, Germany. Halfway into its voyage, air traffic controllers monitoring the flight suddenly lost track of it on their screens—it simply disappeared, without warning, over the North Sea. After an exhaustive search of the seabed in the area where the plane disappeared, the wreckage of the plane—and the bodies of the 55 people killed in the crash—were located and lifted from the ocean.

Investigators then began studying the wreckage in an attempt to discover what had caused the crash. It became apparent that a catastrophic failure had occurred—the tail assembly had torn loose from the airframe, an extraordinarily rare event. Looking at the tail assembly, and at pieces of the wreckage that were found scattered around the main body of the fuselage, investigators were shocked to learn that the bolts and bushings that held the tail assembly to the airframe were not genuine parts—they were substandard counterfeit parts.[1] The disintegration of the bolts in midair had led to the violent separation of the tail, the consequent crash, and loss of life.

While this may be the most well-documented example of a crash due to counterfeit aviation parts, it is by no means an isolated incident. In January 2001, Italian police, working with the FBI and other law enforcement agencies, seized more than $2 million worth of counterfeit aviation parts and arrested six people in a ring made up of three companies. According to the Federal Aviation Administration (FAA), there was evidence that the ring members, New Tech Italia, New Tech Aerospace, and Panaviation, all aviation parts manufacturers located in Rome, had sold parts accompanied by forged papers to Alitalia, AirOne, and Meridiana.

Some of the forms accompanying the bogus parts were altered using white-out; others were photocopied. Used parts were being cleaned, improperly modified, repackaged, and sold. Based on the evidence, the FAA notified the entire industry that this problem may have begun as early as the 1980s. Authorities are looking into possible connections between the aircraft parts sold by the Panaviation ring and past airplane crashes and malfunctions.[2]

In the United States the FAA has jurisdiction over the approval and use of replacement parts. According to the Aircraft Safety Act of 2000 and its implementing regulations, "standard parts" should bear "a mark indicating the part has been produced in accordance with the specification requirements" and should be accompanied by a Certificate of Conformity. Parts that do not comply are referred to as "suspected unapproved parts (SUPs)," or loosely as "counterfeits." However, as the Panaviation case shows, there can be loopholes in ensuring that the markings on the parts are legitimate and actually associated with a (genuine) Certificate of Conformity. The FAA has been heavily criticized by one of its own, former Inspector General Mary Schiavo, in her book *Flying Blind, Flying Safe.*[3] In it, she criticizes the FAA and industry for failing to take strong actions to build accountability and authenticity into the parts program. Her book claims that up to 43 percent of certain types of parts fall into the SUPs category—a chilling statistic, even if many of them are merely paperwork errors.

In 1996, the Air Transport Association established a task force to investigate the use of bar code identification of parts, but nothing has come of this so far. In 1998, the Boeing Commercial Airplane Group issued a "Request for Information for Parts Marking Systems to Deter Unapproved Parts," identifying the purpose of the Request to be: "[primarily] the issue of unapproved parts deterrence . . . [also] part tracking, inventory control, part maintenance history, authentication of spare parts and airplane configuration."[4] Although several companies expressed interest in making proposals, this request appears not to have been pursued. So while parts authentication has always been a concern in the aviation industry, especially since the 1989 North Sea accident, the logistical complexity of identifying and keeping histories on individual parts has proven daunting thus far. There are more than 3 million parts in a Boeing 747. Some of these are very small, like fasteners; others are quite large and subject to extreme conditions, like jet turbines. A secure, automated system for marking and maintaining records on such a collection of parts, as well as the population of potential replacement parts, has not yet been implemented.

The following case involving Bell Helicopter illustrates just how extreme the counterfeiting problem can become, and to what lengths companies may have to go in order to protect themselves. Bell, a subsidiary of Texitron, Inc. has been involved in numerous lawsuits where plaintiffs have injured or killed themselves in craft that they "remanufactured" from parts. One of the earliest cases was *Goldsmith v. Bell,* filed in the late 1980s by the estate of Goldsmith, a mechanic who perished in a helicopter that he had built in his garage. Goldsmith made ("remanufactured") the helicopter using used scrap parts and "registered" it with the FAA using information he obtained from a previously issued FAA dataplate, the official registration of airworthiness for an aircraft. One key problem with Goldberg's registration, however, was that the dataplate came from a helicopter that had previously been destroyed in a crash.[5] That is, Goldberg built his own scrap helicopter, fraudulently gave it a dataplate, flew it, crashed it, and died. Following this, his estate attempted to recover from Bell, the manufacturer of the helicopter from which Goldberg stole the nameplate information.

With the abundance of decommissioned UH−1 ("Huey") helicopters and parts being sold by the military and their close resemblance to Bell's models 204B and 205A−1, the problem of "remanufacturing" was growing during the 1990s. Ironically, the FAA also played a role in creating the problem. Once it inspects an aircraft for airworthiness and issues a dataplate, it never deletes the dataplate from use, even after the aircraft crashes or passes out of service. This information is available to the public, and to "remanufacturers" and counterfeiters. In October 1998, after having to defend several liability suits based on injuries caused by remanufactured aircraft, Bell Helicopter initiated a nationwide campaign to fight back. Numerous companies and individuals were identified as "remanufacturing" Hueys into fake Bell 204Bs. The company adopted an aggressive litigation strategy to attack this part of the problem and filed suit against a number of the parties. Bell also revised the contract that it uses with its Customer Service Facility (CSF) repair stations across the country to include a strong anticounterfeiting provision. These efforts have resulted in an improvement in the situation.

What's Wrong with This Printer?

In 1990, Electronic Data Systems (EDS) began having problems with some of its NEC printers. Some printers were acting erratically and some stopped working completely. EDS complained to NEC, which was experiencing higher than usual warranty repair claims. The malfunctioning units had a variety of problems, but there did not seem to any underlying cause or explanation. Finally, a sharp NEC technician noticed that a serial number of one of the printer ribbon units was unusual; it didn't conform to the company numbering system. This was the starting point, and with more detailed field examination, it became clear that the ribbons in many of these printers were not standard NEC parts. In fact, they were counterfeits. It turned out that the fakes had different electric potential characteristics that damaged the sensitive motherboards of some printer units.

Investigating the bogus ribbons led NEC to identify the source of the fakes, a knockoff factory based in Malaysia. When the company raided the factory, they found quantities of fake NEC parts and packaging, but also substantial quantities of fakes of other printer company products.[6] This prompted the company to look in two directions: (1) to take actions to correct its immediate problem, and (2) to begin working with its competitors to develop industrywide approaches to fight counterfeiting.

On the immediate level, NEC analyzed how to protect its ribbons from future counterfeiting. After surveying its distributors and end users, management concluded that an overt authentication system would work best. Such a system would provide its customers with direct assurance that the printer ribbon was genuine and could be tied into the company's existing product support phone system.

NEC began using a half-inch square Polaroid photopolymer hologram label on the ribbon casing for authentication. The package contained customer instructions describing how users could verify the genuineness of the ribbon. First, they were instructed to examine the hologram visually to verify the 3-D effect, and then, for further confirmation, they could peel the label off, thereby causing the holographic effect to disappear. Once the system was in place, the company informed its distributors about the counterfeit problem and included a notice in each package explaining that the hologram was intended to confirm the genuine nature of the product. An 800 "hot line" phone number was set up for questions and to report questionable products.

The system worked well during the mid-1990s as a deterrent to counterfeiting, more than paying for itself in the first year. Officials estimated annual lost ribbon sales in the United States alone were approximately $750,000 per year, with additional company costs due to service and warranty repairs. The holographic security labels cost approximately seven cents apiece applied to the 600,000 units per year. Figures suggested that the company realized a net revenue increase of more than $250,000, as a result. Even with adding the $10,000 manufacturing modification costs, the security labels appeared to generate returns of more than 5:1.[7]

NEC didn't stop there. It began working with several other printer/copier companies to form the Imaging Supplies Coalition (ISC), a nonprofit group whose charter is to fight counterfeiting and protect its members' IP rights around the world. The Coalition, formed in 1993, has developed a number of tools for accomplishing its mission. One of the most basic is the periodical *Benchmarking Survey on Fraud and Counterfeiting in the Imaging Marketplace.* Nineteen of 40 companies responded to its 1995 *Survey.* An analysis of these results suggested that in 1995, the $15 billion imaging supplies industry was suffering 2.5 percent (or $375 million) in counterfeit sales annually. It repeated the *Survey* again in 1999 and found that this number had increased to $470 million.[8]

As any visit to the local computer shop will demonstrate, the profits in the imaging supplies industry are in the consumables, not the hardware. Toner cartridges are small, high-value products that are easily shipped internationally. There is an active, global secondary market in these products, so legitimate businesses frequently buy discounted lots from closeouts, overstocks, and so on. One of the ISC's key challenges as it formed was to define a program that could help stop counterfeits, but not interfere with the legitimate secondary market. Its answer—*When in Doubt, Check it Out,* which is described more fully in Focus 5.1.

◑ FOCUS 5.1 ◐

THE IMAGING SUPPLIES COALITION

The ISC is one of the most effective trademark-based anticounterfeiting alliances. *When in Doubt, Check it Out* is a flagship program of the ISC. This confidential call center allows industry participants to send in suspect samples to be verified as genuine or counterfeit on a rapid response basis. If the samples are determined to be genuine, no further action is taken. If the samples are found to be fake, the user must give details of the source of the product. The program's feedback loop serves as a confidential authentication and verification system. Detecting counterfeits is difficult, because the packaging and trade dress of most fakes so closely resembles the genuine product. Of the nearly 1000 submissions received for the two-year period 1998 and 1999, about 18 percent were counterfeit. The call center maintains a database of all counterfeits.

The *When In Doubt* program and the ISC have removed thousands of illegal products from commerce since their inception in 1994 and were honored in 1999 by the *Global AntiCounterfeiting Awards*. The program has led ISC member companies to the source of the counterfeit product and has resulted in civil and criminal prosecution in the United States, Europe, Latin America, and Asia. Founded initially to fight counterfeiting in the United States, the imaging supplies industry has extended its activities into other regions of the world. In 1997, it organized a sister organization, the Imaging Consumables Coalition of Europe (ICCE), to operate similar programs in Europe. And, in 2000, these efforts were extended into Latin America and the Middle East. With a need to fight counterfeiting more aggressively, the ICCE has also established a "front" company that trades on the black and gray markets, generating very valuable investigative information.[9]

Automobiles

Not surprisingly, automotive parts and consumables are counterfeited too. In 1996, the U.S. Federal Trade Commission estimated that counterfeits accounted for more than $3 billion per year in losses for the industry in the United States and some $12 billion per year worldwide.[10]

In 1997, the automobile and auto parts industry in America was made up of some 4,400 manufacturers, producing approximately $314 billion in goods annually and $140 billion in replacement parts. The replacement and specialty parts market has undergone substantial change since then. It used to have a well-defined distribution system through dealerships, but over the last decade the system has become fragmented. It now exists as a mix of two–step and three–step parts distribution chains (manufacturer–distributor–installer or manufacturer–wholesaler–jobber–installer). There are now numerous low-cost and specialty manufacturers selling parts to dealerships, aftermarket parts chains, independents, repair/maintenance shops and even auto clubs. Price, authenticity and warranty issues are all problems for the industry. The original equipment manufacturers (OEMs) are making efforts to control the distribution chains by putting pressure on their dealers and other resellers, but this pressure is being resisted.

Counterfeit, inferior, unauthorized, and diverted parts are substantial problems for the OEMs, specialty manufacturers, and for the insurance and repair industries. OEMs suffer lost revenues, brand damage, and bogus warranty claims. Independent manufacturers suffer price erosion and lost market share to knockoffs, while insurance companies have to pay inflated repair claims for inferior parts. This is an international problem.

Stories of counterfeit auto parts are increasing. The greatest public concern arises with fake parts that are critical to safety. A batch of brake shoe linings in Nigeria was made from compressed grass and burst into flames when the brake shoes were tested.[11] Counterfeit bus brake diaphragms that should hold up for over one million cycles were found to fail after as few as eight cycles when tested in the United Kingdom.[12] And, in 1987, seven children died when their bus turned over, due to faulty brakes made with sawdust pads.[13]

A 1999 European Union Green Paper estimated that between 5 to 10 percent of vehicle spare parts sold in Europe are counterfeit. It noted that the counterfeit trade in spare parts was found at all price levels and with all types of cars. The International Transportation Safety Association noted that in 1999 there had been a 59 percent increase in arrests and a 50 percent increase in convictions.[14]

In December 2000, Chinese officials reported the seizure of $2.5 million in counterfeit car parts in eight different cities. The article also said that in 30 separate outlets in Chengdu, 80 percent of the car parts being sold were counterfeits. In some cases it is not just parts, but whole vehicles, that are being knocked off. And, sometimes they are *not* of inferior quality. In July 2001, the *Pittsburgh Post-Gazette*[15] reported that Japanese motorcycles were being copied by Chinese companies at a furious pace. It was estimated that 7 million of the 11 million motorcycles (nearly two-thirds) built in China in 1999 alone were copies of Japanese designs. By using better parts and engineering, it was apparently very difficult to tell the copies from the real cycles being produced by companies such as Honda, Yamaha, and Suzuki. Sometimes it was only slight misspellings of the authentic brand names that gave them away—for instance Honea, Yameha, and Suzaki. With the knockoffs sometimes costing only half the price of the real cycles, sales by Japanese companies in China began to plummet. In 2000, Honda's sales dropped 27 percent and Yamaha's plunged 55 percent. The Chinese copies have also captured 25 percent of the Indonesian market in a two-year period of time.[16]

The concern of the Japanese producers was not primarily liability claims, rather it was loss of sales and market share. This concern extended into the fact that China's newfound expertise might be translated into other products. As the Chief Executive Officer for Honda Motor Company, Hiroyuki Yoshino said, "This trend is not limited to motorcycles. This will expand to auto parts and many other products."[17] Ironically, in this case, Honda decided to practice the old adage: "If you can't beat 'em, join 'em." Honda formed a joint venture with one of the companies (Hainan Sundiro Motorcycle Company) that was producing knockoffs. Now Honda has a partner in China with a vested interest in preventing other Chinese companies from copying the product, because it is now partly the partner's turf. The fact that the Chinese partner could also buy parts at half the price that the Japanese were paying probably helped seal the deal.

The automotive industry has mobilized to fight counterfeits over the past ten years, organizing large sting operations, raids, and, increasingly, using security marking and preventative solutions. In 1987, General Motors embarked on an undercover sting operation with the Federal Bureau of Investigation (FBI). Using the code name Operation PARTS-MAN, GM helped the FBI set up an ACDelco Wholesale Distribution Center in Michigan. The operation ran until the end of 1989. In early 1990, the FBI seized more than $50 million in counterfeit parts and raided a number of organizations making up a counterfeit parts distribution chain. More than 40 different types of parts were seized, including wheels and engine bearings, brake pads, ignition modules, oil and gas filters, air conditioner compressors, spark plugs, wheel trim, mud flaps, window decals and floor mats. At the time, this was the largest nondrug related seizure in the FBI's history.[18]

In 1991, GM Spare Parts Operations (SPO) launched the GM Restoration Parts Licensing Program to help organize its aftermarket parts sales. Prior to this, numerous companies, individuals, and even car clubs were manufacturing, reconditioning, scavenging, and reselling replacement parts for GM vehicles. Similar in ways to the Honda example, GM started drawing these groups into the program on its own terms. The company effectively created a number of watchful allies in its licensees. Once a company signed up as a licensed manufacturer or distributor, it had an economic incentive to ensure that nonlicensed competitors were brought to GM's attention. According to Rod Kinghorn, Senior Administrator for Investigations, the system worked.

On April 28, 1994, somewhat by coincidence, the U.S. Customs Service and Secret Service busted Multiple Auto Parts and Sarine Corporation, two suspected parts counterfeiting operations, for charges related to the counterfeiting of U.S. currency, as well as the counterfeiting of GM parts. This bust netted more than $1 million in bogus parts and the company appeared to be an $8 million per year counterfeit parts operation. Sultan was convicted on January 18, 1995, on seven counts of trafficking in counterfeit goods. Garbis Jerjerian, the owner of Sarine, escaped.[19]

With the experience gained over more than 12 years, GM introduced a new authentication program in late 1996. This program was tied to its strategic enforcement approach of applying its limited enforcement resources to the effective prosecution of major offenders. In part, the timing was chosen to align with the company's introduction of its new ACDelco logo. The company began applying an undisclosed, covert authentication device to some of its most frequently counterfeited products, suitable for marking both parts and packaging, but not detectable without specialized equipment.

Of course, GM is not the only car company affected by counterfeiting. In 1990, Ford of Europe estimated that 4 percent of the Ford replacement parts being sold were counterfeit or unauthorized. In 1996, under the direction of Steffen Doener, the company implemented a new test program to fight the problem. After its first year, in 1997, Doener reported the program was "very, very successful," so much so that his Ford European Parts

Brand Protection Group gained a "generous working budget" to replace its original "tiny" funding. The Group took over coordination parts and service, building teams from marketing, general counsel, the parts purchasing departments, and the parts security departments, in each country on a Pan European basis. It developed its own investigative force that began working with the World Customs Organization (WCO), European Customs organizations, and Ford dealers. All turned out to be valuable sources of information about fake parts. The teams also conducted unannounced inspections at dealers and trade shows, and conducted "trap purchases" if they had specific information to investigate.[20]

At the same time, Ford rationalized its parts labeling to improve the authentication contribution of labels. Many different label types were replaced by one standard type of label, which incorporates anticounterfeit/authentication features. Ford buys millions of parts labels but, as Doerner pointed out, it will only spend fractions of a penny for each one. Nevertheless, these labels are also contributing to the fight against counterfeits.

More recently, the world's leading car companies have begun to combine efforts. On October 19, 2001, Ford Motor Company's Automotive Consumer Services Group, Mopar Parts Division of DaimlerChrysler AG, and General Motors Service Parts Operations announced that they had joined together in forming the Global Industry Network. The Network is dedicated to assisting law enforcement agencies and the government in enforcing existing laws, strengthening patent and trademark protection laws, and notifying vendors of counterfeit parts. Company officials referred to recent counterfeiting actions including General Motors' raid of 14 counterfeit retailers and four printing operations in the Middle East and China, and Ford's identification of more than two dozen counterfeiters in Mexico, Argentina, and Brazil. In the Network's inaugural press release, Mike Jordan, president of Ford Automotive Consumer Services Group, said, "Now, everything is fair game [for the counterfeiters]. If it goes into or onto a vehicle, it's at risk of being counterfeited. Parts such as steering and suspension components, ignition modules and brake pads—items that have a direct bearing on the safe operation of our customers' vehicles—are being sold by counterfeiters without the benefit of testing for quality, safety and durability."[21] To date, however, there seems to have been more progress in Europe than in North America.

There should be no underestimating the ingenuity, either of the counterfeiters and cheats, or of the countermeasures that industry uses to fight back. Automotive fluids, gasoline, and other consumables are also counterfeited regularly. In the high stakes auto-racing world, a slight increase in the energy content or burning characteristics of fuels can make a difference in a driver's acceleration or speed. This creates the temptation to cheat by adding unsanctioned materials. In June 2002, Sunoco, the world's largest manufacturer of racing gasoline, announced it would begin marking all of its U.S. racing fuel with a sophisticated suite of authentication markers. The near infrared markers, made by Isotag, are invisible but allow race officials to instantaneously authenticate fuel at the race site using a handheld reader.[22]

In Africa, the issue is adulteration or mixing of kerosene into gasoline in order to cheat tax collectors and illegally increase the profits of refiners. The problem was particularly acute in Kenya, where fuel is refined for both the domestic and foreign markets. Refined fuel for export is taxed with a duty, whereas domestic fuel is duty-free. Fraudsters capitalized on this situation by adding untaxed kerosene to the automotive fuels refined for export and diverting the excess pure gasoline back to the domestic market. This approach allows the refiners to "sweeten" their profits to the extent of the unpaid duty. Biocode, a product security company, working with a group of African fuel authorities, is on the way to solving this problem. Different biological taggants are added in known concentrations to all refined gasoline and kerosene. The export and domestic fuels can then be checked in shipment and at retail to determine whether mixing or adulteration has taken place. Fines are imposed if it has. Since introducing the fuel-marking program, the percentage of sites selling illegal fuels has dropped by 50 percent.[23] Biocode indicates that East African governments have realized more than $100 million in increased tax collection.[24]

Electrical Product Safety

Safety certification of electrical parts is a fascinating illustration of the upper-left cell of the Harm Matrix. It shows that counterfeiters are interested in creating and selling "passable products," that is, items that will be accepted by the relevant buyer. This may, or may not, involve focusing exclusively on the manufacturing and distribution chain.

For more than 100 years, the U.S. hallmark for safety in electrical appliances has been the Underwriters Laboratory (UL). Interestingly, UL does not manufacture a product. And yet, it has faced a potentially life-threatening counterfeiting problem, which it has fought with a "zero tolerance" policy and the use of effective security technology.

UL is a nonprofit organization established in 1894. It is the world's oldest and largest product safety certification organization. Its safety certification labels are affixed to more than 14 billion products annually. Backing this certification is UL's rigorous program of construction evaluation and safety testing, including unannounced inspections in the factory and in the marketplace.

In the early 1990s, UL became aware that some electrical products were being imported bearing counterfeit paper UL labels. In one tragic case, a little girl was electrocuted by licking an incorrectly wired, falsely labeled Christmas candle. In others, house fans burst into flames, threatening the customers' property and safety.[25]

Never having confronted the problem of its certification labels being counterfeited before, but recognizing that most of the electrical products that it certified were manufactured overseas and imported into the United States, UL contacted U.S. Customs in 1995. Inspections revealed bogus labels on products entering through a number of ports. As a nationwide problem, the project was assigned to the Customs Office of Strategic Trade (OST), where Mark Goins was put in charge. OST concluded that the public health nature of the threat, coupled with the frequency and scope of the problem, warranted an unusually aggressive response.

Customs concluded that the vast majority of problem products were being imported from China, and the scale of the problem required action by Customs at all ports on a simultaneous basis. This represented U.S. Customs' first such all-port IPR Intervention. The task was complicated by the fact that there is no legal requirement for electrical equipment to bear UL labels (however, if they do have such a label, it is a crime for the label to be counterfeit). Customs developed and used an automated method for targeting shipments and ultimately inspected thousands of labels.

This project required extensive training and coordination between Customs and UL. Brian Monks, a UL engineer who had been involved in product certification and some forensic examination work, managed the UL side. Inspectors, special agents and import specialists in all of the top 10 ports were trained. Officers in all of the other ports received training materials, and all ports received continuing support throughout the Intervention. More than 1,000 Customs officials were involved.

During the course of the Intervention beginning in May 1997, more than 3 million fraudulently labeled electrical products, worth more than $50 million, were seized. This collection filled more than 250 ocean freight containers. Many of the products posed serious health and safety risks. Products including lights, fans, electric surge protectors, and other items were improperly grounded, or wired with incorrect polarity. The U.S. Consumer Product Safety Commission was asked to help with the defective products already in the United States. Ultimately, it recalled more than 50 container loads of hazardous electrical gear including more than 800,000 fans with the potential to catch fire.[26]

UL has a "zero tolerance policy," and never gives permission to release seized products bearing counterfeit labels. This approach got the attention of international traders and U.S. retailers alike. UL has gone beyond having Customs seize products. It has made major efforts to build public awareness. Both UL and Customs have issued press releases and written articles on their successes. On October 9, 1997, piles of mislabeled Christmas tree lights and other products were crushed by a steamroller, as part of a national media event.[27]

UL also took its fight to China through the U.S. Trade Representative (USTR) and to Chinese customs inspectors. Negotiations were opened between the USTR and China's Foreign Trade Minister on the issue during 1998. Also, during 1998, Chinese authorities conducted 55 raids on counterfeiting shops, leading to a number of arrests and hundreds of thousands of dollars in fines.[28]

At the same time, UL began working with Customs and started to make its labels more difficult to counterfeit. In November 1996, UL mandated use of the holographic labels for products imported from China in fifteen product categories (including power supply cords, current taps, fans, incandescent fixtures, night lights, work lights, time and photoelectric switches, power taps, transformers, surge suppressors, and power cords). It has since added more categories to this list. The labels are supplied through UL to the Chinese manufacturers of its licensees via a tightly controlled distribution system.

In March 2000, UL was recognized for its efforts and received the *Global AntiCounterfeiting Award* for outstanding accomplishments by a company.[29]

FROM PARTS TO THE WHOLE

Parts counterfeiting illustrates several issues that must be addressed as companies and governments attempt to solve the problem. The distribution and service delivery chains involved in replacement parts and consumables are often more complex than in the case of new products. The parts can generally be purchased from the OEM, or one of its authorized distributors; but can also be obtained through the secondary market, used parts, nonauthorized repairs, do-it-yourself repair, and dealers. And, of course there are a myriad of commercial exchanges, sales, closeouts, web sourcing, and other transactions that go on between, and among, these players.

The implication of this complex marketplace is that it is much easier for opportunists to insert counterfeits into the distribution chain than it would be in a tightly controlled new product sales chain. That is, the criminals have more opportunities to find weaknesses. Likewise, manufacturers and brand holders have less control and will often find it more difficult to police the market. For example, the manufacturer of a branded fashion apparel line may well be quite selective about the distributors, agents, and retailers through which it sells its goods. It may require each authorized party to sign contracts pledging not to buy from the gray market, to allow unannounced inspections of inventory, to account for sales, cancellation for breach, and so on. It can then include a covert information-bearing microthread, for example, in the labels of each of its garments (not disclosing this fact to its channel partners) and can have field investigators randomly check the inventory. By taking these measures, the company is in a relatively strong position to monitor the behavior of its distribution chain and to punish offenders that deal in counterfeits.

Virtually none of these conditions are likely to be available in most parts, consumables, and service markets. The OEM is unlikely to be able to identify, let alone contract with, all those who might be supporting users of its products. The marketplace is very unlikely to agree to inspections. And, if distributors are caught dealing in counterfeits, termination of the relationship with the manufacturer may not be deemed to be a significant threat.

Different industries also tend to have different legal and business contexts. In the United States, the FAA is responsible for authorizing the production, sale, and use of most critical aviation parts. Though this system does not function perfectly, at least there is a regulatory authority and a system in place. Now consider the computer industry. Except for certain telecommunication applications and electromagnetic emission standards, there are virtually no standards or regulatory authorities that oversee the marketplace. Price/performance and competition rule. The type and extent of regulation in each parts category will affect how and whether counterfeits can be controlled.

The FAA has the authority to initiate proceedings and promulgate legally binding rules to control counterfeiting. Indeed, it has a Suspect and Unapproved Parts task force made up of industry and agency members that have looked at the advisability of doing just that. The information technology industry is in a very different position. Recently, a number of leading information technology companies formed the Anti-Gray Market Alliance (AGMA) that is dedicated to fighting diversion and counterfeiting. It is working to characterize the extent and nature of counterfeiting in the industry, and on industry best practices for use in fighting back. The point is that the basic approach to solving the problem for any industry will depend, in part, on its legal and business context.

This chapter ends, as it began, by observing that the one unusual challenge that the parts industries must face in fighting counterfeiting is that, frequently, the purchasers or users do not, or cannot, focus on the actual product as closely as they would a new product purchase.

CHAPTER 6

Copyright and Digital Products

PIRACY OF COPYRIGHTED PRODUCTS

In China, Microsoft is launching the authentic version of Windows XP on November 9 [2001], *with a price tag of 1,498 yuan ($180). On the streets of Shanghai, meanwhile, XP has been selling for about 20 yuan for weeks. This is hardly shocking in a country in which roughly 95 percent of all software is pirated.*[1]

This chapter deals with a variety of products that are usually covered by copyrights. We are talking about products such as books, photographs, songs, plays, paintings, movies or DVDs, software, and audio records, tapes, or CDs. A copyright protects the creative works of authors or artists and gives them exclusive rights to reproduce, display, perform, distribute, or sell their works. In this way, a copyright can be useful in preventing the illegal copying of the work involved. Note, however, that it is more the form than the knowledge that is being protected. The copyright holder also has rights to derivative works. You cannot copyright an idea (e.g., to make a movie about the sinking of the Titanic), but only the tangible expression of that idea (i.e., the movie itself). Thus, if a company has valuable knowledge that is embedded in a process or product that they have written about in a scientific article, they will also need a patent to protect that knowledge; the copyright would merely prevent the copying of the article. However, an artist can grant or sell the right for someone else to use, copy, or distribute their work. The major international agreements dealing with copyrights are the Universal Copyright Convention (UCC) and the Berne Convention, in which signatory countries agree to honor the laws of other signatory countries. Chapter 13 discusses copyright protection in greater detail.

		Low	**High**
Deception Level of deception inherent in the sale of the product	**High**	A poorly reproduced audin tape in an official and sealed package.	A good reproduction of a painting by Renoir being auctioned by a reputable firm.
	Low	A bad copy of the movie *Titanic* on an unlabeled video tape.	A copy of *Microsoft Office* software on an Iomega zip disk with no documentation.

Low   **High**

Quality

Quality and functionality
of the counterfeit product

EXHIBIT 6.1   **Harm Matrix for Digital and Copyright Goods**

Let us again turn to the Harm Matrix (see Exhibit 6.1) to help sort out the various types of counterfeits and pirated products in this diverse realm of copyrighted products. These products are increasingly available in digitized form, making quality copies even easier to make.

For the industries involved, the biggest problem is the lower-right cell. This is where product piracy is rampant. This is not problematic for the consumers for exactly the same reason that it is a problem for the producers. The cost to duplicate an expensive software program is practically

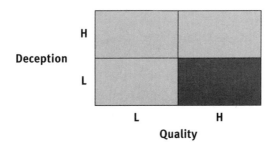

nil compared to its sale price. Customers are rarely deceived; they know they are not buying a licensed version of the software. Yet, they receive a product that has a high level of functionality. It does what it is supposed to do. The only real problem for consumers is if something goes wrong with the program. They will not be able to get any technical support from the company, nor will they be able to receive cheap updates. For computer software (as with some other products in this category), the value is not in the physical product (the disk), but rather in the information on the disk. That is also where the investment is for the company producing software, and it is that research and developmental investment that they must recoup.

Likewise, in the lower-left cell of the matrix, consumers again don't suffer much harm. If they buy what they know to be a poor copy of a popular movie, at least they can say they saw it. They get what they paid for and what they expected. However, for the producers, the story is the

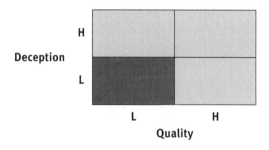

opposite. The expense is in the production of the movie. Even the cheapest movies today are likely to cost several million dollars to produce; many cost several hundred million. The only way to recover that investment is to be able to sell the right to enjoy your creative work to someone else. When that movie is pirated, copied, and sold illegally, it comes straight off the bottom line for the creators and producers.

One could also argue that consumers may not suffer much harm in the example depicted in the upper-right cell of the matrix. It is true that consumers are unaware that they are buying a fake or unauthorized copy. However, if it performs well relative to the consumers' purpose in buying

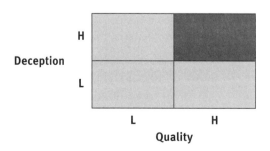

it, perhaps not much harm is done. If it looks like a Dali, and my friends and I think it is a Dali, then who is harmed? But, of course, if the fake is discovered, then consumers lose even the psychic value of ownership, not to mention that the resale value will take a nosedive. The question is whether Salvador Dali (or his estate) is harmed. In this example, there is probably not much harm done. However, we could extend this example to good quality software, where the product and information, as well as the packaging and documentation, have all been exquisitely copied. In this case, the producers suffer from lost market share and the damage to their reputation when they refuse to stand behind what the consumer firmly believes is an authentic product.

Finally, the upper-left cell represents an example where consumers stand the best chance of suffering harm—economic harm, not physical. It is again a combination of the consumers being deceived, coupled with

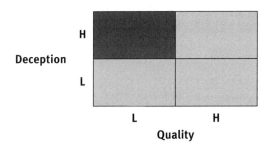

a product that does not function as intended. One author once purchased an audiotape from a street vendor in Taiwan. It was nicely packaged with the same label and cover that he had recently seen in the States. It was even sealed with a cellophane-type material. The first time he played it the audio quality was terrible. The second time he played it the tape came unwound in his machine and broke. He thought he had bought the real thing for a great price. Actually, he bought a terrible product at a terrible price, since any price greater than zero would have been a bad deal. Legitimate producers can suffer harm in this case. Had the author not been able to find this "great deal" on the tape he wanted, he would probably have purchased it at the regular price when he got home. Since the one he bought now had to be replaced, one could argue that the producer may, or may not, lose market share in this example. Actually, the author didn't replace it; he just had a bad feeling about that recording group after his bad shopping experience. Sure, he knew it wasn't their fault but he had to blame someone, didn't he?

THE INTERNET HAS ENHANCED THE PROBLEM

The Internet medium makes the act of plagiarism much easier, much faster to accomplish. Instead of having to take the time to retype content, copyright violators can now simply use copy-and-paste tools to steal material. And because there is so much information posted on the Internet, it's become a huge headache in terms of policing content.[2]

In fact, that is exactly what the author has done with the above paragraph. Through a particular search engine, he was able to find an article from *Folio: The Magazine for Magazine Management.* He printed and saved the article, then cut this paragraph out and pasted it into this chapter.

And so it goes. Once a piece of work (book, song, picture, movie, or article) is digitized and made available on the web, it is extremely easy to copy and make it available to a number of people all at once. There is a misconception that once something is available on the Internet that copyright legislation is no longer applicable. But, as the recent case against Napster by the music recording industry has clearly pointed out, that is not the case. Nevertheless, copyright infringement has become much more difficult to police now that the Internet has arrived. The Internet is fast and fairly anonymous. It has resulted in a cultural sea change regarding the rights of creators in conflict with the desires of consumers. Copyright infringement is facilitated by the possibilities of this new technology.

SEVERAL TYPES OF PRODUCTS ARE AT RISK

A variety of creative works are protected by copyrights. Chapter 13 discusses copyrights and the protection of certain types of intellectual property in more detail. The major areas of copyright infringement are discussed below.

Computer Software

When speaking of computer software, there is some confusion in the literature as to the various types of pirated software. Software can be pirated by "end-user copying," when someone installs software on more computers than they are licensed to do (e.g., home and office, or several office machines). Commercial copying and compilation are also problems. "Downloading" software from Internet sites without the express permission of the copyright holder is also a form of pirating. Another type of pirating is referred to as "unauthorized license use." This could happen when software is specially priced for academia, but somehow gets directed into the nonacademic market. And finally, there is "counterfeit" software. However, some use this term to refer to software that is made to look like the real thing in terms of its packaging, but may have little functionality at all. Others define counterfeiting (as applied to software) as "the illegal duplication and sale of copyrighted software." For others, unauthorized copying and selling is called "bootleg" or "pirated" software.

According to industry organizations like the Software and Information Industry Association (SIIA), software piracy accounted for an annual $11 billion loss in revenues to legitimate producers worldwide back in 1998. They further claimed that one in four installed business applications in the United States at that time was pirated software. Could you afford to have someone steal one-quarter of your business? Another study jointly commissioned by the Business Software Alliance (BSA) and the Software Publishers Association (SPA) concluded that, in 1997, 40 percent of new business applications installed worldwide were stolen. Could you afford to have someone steal 40 percent of your new business?[3]

Software producers are not the only losers. A 1998 study by PricewaterhouseCoopers suggested that if software pirating could be reduced to reasonable levels, the industry could double the number of jobs it creates worldwide from 1 million to 2 million. This would mean an additional 200,000 jobs in the United States alone. Likewise, a study commissioned by the Business Software Alliance, and conducted by Nathan Associates, estimated the losses to the United States' economy in a single year were 109,000 jobs, $4.5 billion in wages, and $1 billion in lost tax revenue.[4] The elimination of software piracy by 2005 would mean an additional $25 billion in revenues for governments worldwide. Furthermore, software piracy stifles innovation when creators cannot benefit from their own creation, at least to the extent that makes them willing to take the risks in the first place.

Perhaps to a greater extent than with other products in this category, software piracy is increasingly linked to organized crime. Organized crime produces counterfeit software that is sold, not only through the black market, but also through legitimate resellers. On-line auctions have made it even tougher to catch the counterfeiters of software. A raid in Paramount, California, exposed an organized crime ring and $56 million worth of bootleg Microsoft software. They also found a $1.5 million CD-ROM replicator that was "as big as a high school classroom."[5] Related companies were busy counterfeiting the Microsoft boxes, labels, and certificates. Organized crime can afford the very best. It's the old adage that it takes money to make money, or to steal money.

◑ FOCUS 6.1 ◑

THE BUSINESS SOFTWARE ALLIANCE

There are many industry organizations that can be helpful in the fight against counterfeiting and pirating. The Business Software Alliance (BSA) is the organization serving the hardware, software, and Internet sectors, which are among the fastest growing industries in the world. The BSA plays a research, education, and advocacy role as it relates to these industries. Some of the best known companies in the worldwide technology sector are members of BSA and/or its Policy Council; they include Adobe, Apple, Borland, Compaq, Dell, IBM, Intel, Intuit, Lotus Development, Microsoft, and Symantec.

BSA commissions an annual study of software piracy by the International Planning and Research Corporation (IPR) for its corporate members. Only business software such as databases, word processing, and spread sheets are included, along with other professional applications and utility programs. The study defines software pirating as "the amount of business application software installed . . . without a license." The results indicate that the amount of piracy decreased for four straight years from 1996 through 1999; however, it has increased the past two years. The lowest rate of piracy reached in 1999 was 36 percent, but that figure

(continues)

FOCUS 6.1 *(Continued)*

increased to 40 percent in 2001. The dollar losses due to piracy actually declined by nearly 7 percent between 2000 and 2001, though they were still estimated at nearly $11 billion. However, this was due to the impact of a strong dollar (thus lower prices when converted to dollars), and to the decreased demand due to the weakening economies around the world. Nevertheless, dollar losses were again highest in the Eastern European region at roughly $4.7 billion. However, the three countries with the highest piracy rates were from Asia; they were Vietnam (94 percent), China (92 percent), and Indonesia (88 percent). Can you imagine trying to sell a product where only 6 percent of the market is legitimate? Furthermore, results suggest that in bad economic times, compliance with legitimate licensing agreements may be considered a luxury which is quickly abandoned, augmenting the problem even further.

In fighting the problem, Microsoft Corporation has often gone after the resellers of fake software. They hope that by starting with the little guys they will be able to work their way up the chain and nab the big guys. However, the resellers complain that it is impossible for them to know whether the product is legitimate. Some products even come with fake certificates of authenticity. Others claim that software sales represent such a small percentage of their revenues that it would be stupid to intentionally sell counterfeit software. Microsoft counters that consumers can solve the problem by only purchasing through authorized Microsoft distributors. If consumers continue to buy from suspect sources, particularly after receiving a warning letter from Microsoft, then they may not be the innocent victims they claim. Microsoft claims to receive more than 25,000 new reports of piracy every year.

On-line auctions of software through sites like eBay and Yahoo have complicated the problem further. One report noted that a search on eBay found 340 classified ads selling software at far below the retail price. A representative for Adobe stated that their own research indicated that 70 percent to 90 percent of the software sold on auction sites is pirated. However, the auction sites claim it is impossible for them to determine what is and is not legitimate. After all, they are just providing the marketplace. And so the buck gets passed along, and the consumer gets left holding the bag (with the fake product in it). Again, the big problem for the software producers is when consumers call them to fix a problem with their software, only to be told that it is not authentic. When the company refuses to service the counterfeit goods, the customer often becomes irate. Consumers feel that it is the company's responsibility to prevent counterfeits, and if the company can't do this, then they feel the company should service the fake product anyway.

◑ FOCUS 6.2 ◑

ETHICS AND INTELLECTUAL PROPERTY RIGHTS

If we separate ethical questions from legal ones, then there certainly are some legitimate ethical concerns in the protection of intellectual property rights (IPRs). After all, IPRs are essentially private rights that accrue to the creator, or the licensee or right holder when they have been transferred. These private rights may be at odds with what is perceived as the public good. This is probably most obvious with products such as pharmaceuticals (which were discussed in Chapter 4). Is it more important to protect corporate patents or to make sure that beneficial medicines can be made available to the people who need them at a reasonable price? Most recently, this issue has been raised regarding AIDS drugs for Africa and regarding Cipro for protecting the U.S. population from the anthrax threat. While the general populace may appreciate the need for protecting private rights in order to compensate for past creativity and to stimulate future innovation, they may not feel that these rights should dominate when a critical public threat is present.

With something like software the conflict between private and public rights may not be as evident as it is with pharmaceuticals (that is why we decided to discuss the issue in this chapter.) Software is often quite expensive to develop but incredibly cheap and easy to duplicate. Much like pharmaceuticals, the price reflects the high development costs. Thus prices remain relatively high, particularly for consumers in the developing world. Yet in this new computerized economy, many people in the developing world contend that the progress of their societies depends on affordable access to the tools required in this new environment. Without such access, it can be argued that the gap between rich

(continues)

FOCUS 6.2 *(Continued)*

and poor will continue to widen. It is difficult for such consumers to understand how the private rights of big software companies and the financial harm to such corporations should outweigh the public rights of people who need their product to compete economically, yet cannot afford the seemingly exorbitant price being asked.

It is in this context that some have come to see "pirating" as a "Robin Hood crime." By stealing business software from the rich and providing it to the poor (at reasonable prices), the pirates are seen by many as heroes rather than villains. Others feel that if software providers were willing to make their products available at much more reasonable prices, then even consumers in the developing markets may prefer to buy authentic products and get the service and access to updates which come along with them. However, the price that would seem "reasonable" is no doubt a small fraction of the existing price. Likewise, as prices in different markets become significantly different, a problem with gray markets develops where third parties will buy in the low-priced markets and sell in the high-priced ones in order to capture that differential for themselves. The problem of gray markets is discussed further in Focus 7.2. The challenge is to find an ethical solution which protects both private and public rights!

In some of the less developed countries, or those facing severe economic problems, the counterfeit situation is huge. The Software and Information Industry Association (SIIA) estimates that nearly 100 percent of business software in Russia, China, Vietnam, and Indonesia is counterfeit. However, corporate bootlegging seems to have declined somewhat in other parts of the world as the legitimate price of software has declined. At the same time, illegal Internet sales of bootleg software seems to be on the rise at the person-to-person or C2C level. In August 1999, a student at the University of Oregon was arrested for posting, to be downloaded from his site, thousands of copyrighted software programs, digitally recorded movies, and music recordings. He could have received a fine of up to $250,000 on top of a 10-year prison term.[6]

With the advent of CD-recording capability, copying the software to disk has become available to the little guy. Now the problem is the packaging and the certificates of guarantee. Microsoft's "Certificates of

Authenticity" apparently contain at least ten different protective features, produced at no small cost. However, it was reported that break-ins in Ireland and Scotland in 1997 supplied counterfeiters with enough authentic Microsoft guarantee certificates to last several years.[7]

◑ FOCUS 6.3 ◑

MICROSOFT

THE ALBUQUERQUE GROUP: December 7, 1978
Top row: Steve Wood (left), Bob Wallace, Jim Lane. Middle row: Bob O'Rear, Bob Greenberg, Marc McDonald, Gordon Letwin. Bottom row: Bill Gates, Andrea Lewis, Marla Wood, Paul Allen.

You have to watch out who you hang around with; you could end up a multibillionaire! The guy in the lower left corner is Bill Gates, born in 1955 and now the Chairman of Microsoft Corporation. The company had its roots in a partnership that Gates formed with his childhood friend Paul Allen (also in the picture). Microsoft was incorporated in Washington in 1981. Now, just over 20 years old, it is one of the largest companies in the world. In fiscal year 2002, Microsoft had net income of $7.83 billion on revenues of more than $28 billion. Total assets were over $59 billion, and as of July 1, 2002, the company had more than 50,000 employees. The company has grown through mergers, acquisitions, and

(continues)

strategic alliances. It now has 118 subsidiaries (107 are wholly owned) operating in nearly 80 sovereign countries or regions around the globe. In 2001, 27 percent of Microsoft's total revenue came from outside the United States. We saw in Exhibit 2.3 that Microsoft was second only to Coca-Cola as the most valuable brand in the world in 2002, with a brand value in excess of $64 billion. It is by far the most dominant player in the computer software market.

More recently, the company has faced lawsuits by the government and some competitors for monopolistic practices, but to date the company has survived those challenges quite well. A much greater threat (than antitrust concerns) has come from software counterfeiters and pirates. Microsoft uses a variety of methods, including private investigators, and has brought hundreds of lawsuits over the years against retailers and distributors of counterfeit and pirated software. However, on-line auction sites have made the distribution of pirated software even easier. In some cases, everything is either pirated or counterfeited—the software, the packaging, the user manual, the labels and holograms, and even the certificates of authenticity. Disks containing software valued at hundreds of dollars in the retail market can be duplicated for less than 50 cents each. As an example of the magnitude of the problem, Office 2000 Professional which retails for over $500 in the United States was available in Hong Kong and Singapore for less than $20, a week before it officially debuted.[8]

While fighting counterfeiters can be expensive, Nancy Anderson, Senior Corporate Attorney at Microsoft Europe, reported that they realized a return of 5-10 times on their investment—and that was in 1996. And that does not include the huge increases in legitimate jobs and tax revenues that result from successes in the anticounterfeiting fight.

Paintings

For much of history, whether a painting was an original or a copy was not of much concern. In many ways, imitation was the highest form of flattery. The first painter to actually sign his paintings was Giotto (1266–1337). Later, it became more common to sign paintings, but it was still not always clear who the actual artist was. This was because a more famous artist such as Rubens headed a studio that had several pupil assistants that actually did some work on the paintings to which the Old Master eventually attached his name. The master could have been solely responsible for the painting, he could have finished the painting after some preliminary work by his apprentices, or he could have only supervised the work of several other experts on a particular painting.

Today's counterfeiting of artwork is often the result of an unknown artist producing a painting "in the style of" a well-known artist and then forging the signature of that artist. There are two types of such forgeries. With "pastiche," artists supposedly interpret works by a well-known artist, copying the style and brush strokes, but applying the technique to a different subject. With "mosaic," artists copy elements from several works of a well-known artist and combine them into a new work. In either case, it is the forged signature attributing the work to the well-known artist that is intended to deceive the buyer and, therefore, results in the fraud. In faking the signature, the artist is attempting to usurp the value of that individual's brand and deceive the buyer—counterfeiting by our definition.

The legality of such copies (even those including the famous artist's signature) varies from country to country. For example, in France it is not illegal to copy the signature of an old master if the work is in the public domain. In fact, galleries have opened in France and Italy to display such copies, signature and all. Similarly, action cannot be taken against a copyist if the materials, size, or colors are different from the original. Therefore, counterfeiting of famous paintings presents some unique problems that do not seem to be present with other types of copyright-protected goods.[9]

There have been several high-profile cases of forged artwork. One of the best known was by Hans Van Meegeren. He forged several works which he attributed to the great Dutch Masters of the seventeenth century, including Vermeer, Hals, Hoogh, and Terborch. It was said that part of his motive was to be able to demonstrate the incompetence of the art experts by successfully passing his works off as originals of the masters. He often found periods of time during a famous artist's life about which little was known. He would then create works for that period that would fill in the gaps of that artist's productivity.

A second famous case involved Fernand Legros who became a dealer of fakes. He had many forgers who worked for him; one of the best was Elmer Hoffman, known as Elmyr de Hory, who claimed to have produced over 400 masterpiece imitations. It is thought that his works alone sold for more than $60 million. However, Hory never signed his works. It was another fellow that worked for Legros, Real Lessard, who added the forged signatures to Hory's works. Hory committed suicide before he could ever appear in court. Legros, after fleeing to Switzerland and then Brazil, was finally apprehended and sentenced to two years in prison. Lessard actually published a book in which he claimed nearly all of Hory's fakes as his own. One American collector, Algur Meadows, had purchased 58 paintings sold by Legros. His $55 million worth of paintings were eventually revealed to be fakes.

Often these forged paintings became legitimized by being introduced in shows and galleries along with authentic paintings by the famous artist. In 1967 at the National Gallery in Ottawa, it was reported that of 187 paintings, 85 were fakes and another 70 were suspect. In another case, Ellen and Jan Van den Bergen were arrested in France in 1994. By that time, they had spent about 16 years putting into circulation fake Chagalls, Dalis, Klimts, Miros, and others. Along with fake paintings officials found 200 fake certificates of authenticity. Did you ever wonder how you could be sure that certificates of authenticity were indeed authentic? Now you know—you can't. In fact, Henri Haddad (aka David Stein) revealed that he had sold more than 300 fakes between 1963 and 1967 for more than $2 million; he signed the certificates of authenticity himself.

A British forger, Tom Keating, claimed to have faked more than 200 paintings that he passed off as Constables, Goyas, Krieghoffs, Degas, Gainsboroughs, and Turners. Another forger, Edgar Mrugalla, put into circulation over 2,360 fakes worth $60 million by the time he was arrested in Germany in 1988. The problem is immense. In the seven years between 1980 and 1987, it was estimated that Americans paid between $600 million and $1 billion for fake Dalis. However, some claimed that Dali himself augmented the problem by signing paintings by others when he could no longer paint himself.[10]

Songs

Like films, the music industry has been plagued by the unauthorized duplication of audiotapes and CDs. In March 2001, *The New York Times* reported that the Secret Service found a large CD counterfeiting operation in Queens and Manhattan. The operation had enough equipment (which was seized) to produce more than three million CDs a year.[11] The recent controversy involving Napster is more of an open sharing arrangement, but nevertheless an infringement of copyrights.

What would you think of a company that went from zero to 38,000,000 customers in less than a year with no advertising? However, despite that meteoric rise, the company never really made any money. That is quite different from most of the other companies and industries we have been discussing in this chapter. Counterfeiters are definitely in it to make money, and they do it, in this case, by infringing on the copyrights of others. Napster also violated (maybe bypassed is a better word) the copyrights of the artists and recording studios whose songs it made available to others. At least, this was the view of 18 different record labels, including some of the biggest in the industry—BMG, Sony, Warner, Universal, and EMI. They filed a lawsuit against Napster in 1999, and the courts have basically upheld their complaint.[12]

But again, what Napster did was not illegally copy others' songs; rather it simply made them available through a rather ingenious file-sharing website. Napster not only made physical products obsolete (i.e., tapes, CDs, records) and the physical distribution system to deliver them to customers; it also relegated copyrights to the dustbin. The copyright holders no longer held exclusive rights to benefit from the use and distribution of their works. Copyrights were a type of property right that had long been considered sacrosanct in this country, and it made little difference whether someone else was benefiting financially from bypassing those rights. The copyright holders were losing money, and that was that.

The dilemma is how to protect copyrights while allowing music fans to listen to what they want, when they want. Radio doesn't allow that, and buying your own CDs means a fairly substantial upfront investment for what might be fairly temporary desires. That's why audiophiles have stack upon stack of CDs that haven't been listened to since the first month they were purchased. If the big record companies get together they could offer an on-line subscription service that would protect copyrights, bring in income, and offer a much cheaper alternative to the listening public. But, it needs to be a collaborative venture. Just as consumers would not buy a TV that only broadcast shows from a single network, music lovers will not subscribe to a website that only plays the music of a single recording company. One might question why the big recording companies didn't jointly buy Napster and make it their portal? Then all of their offerings could have been available through that single portal for a very reasonable monthly subscription price. Some estimates suggested that Napster could have been purchased for $20 billion, and that the recording companies could have doubled their $13 billion in annual CD sales in a couple of years.[13]

Actually, it sounds like the major record labels are coming to terms with this new reality. A recent *NYTimes.com* article says: "Three years after Napster unleashed the first wave of music-trading over the Internet— and a full year after the company was shut down by a court order—the labels are coming to terms with the notion that Internet file-sharing is reshaping their business, and they must compete with piracy or risk losing a generation of customers. The Universal Music Group plans to announce today that it has licensed its catalog to Listen.com, making Listen.com the first to provide customers access to the catalogs of all five major labels over the Internet for under $10 a month."[14]

After a 5 percent decline in worldwide sales in 2001 and a continuing decline in 2002, the music sellers are increasingly convinced that "digital piracy" is the culprit. Furthermore, there is an increasing realization on their part that "sharing" music over the Internet is becoming the accepted cultural norm, and the old notion of "creative rights" is being replaced by this new right to listen to whatever music listeners want, when they want it.

The President of the eLabs division of Universal, Larry Kenswil, logically concludes, "We could be 100 percent correct morally and legally that it is wrong to trade copyrighted files, but from a business standpoint it doesn't matter. We need to construct legal alternatives."[15]

Movies

In Chapter 1 there was a reference to a recent bust in Brooklyn where a man and his uncle were caught counterfeiting DVDs. The excerpt from *The New York Times* article was:

> *A man and his uncle, accused of running a pirating operation out of a store in Brooklyn, were indicted yesterday in the biggest DVD-counterfeiting case in the five-year history of the format in the United States, federal officials said. The*

authorities say they found more than 30,000 bootleg DVD's, some of them
popular movies like Cats and Dogs, The Grinch *and the* Godfather *trilogy,*
along with 30,000 compact discs by musical performers like Jennifer Lopez, R.
Kelly and Santana, in a cottage factory run by Abdulla Qaza, 19, and his
uncle, Khalid Ghnaim, 33. The discs had a retail value of about $1 million, the
United States attorney's office said. Both men were charged with copyright and
trademark infringement and conspiracy and face up to 10 years in prison and
$2 million in fines if convicted.[16]

Several things are interesting about this story. First, it took place in
Brooklyn—not Beijing, not Bangalore, not Bangkok, but Brooklyn. In
some respects, this was a very small-time operation—a young man and
his uncle. The article goes on to note that DVDs only hit the American
market in 1997, yet here is this mom and pop (ok, boy and uncle) operation duplicating this new technology within five years and distributing
the counterfeit products through street vendors in the New York metro-
politan area. The authentic products usually cost $20–$25, but these
were selling on the street for half that price.

Here is the vicious cycle. The article says "by cutting into the revenue
of the legitimate entertainment businesses, bootleggers end up driving
up the prices that law-abiding customers pay."[17] Why is that? Because it
costs money to adequately protect what is rightfully yours—your intellectual property (which, in this case, is your creative property.) The later
chapters in this book discuss in detail the many ways available to seek
protection; you can establish an internal management structure with the
sole purpose of brand and IP protection. Of course, this is not free. Or,
you can hire private investigators, and possibly undertake legal action if
the investigators are successful. Also not free. There are a variety of technological solutions to the counterfeiting problem—for a price. Well, you
get the picture. But, the legitimate producers will pass along these costs
of protecting their rights. In part, this is what will drive up the prices to
law-abiding customers. Of course these higher prices for the authentic
products only serve to widen the gap between legitimate and counterfeit
products, which in turn increases the incentive for counterfeiters, bootleggers, and pirates to enter the market. And so forth, and so forth.

Some films like *The Blair Witch Project* appear on the internet as MPEG
digital files before being released in theatres; this kind of illegal release
can cost American movie producers as much as $3 billion annually.[18]

Another article claims, "Just days after *Harry Potter and the Sorcerer's Stone* broke opening-day records in London and New York, pirated copies of the film are already being sold along the streets and alleys of Beijing."[19]

◖ FOCUS 6.4 ◗

IS IT FAIR USE OR INFRINGEMENT?

A good example of how technology has made the legal issues surrounding copyright infringement more complex is represented by a small company in Greeley, Colorado, called Family Shield Technologies, Inc. They decided that "fair use" included allowing people to watch only those parts of a movie they wished to see, and they created a technology to make that possible. Their software, which you can download from their website for a fee, allows you to blank the screen for nudity or violence, or to mute bad language from the sound track. There are eight different types of shields that can be applied.

Movie producers are screaming foul. After all, copyright laws (at least in this country) prevent someone from altering your creative work and benefiting from it financially unless they have been authorized by the creator (small "c"). Copyright holders are claiming their exclusive rights are being violated by editing companies such as Family Shield.

However the law also allows "fair use" of copyrighted material as long as one is not making money from the creations of others. The executives of Family Shield contend that they are not making any alterations to the more than 100 films for which they have created shields. According to them, they are simply allowing people to watch whatever parts of a movie they want to watch. The inventor of the shield technology even contends, "In fact, more people will see the movies with this technology, than would see them without it."[20] But the producers counterclaim that by omitting certain scenes and certain language, their works have indeed been altered and the movie that people end up watching may be quite different than the one they created. It is not the same as the issue with Napster. There consumers were able to acquire copyrighted material for free, whereas here the consumer still has to pay for the movie, but then can alter it for personal viewing in their own homes. Is this free speech or copyright infringement? The courts have yet to decide.

A plant in Fujian Province was finally shut down by the Chinese; it had been producing about 80,000 illegal copies of video CDs per day, according to the Xinhua News Agency.[21]

Just as Napster allows the free sharing of music recordings, *Scour.com* can be used to download free movies from the Internet. Someone reported searching for *American Beauty* and *Gladiator* and said they found several sources for free downloads. However, downloading movies is much more time-consuming than downloading songs because video files are much larger. In fact, depending on your computer modem's connection and transfer speed, it may take four to five times the length of the movie.[22] Nevertheless, according to the Motion Picture Association of America, as many as 450,000 movies are downloaded every day, which in turn cost studios an estimated $3 billion every year. Four out of 10 movies never recoup their original investment, which in 2000 was over $80 million per film.[23] Of course, once you have got it, you have got it for good—and for free. Frankly, $5 at Blockbuster sounds like a better use of one's time. Time is money. Anyway, as you would guess, *Scour.com* has been sued by The Motion Picture Association of America (among others) in order to prevent the violation of copyrights their members hold. Also, not surprisingly, *Scour* claims to be protected by the "safe harbor" clause of the Digital Millennium Copyright Act of 1998.

Books and Articles

In early 2001, the Association of American Publishers, using undercover investigators, found $14.5 million worth of counterfeit books in a warehouse outside of Seoul, Korea. Included were about 600,000 books involving 2,000 different titles from several different publishers. The President of one of Korea's largest book distributors was arrested and held without bail. One month earlier in India, a similar raid turned up 20,000 counterfeit copies of books by popular authors such as Clancy, Ludlum, and Rowling.[24]

In China, Ms. Wang Ruiqin of People's Literature is betting that Harry Potter will eventually be as big there as it is in the United States. She won the right to publish the Harry Potter books over ten rival companies. She published the first three books as a set; the initial print run was to be 600,000 sets. The sets were to sell for about $10, which is quite expensive by Chinese standards. She was to pay a 10 percent license fee for each book sold.

While Ms. Wang was concerned about the current campaign against "feudal superstition" in China, which might diminish the appeal of the Potter books, her bigger concern was piracy. Unauthorized copies of the books were available in kiosks well before her planned release date. Even one of Beijing's biggest bookstores said it would have the books available before her release date.

Ms. Wang's company had a similar problem a few years earlier when it published *The Bridges of Madison County* in Chinese. At the time, she estimated that pirated copies outsold the authorized versions by 3 to 1. Someone even wrote an unauthorized sequel in which the lovers were reunited in Japan; that's some bridge!

The author will indirectly lose money since the official licensee in China will not sell as many books in China due to the pirates, and therefore won't pay as much in license fees as would otherwise be the case. Sometimes, it helps to have a local licensee, because then you have an insider who is losing money as well and, therefore, has a vested interest in seeing that this kind of illegal activity is prevented. Local police are more likely to aid a local firm than an invisible foreign firm. For her part, Ms. Wang decided to have the Harry Potter trilogy printed on a special light green paper. She felt she could then turn to the media to help her educate the buying public to recognize the real version from the pirated version.[25] The question—again—is whether the buying public cares.

Whether the pen is mightier than the web is very much an open question, at this point in time. The ease with which the written word can be digitized presents some interesting legal questions. The Copyright Act of 1976 states that publishers can reproduce and redistribute a particular work as part of "the original collective work; any revision of that collective work; or any later collective work in the same series." Thus, when electronic databases like *www.nytimes.com* or *www.UnCover.com* republish an article from a particular periodical, they claim it is permitted as a legitimate revision of the original article. However, some authors, particularly freelancers, say that when this happens on-line publishers are using their work without their permission. By including someone's work in their database, it can be argued that the on-line publishers are benefiting from that work, if only because they can claim more citations. Since the copyright law does not directly address methods and media, the courts are wrestling with this dilemma.

One such case is *Tasini v. The New York Times.*[26] Tasini is president of the National Writers Union. He lost in the first round, but won on a reversal in the Second U.S. Court of Appeals in New York City. The court agreed that a publisher can not grant rights to an electronic aggregator such as Nexis to distribute a work without the permission of the author. Another case *(Ryan v. CARL Corp.)* resulted in a $7.5 million settlement in favor of the plaintiffs, some freelance writers suing *UnCover.com*. Now some publishers are getting their freelance writers to sign away their rights to sue for copyright infringement and granting republishing rights as part of the agreement to publish their works.[27]

Digital book piracy has finally gotten the attention of the book publishing industry, much as it did earlier in the music and film industries. *Harry Potter and the Goblet of Fire* were available at no cost on the Internet only hours after being released to bookstores. Harlan Ellison is a 66-year old "imaginative fiction" writer who has brought several lawsuits to prevent the release of pirated copies of his work on the Internet. He has had some successes and some failures. One of the failures was a suit against America Online for aiding the illegal distribution of his work. However, the court found AOL innocent, according to the Digital Millennium Copyright Act and the "safe harbor" clause. This states that Internet access providers are not responsible for what can be accessed through their portals, as they are only providing the conduit and not the content.[28]

Photographs

Photographers have had many of the same issues regarding copyright infringement. Jerry Greenberg sued *National Geographic* when some pictures he had shot for them as a freelance photographer were included in a CD-ROM set covering 108 years of the magazine. Since the set included a separately copyrighted search engine, Greenberg's contention was that this constituted a new derivative work and therefore violated his copyright. However, the District Court judge ruled against him.

WHAT IS BEING DONE TO COUNTER INFRINGEMENTS?

There have been a number of approaches to fighting the growing losses to copyright holders. These have included government action, legal action, investigative services, and utilization of a variety of security devices. We will briefly discuss each of these approaches only as related to copyright material, as they are covered in more depth in other chapters.

Government Action

In the 1980s, the overseas pirating of American copyright-protected products became particularly onerous. While the problem was acute in a number of countries, Korea became the focus of the American government's efforts to combat the problem.

In their case *"The U.S. Korea Dispute Over Intellectual Property Rights,"* Michael Ryan and Justine Bednarik note:[29]

> USTR [United States Trade Representative] also received complaints of extensive copyright piracy concerning books, records, and cassettes, films and video cassettes, and computer software. The International Intellectual Property Alliance, a consortium of associations representing the publishing, music, motion picture, and software industries, charged the Korean copyright law offered little protection of foreign copyrights. Videocassette piracy was rampant in Korea. While the Motion Picture Law was intended to provide some protection, it was rarely enforced. Other trade barriers such as quotas and import delays discouraged and slowed the importation of U.S. works and left the door open for pirates to fill the demand for Hollywood films. Book losses, that is, unauthorized reproduction of U.S. literary works, were estimated at $70 million in 1984. Legitimate importation amounted to only $8 million. Over ninety percent of the English language textbooks used in Korean universities was pirated, and entire textbooks were frequently copied and distributed. It was estimated that sales of pirated tapes and records made up sixty percent of the Korean market, amounting to $40 million in lost revenue annually for American intellectual property (IP) holders. Similarly, copies of computer software were readily available and estimated losses were increasing rapidly from a base of $20 million in 1984.
>
> These American industries asserted that they were losing in total about $150 million annually in Korean markets to pirated products and that the losses were increasing each year as the markets grew and as pirating practices became more prevalent. They pointed out that Korea was not a signatory to any multilateral

treaty or to a bilateral treaty with the United States that would protect foreign copyright holders. USTR was urged by the alliance to press Korea to pass a new copyright law, accede to international copyright agreements, and to enforce the new laws vigorously.

If these don't seem like huge figures, remember it was the early 1980s, in a single country, for copyright holders in a few related industries. In the late 1980s, there was increasing pressure on the U.S. government from several industries that felt violations of their intellectual property rights were costing them billions. Intellectual Property Rights (IPRs) became perhaps the biggest issue for U.S. trade officials, as they began to see IPRs as just as important as tariffs and quotas. The government took a number of steps to counter the threat to American IPRs. They made them a major issue in the Uruguay Round of multilateral negotiations under the auspices of GATT (the General Agreements for Tariffs and Trade). They also began to link IPR protection to the GSP (Generalized System of Preferences), which gave special tariff reductions to goods from designated developing countries. The Trade and Tariff Act of 1984 was amended to give the Executive Branch greater power to impose compensating trade restrictions under what was known as "Section 301" (of the 1974 Trade Act).

Many countries were cited as being weak in the enforcement of IPR protections, among them Brazil, Korea, India, Indonesia, Saudi Arabia, Taiwan, and Thailand. However, it was Korea on which the government selected to focus its immediate attention. However, in Korea, there was a very different cultural attitude toward the importance of protecting the intellectual property rights of others. The Koreans felt they were entitled to benefit from the creations of others. Perhaps this attitude stems more from economic than cultural differences. In fact, the United States itself refused to sign the first multilateral agreement (the Berne Convention) in 1886 because it felt entitled as a developing country to benefit from the creations in the then more developed world. Apparently, for less developed countries the concern regarding IPR is access, not protection.

This U.S. government pressure was somewhat successful in getting the Koreans to pass new laws and to step up enforcement of existing laws. Being a major trade partner for Korea, the U.S. government is no doubt more successful than others would be in leveraging its influence with countries where serious copyright violations occur. More recently, on March 13, 2001, the Bush administration threatened to impose Section

301 trade sanctions against Ukraine unless that country makes substantial progress in eliminating the production and export of illegally copied music, software, and other copyrighted material. The U.S. recording industry has estimated that the Ukraine has produced and exported between 60 and 80 million compact disks over a 2-year period.[30] Such piracy is estimated to cost the U.S. record industry about $200 million each year. U.S. threats may carry additional weight, as the Ukraine seeks membership in the World Trade Organization. For more information on government actions, refer to Chapter 13.

Legal Action

Perhaps the most applicable new law to this field is the Digital Millennium Copyright Act of 1998. Many seem to see this law as strengthening the position of copyright holders at the expense of the "open-access" position. The law took full effect in 2000 with maximum penalties of $1 million or 10 years in prison.[31]

Another piece of legislation, The No Electronic Theft (NET) Act, is getting similar criticism from some quarters. The new law was passed following the dropping of an indictment against a college student (David LaMacchia) for distributing copyrighted software over the Internet. The NET Act does a couple of questionable things. It expands the meaning of "copyright infringement" as it has been understood in previous legislation. It does this by making the mere distribution of copyrighted material by electronic means an infringement. It doesn't have to be printed anywhere, or even be stored on a hard drive, in order to violate the law. The White Paper upon which the new law was based even suggested that viewing such material on the Internet was a violation. But perhaps the bigger concern with the law is the criminalization of behavior in some cases. The law makes a distinction between "misdemeanor behavior" and "felony behavior" based on a retail value of $2,500. If someone distributes material with a retail value of more than $1,000, but less than $2,500, it is a misdemeanor; above $2,500, it is a felony. This seems a thin distinction and a relatively low value for determining criminal behavior. The retail price for software is often far in excess of the street value, and its value is likely to decline sharply over time. Some have felt that the plausible threat of being convicted of a felony will lead to a plethora of plea agreements to misdemeanor charges.[32]

Nevertheless, these are some of the many new legal weapons available to copyright holders in their battle against infringement of their intellectual property rights. They are exemplary of the struggle to protect such rights in the new electronic age where intellectual property can be reduced to digital form and distributed globally, both quickly and cheaply. It depends on which side of the "access versus protection" debate you support that determines whether you see such legal developments as a sin or a savior.[33]

According to a recent *Wall Street Journal* article,[34] legal action is apparently becoming the remedy of choice among major music companies. In the past, they have taken legal action mostly against those "for profit" operations that have pirated copyrighted music. They have also targeted peer-to-peer operations like Napster and Morpheus in the past because of the sheer volume of copyrighted material they have made available. Morpheus, a file-sharing application, has apparently been downloaded more than 95 million times. But now the strategy is also to go after individuals who are providing the most songs to other peers. However, the fear is that when these individuals are not making profits from these sharing schemes, the industry may alienate many of its biggest group of fans. Now that AOL (America OnLine) and Time Warner, Inc. have joined forces, actions by the Warner Music Group against individuals who are adversely affecting music sales could be the same people who are customers on the AOL side of the business. Dilemma! Dilemma! For more information on legal remedies, see Chapter 11.

Investigative Services

Microsoft has successfully used the services of a private investigator. In October 1996, they hired a former San Diego police officer named Fred Matthews. Through some excellent detective work, Matthews found a plant near Cambridge, England that was using some sophisticated equipment to duplicate Microsoft software CD-ROMs. He was unable to get the Cambridge police to participate in the investigation. He learned of a shipment of pirated software to Germany from the Cambridge plant. He was unable to stop the shipment before it left the United Kingdom, but he was able to get German customs officials to seize the shipment. Some $60 million worth of counterfeit software was found on a single truck. Though he was still unable to get the police to raid the plant in Cambridge, he was able to get a civil search warrant and along with Microsoft lawyers, he conducted his own raid on the plant. The plant owner, a Texan named John Staud, was sentenced to four years in a German prison, and faces further prosecution in Britain.[35]

This example demonstrates that private investigative services can be quite helpful in locating the source of pirated goods, collecting evidence for legal actions, and even aiding in the apprehension and conviction of the perpetrators. Usually private investigators are more effective if they can gain the support of local law enforcement personnel to assist with these tasks. However, as this example also points out, this doesn't always happen. For more information on utilizing investigative services, see Chapter 10.

Security Devices

The authentication industry continues to develop new technologies that can be useful tools for reducing the incidence of pirating and counterfeiting of copyrighted material and products. We discuss some of the more effective tools in Chapter 12. Some technologies that are directly relevant to copyright and digital products include:

- *Digital Watermarks.* These are patterns of digital bits that are incorporated into the master copy of a CD or DVD, such as the technology provided by Digimarc, an Oregon-based company. However, the information represented by this pattern of bits can only be transferred from the master to a copy. Illegal copies made from other copies, and not the master, will not have this imbedded information. Thus, any suspect disk can be checked to see if it includes the hidden information. If not, it is known to be an illegal copy. To be effective, a digital watermark must not interfere with the product's use. Similarly, it should not be removable from the legitimate product and should be able to be decoded by authorized personnel. Digital watermarks have become more necessary with the development of fairly cheap CD-ROM "burners" that can easily and quickly make copies of disks.

- *Magnetic Taggants.* These are magnetic metal film tags that are affixed to the product, package, and/or instructions. The advantage of these magnetic tags is that they can be read from a distance with magnetic scanners. Thus, there does not have to be line-of-sight observation of the product. In fact, there doesn't have to be any contact with the product in order to check its authenticity. Furthermore, the checking or scanning can be done in a covert way. Scanners can look like cell phones, for example, so that others will not be aware that the product is being authenticated. Not having to physically examine each and every product has significant advantages when such physical examination could damage the product, or even the packaging. Another advantage is that more than just a sample of the product can be examined indirectly. When samples are selected for inspection, you may never be quite sure that the sample selected contained any of the bogus products. Obviously, the bigger the sample, the better the chances of finding any unauthorized products, but in most cases bigger samples are both more time-consuming and more expensive, and increase the chances of the product being damaged.

- *Optical Variable Devices (OVDs).* These are often commonly known as holograms, though there are several different types and many are not, strictly speaking, "holograms." There are "2D/3D holograms," "3D holograms," "stereograms," "kinetic gratings," "dot matrix kinetic gratings," "ebeam images," and combinations of the above. The distinction between these various OVD devices is probably of little concern to the reader. These devices are less covert than either magnetic taggants or digital watermarks. Thus, they have a different purpose in preventing pirating. They allow the consumer to verify the authenticity of the product, assuming the customer cares. Some of these technologies also can be simulated by counterfeiters. Thus, low-end holograms of the "2D/3D" variety are more easily replicated by the more sophisticated pirates. Higher-tech OVDs will obviously be less easily copied, but they cost more as well. For most security devices, this is the tradeoff—effectiveness and difficulty of duplication versus cost. However, hologram manufacturers are increasingly incorporating covert messages or symbols within the hologram that can only be detected by specialized equipment. Holograms and OVDs remain some of the more cost-effective security devices available.

- *OVDs Embedded in CDs and DVDs.* 3dcd, a joint venture between Applied Optical Technologies and Technicolor, produces a sophisticated version of CDs and DVDs where the OVD is embedded underneath the surface of the CD or DVD. Without the highly sophisticated manufacturing equipment necessary to make these products, counterfeiters are reduced to attempting to simulate the OVD via other means. The 3dcd product provides overt authentication to consumers, a major advantage of holograms and OVDs. 3dcd is also a relatively unique authentication product in that the authentication technology is directly incorporated into the final manufactured product rather than applied to the packaging or onto the outer surface of the product.

- *Digital Signature Authorization.* Microsoft has recently announced Palladium, which is a computer architecture that will only allow digitally-signed software to execute. With this authorization, only programs and content which have been thus certified can run on your computer. However, as a recent *New York Times* article cautions, "At the level of bits, censorship and digital-rights management are technologically identical."[36] This technology offers a new method for controlling after-purchase use of a product. The jury is out on whether this is necessarily a good thing, particularly for the consumer.

Multilateral Institutions

Finally, there are a variety of bilateral and multilateral treaties that have been signed with the intent to protect intellectual property rights (IPRs) such as copyrights. These treaties are being recorded and monitored primarily by WIPO (the World Intellectual Property Organization), part of the United Nations system that is headquartered in Geneva. For a more complete discussion of WIPO, of what copyrights cover, and how they are protected, see Chapter 13.

Certification

Perhaps one of the newest approaches in the battle against digital pirating is "certification." The International Recording Media Association (IRMA) has launched an Anti-Piracy Compliance Certification Program. It is a self-administered program similar to the quality certification program offered by ISO9000. IRMA has more than 450 members who are either copyright owners, equipment manufacturers, or replicators. Companies wishing to be certified must pass an audit assuring that their internal procedures meet rigid management and operational standards. Right-holders have considered allowing only IRMA-certified companies to copy their content. If that happens, then the certification will be a necessity in order to be a major player in the industry.

This concludes a discussion of the specific industries that are most impacted by counterfeiting. The next section of this book provides a detailed discussion of the winners and losers from an economic and social perspective.

PART THREE

The Economic and Social Consequences of Counterfeiting

Counterfeiting is often viewed as a victimless crime. Some consumers believe that purchasing fake handbags or watches means they get a "great deal." Others believe that many luxury brands are overpriced to begin with and that brand owners will get their "comeuppance" by having counterfeits of their goods sold in the market at low prices. The result is that often there is little concern about fake products in the marketplace.

It is clear, though, that some counterfeits have very direct and harmful consequences. The harm wrought by counterfeit products affects a number of different parties—brand owners and the brands' consumers, employees, distributors, and investors, as well as governments and legal and law enforcement authorities. The economic and social consequences of counterfeiting to these and other parties can be very damaging.

CHAPTER 7

The Economic Consequences of Counterfeiting

HARM EXTENDS TO ENTIRE ECONOMIES AND SOCIETIES

More than 30 lawsuits have been filed in the past several years by John Paul Mitchell Systems to halt the sale of phony hair care products. Fortune 500 companies are spending millions of dollars per year to prevent counterfeiting of their products. Versace has been training New York Police Department's Peddlers Task Force to recognize counterfeit Versace accessories. Some films like *The Blair Witch Project* appear on the Internet as digital files before being released in theatres; this kind of illegal release can cost American movie producers as much as $3 billion annually. The National Football League has begun using special hologram hang-tags to prevent the illegal sale of its licensed sports apparel. A man is being sent to prison for the sale of fake Pratt and Whitney aircraft engine parts, while on probation for the same offense. It is now estimated that approximately 5 to 7 percent of all world trade (some $250 billion per year) is in counterfeit goods. Some think of counterfeiting as a victimless crime; others would strongly disagree. So, who does lose as a result of international counterfeiting?

Well, just about everyone loses but the counterfeiters, until (and if) they get caught. But even then the reward is far higher than the risk — perhaps millions of dollars versus only months in prison. Several parties suffer losses because of international brand-name counterfeiting. Obviously, there are some parties who also benefit, and thus the problem. Previously we have focused primarily on the harm done to brand holders and consumers. In fact, whole economies and societies can be harmed. Thus, it is appropriate to expand our Harm Matrix by one dimension to incorporate the level of harm to the individual, the company, and the society. Exhibit 7.1 shows the expanded Harm Matrix.

This chapter describes the winners and losers, and what they win and what they lose in economic terms. We'll start with the losers.

AND THE LOSERS ARE . . .

It should be clear from previous chapters that brand owners and consumers often suffer considerable harm from counterfeiting. However, employees, distributors, retailers, and others associated with legitimate businesses also suffer. In fact, the harm extends to governments at all levels, and even to entire societies.

Brand Owners

Obviously a major loser is the *creator* or *"right holder."* This terminology may seem a bit confusing. We usually think of the creator of a good or

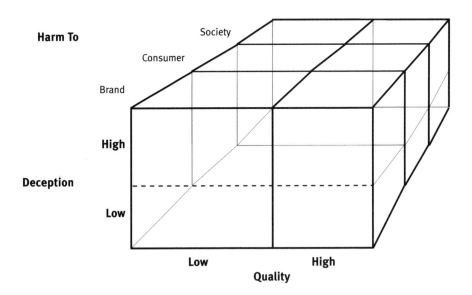

EXHIBIT 7.1   **The Expanded Harm Matrix**

service as the one who will be most hurt by product counterfeits that attempt to imitate their creation. However, in many cases, creators transfer the rights to their original creation. They could sell the brand name, or they could license another party to produce their brand-name creation. When unauthorized products are introduced that attempt to capture the value of the legitimate brand, these right holders can also be harmed.

For the companies mentioned at the beginning of the chapter, imitation is not the highest form of flattery. Indeed, they are all examples of companies trying to protect some of their most valuable assets—the value inherent in their brands, their trade names, and the revenues from the sale of the products themselves. How does one know when something is authentic. How do producers protect their brand, their product, and ultimately their intellectual property?

Intellectual property is the catchall term for "property" created from people's creative abilities, intellect, and promotional efforts. Immediately, one relates intellectual property to *patents* (which cover new inventions), trade names (like Xerox or Kodak), *copyrights* (covering things like books, movies, songs, software, and photographs), *trade secrets* (like Coke's 7X formula), as well as *trademarks* and their associated *brand names* (McDonald's and the Golden Arches). In most countries, intellectual property cannot simply be seized by someone else for their own gain, although the rights to intellectual property can be licensed or sold. This is a clear indication of the value placed on intellectual property.

The protection of intellectual property has, in modern times, been the province of corporate and government legal departments, law firms, and the courts. Increasingly, however, lawyers alone are unable to deal with infringements on intellectual property and particularly with outright counterfeiting on a large scale. Not only is it difficult to enforce intellectual property rights in many countries, but the explosion of counterfeiting as a sophisticated, worldwide activity demands new types of solutions. This is particularly the case where counterfeiters are able to make such good copies of products that, in some cases, the legitimate producers are unable to tell the counterfeit products from their own.

The most obvious losses are the sales, and related revenues, which are lost to unauthorized producers of the product. As one example, the law enforcement officials in Great Britain smashed a counterfeiting ring selling fake perfume valued at more than £5 million (roughly U.S. $7.5 million). They report that over 1.5 million fake perfume bottles were imported from Slovenia and Croatia (part of the former Yugoslavia). They were filled with cheap perfume essences obtained from Germany; then the bottles were labeled with well-known brand names such as Chanel, Samsara, Armani, Eternity, Knowing, White Linen, Beverly Hills, Dune, and Paris. These products were destined to be sold in the British market for about £12 a bottle. This is a single example of the potential lost sales to the legitimate producers of these products. Potentially, this loss was nearly £18 million (U.S. $27 million) of a single product, in a single market, at a particular point in time. In this case, the counterfeiters were apprehended, though the problem had existed for years. But think of the several cases where the fakes were not discovered and of the resulting loss in sales and revenue for those producing the real thing.

The problem is particularly acute in China. *Business Week*[1] noted some of the corporate victims. Gillette believes that one-quarter of its Duracell batteries, Parker pens, and Gillette razors have been pirated in China. Bestfoods estimates losses in the tens of millions of dollars from fake Skippy Peanut Butter and Knorr boullion. And Yamaha is convinced that of certain models of motorcycles and scooters, 5 of every 6 in China are knockoffs. Focus 7.1 reports on more severe consequences where the brand was actually hijacked by the counterfeiters.[2]

Statistical horror stories abound about the damage particular industries suffer due to counterfeiting. The Business Software Alliance (BSA) estimated that pirated software cost its industry nearly $11 billion in retail sales in 2001.[3] Software is easy to copy and the cost of a disk is negligible when you don't have to recoup development costs. The Recording Industry Association of America (RIAA) is fighting back against "digital jukeboxes" which allow you to download music free of charge from the Internet; there are estimated to be billions of unauthorized downloads per month.[4] According to the International AntiCounterfeiting Coalition (IACC), automobile manufacturers are losing $12 billion annually, and the equivalent of 210,000 jobs, to counterfeit parts.[5] There are estimates that the unlicensed manufacture of medications is running in excess of $10 billion a year.[6] Without having to recoup research and development costs, many counterfeiters can enter the market with a similar product in less than 2 percent of the time and less than 1/1000 of the

FOCUS 7.1 ◑

THE BRAND HAS BEEN HIJACKED!

The Beijing Study (done by the China Anti-Counterfeiting Coalition and reported in *Authentication News*) illustrates how a "well-established and well-known brand" was taken over by counterfeiters. Figure 1 shows that, from August 1995 to March 1998, the "brand's" share of the market declined slightly, but the amount of genuine product dropped precipitously. The vertical scale in the figure represents market share of the brand in that product category. The difference between the market share and the genuine product shipped is a measure of the amount of counterfeit product in the marketplace.

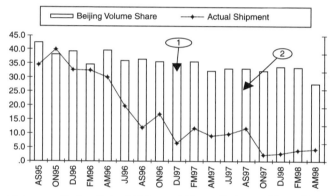

FIGURE 7.1   **Actual Shipment Versus Volumes Share Data**

The "Beijing Volume Share" bars show the amount of the brand (both authentic and fake) in Beijing at the particular time. The "Actual Shipment" line shows the amount of genuine product that the company shipped during the period.

Between August 1995 and March 1996, virtually all the product in Beijing was genuine. By August/September 1996, the brand still held some 37 percent of the product category but genuine product only represented about 12 percent of the total or only 33 percent of the brand's sales. The brand owner introduced a minor price increase in December 1997 (#1) and a larger increase in August 1997 (#2). While the brand market share declined only slightly, genuine product in the market dropped to below 5 percent—the brand itself was still relatively strong, holding a 30 percent share of the product category, but only about 17 percent of the brand was authentic; more than 80 percent was counterfeit.

cost of manufacturing the original. Estimates by the World Health Organization and others involved in the pharmaceutical industry suggest that 5 to 7 percent of the world's medications may be counterfeit; for Latin America the figure may be as high as 25 percent, and for Africa 60 percent.[7] A study by the International Trademark Association estimated that a group of participating manufacturers lost an average of 22 percent of their sales as a result of trademark infringement and counterfeiting.[8] Counterfeit products have cost 750,000 U.S. jobs in recent years.[9]

However, authentic products and counterfeit products are not always perfect substitutes for each other. Therefore, it is often difficult to determine exactly how many sales are being lost to the counterfeiters. In other words, if someone buys a Gucci handbag because of the low price (even though they suspect it is not genuine), that does not necessarily suggest that Gucci lost a sale, because without the extraordinarily low price that same consumer might never have purchased a Gucci bag. Yet in cases where the purchased counterfeit really did substitute for a purchase of the authentic article, the revenue loss to the brand owner is probably greater than you might think. It is not the average profitability that is lost, but rather the marginal profitability, which may be much greater. As sales increase, the fixed costs get spread over more and more items, and the profit per item increases, as well.

Counterfeiters increase the supply of seemingly comparable goods in the marketplace. At the same time, counterfeit products drive down the demand for products from legitimate producers. This combined effect results in significant downward pressure on the market price for the goods. If the producers of authentic goods reduce their prices to compete with the counterfeits, then the brand is devalued because it appears not to warrant the premium price for which brands are developed. If they do not reduce prices to compete with the counterfeits, then the discrepancy between real and fake products gets even wider. This, in turn, attracts more counterfeit activity as counterfeiters attempt to co-opt the brand premium for themselves.

This is, in essence, what happened on April 2, 1993—a day still referred to as "Marlboro Friday." On that day, Phillip Morris (owner of the Marlboro brand) announced that it was cutting the price of Marlboros by 20 percent in order to compete with the bargain brands. These were not counterfeits but rather bargain brands. Nevertheless, the effect was the same. In her book *No Logo,* Naomi Klein[10] notes that many felt that brands in general died that day. After all, the Marlboro Man ad campaign was launched in 1954 and was the longest-running campaign in history. When an icon of the brand business was willing to compete on price rather than image, what did that say about the value of the brand? IBM was forced into similar price cutting in order to compete with the much cheaper clones flooding the marketplace. Indeed, economic pressures can often cause consumers to elevate price considerations over brand loyalty, as was the case in the early 1990s. However, the most recent economic downturn has not always had the same impact; Starbucks was the fastest growing brand in the world in 2001.

Another loss may be royalty income. In many cases, original creators eventually sell the rights to produce and/or sell their branded product. The value to the licensee is based on the value of the brand that has been developed previously. Normally, the original licensor benefits from the licensing agreement by obtaining a royalty from the licensee that is based on the number of items produced and/or sold. Thus, when counterfeiters adversely impact the sales that the authorized producers are able to make, they also impact the royalties which the authorized producers are going to be able (or willing) to make to the original right holder.

For the most part, counterfeits don't "grow" the market. True, someone who buys a fake Rolex for $50 would not otherwise be a customer. However, in most cases, someone buying fakes represents lost sales to those selling legitimate products. Therefore, counterfeit sales represent a direct loss of market share for legitimate producers. Furthermore, counterfeits tend to pull market prices down, thus reducing revenue from the sales of authentic goods. A double whammy—fewer sales at lower prices.

There is also damage to the more difficult-to-measure intangibles we call reputation or goodwill. In many cases, the end consumers are unaware that they have purchased counterfeit goods. Therefore, when the product does not perform as expected, or as the consumer has come to expect from previous usage, then the reputation of legitimate producers is damaged. Even if consumers later become aware that the product was not authentic, they may still blame the legitimate producer for the damage done. Again, the brand represents a good-faith promise of performance and service. When that promise is not fulfilled, consumers may not care who is at fault. In such a situation, it is the reputation and goodwill of the legitimate producer that may be seriously damaged.

Another intangible cost is the diminution of the brand. How valuable are brands, and are they worth protecting? One relevant indicator of the value can be found in the contribution margin of powerfully branded products, which is the premium the brand commands in the marketplace. But even the most attractive margins for legitimate products pale in comparison to those from counterfeit brands. We saw in Chapter 2 just how valuable some brands are. The top five brands in Interbrand's[11] 2002 ranking all had values in excess of $30,000,000,000 (that's billion). They were:

Coca-Cola	$69.6 billion
Microsoft	$64.1 billion
IBM	$51.2 billion
General Electric	$41.3 billion
Intel	$30.9 billion

In making its valuation, Interbrand considers the economic profit generated by the brand, future economic earnings the branded business is expected to generate, the role of the brand in the earnings, and the risk profile of the earnings. It is worth noting that the brand value for Coca-Cola was equal to over half of the company's total market capitalization in 2000.

Obviously, it is important to protect a brand with this amount of value to a firm. There are no doubt hundreds of thousands of brand names whose worth is in the thousands or millions of dollars, rather than billions, but worth protecting nonetheless. In many cases, a brand may become more important than the product itself. It is a symbolic promise to loyal customers of quality and performance consistent with their expectations. The brand is, in many ways, a contract. As with any contract, there are penalties incurred when it is broken. Counterfeiters can do great damage to that contract and the promise that the brand offers. If the estimate of Microsoft's value is correct, then even a 5 percent reduction in the value of Microsoft's brand by counterfeiters represents an economic loss of over $3 billion.

And what about that lost R&D? The research and development costs of new products can be substantial. For products like pharmaceuticals, the R&D costs could be in the hundreds of millions, or even billions, of dollars. In pricing the product, the seller must recoup these very substantial R&D costs. This per unit overhead expense will be based on the estimated sales volume. As counterfeits cut into those initial sales estimates, then the projected R&D costs may not be recovered. Of course, the seller can increase the price even more by including an even higher per unit R&D component, but this only exacerbates the problem by increasing the price differential between the legitimate and illegitimate products. After all, the counterfeiters's major competitive advantage lies in the fact that they don't have any R&D expense to recoup.

◑ FOCUS 7.2 ◑

WHO IS HELPED AND WHO IS HURT BY GRAY MARKETS?

Gray markets do not necessarily involve counterfeit products, but many believe they are a key means for the distribution of counterfeits. Gray markets refer to products being sold more cheaply through unauthorized channels of distribution. This occurs in many cases because producers use a demand-based pricing approach that considers what the market will bear, rather than a cost-based approach or a standard worldwide pricing approach. For example, if you decide to sell your product at a substantially lower price in developing markets than in more developed markets, then others will see an opportunity to buy your product in the low-priced markets and sell them in the high-priced markets. In other words, they will take advantage of the price differential by moving your products and distributing them through their own unauthorized distribution channels. This assumes that the price differential is greater than the transportation and distribution costs to the high-priced markets. These are often referred to as "parallel imports." Parallel sales are legal in the United States but illegal in the European Union (except between member states).

For example, at one point Levi's 501 jeans were selling for twice as much in France as they did in the United States. So some enterprising traders bought them in the United States and exported them to Paris, undercutting the authorized distributors. In such cases, brand holders are hurt because they do not capture the higher market price for themselves. Of course, they make other arguments as well. They claim that consumers may suffer because they may not get the genuine article,

(continues)

FOCUS 7.2 *(Continued)*

or that they will not have the same after-sales service as they would if purchased through an authorized dealer. Advocates claim that consumers gain more than they lose; they get cheaper prices and more choice. Some acknowledge that this may increase the chances of actually buying a fake branded product, but maintain this is really a separate issue. Authorized distributors are almost certainly harmed; they lose sales and may be hit with demands to service products they did not sell. Governments may also suffer because of impact on the balance of payments and possible lost tax revenue. The latter is particularly true for gray market cigarette sales where the price differential is caused primarily by differences in taxes on the product by the governments involved.

Proponents of legalizing parallel imports argue that consumers have access to cheaper products. This is a potentially compelling argument when dealing with necessities such as pharmaceuticals, but even with branded consumer goods like clothing, without looking more deeply, consumers find it difficult to understand how the increased competition of parallel imports can be a bad thing. Critics of parallel imports, however, appear to be correct when they point out that diversion channels are the main vehicle for the distribution of counterfeits where they can be easily blended with legitimate products.

In addition to all of the costs mentioned above, brand holders may also incur increased costs in order to protect themselves from counterfeits. Brand holders could actually incur legal liability for death or injury to those using counterfeit products. In any case, there may be legal costs of protecting against liability claims arising from faulty products, because a legitimate producer may be held liable for damage or harm done by illegitimate products. At least, this is the conclusion by Arthur Best of the University of Denver's College of Law.[12] He contends that tort law would be likely to support a victim's claim against a producer of legitimate goods if harm from a counterfeit product "was foreseeable, the enterprise had a role in creating the risk of crime, and it failed to take reasonable steps to reduce that risk." In any case, there will be the legal costs of defending against such claims. There are also increased surveillance costs and the costs of lobbying one's own government, or foreign governments, to take action when appropriate. Finally, there are the costs of proactive measures such as the use of holograms. Granted, these may be less costly than dealing with the problems which might otherwise occur, but there is nevertheless a cost involved.

Customers

The customer is often another loser. While it is clear that the original creator or the current right holder can suffer damage from counterfeits, it may be less obvious that the customer can also be harmed. After all, counterfeits often appear to hold down prices for consumer products or for services that utilize counterfeit components. However, consumers can be harmed in several ways:

- *Did You Get What You Paid for?* Customers rely on trademarks and brand names to provide an expectation of product quality and service that is almost surely missing with phony, cheap knockoffs. As was discussed above, companies invest millions in building brand recognition, and brand names themselves can often be one of the most valuable assets that a company owns. However, it takes more than mere investment to build brand reputation and loyalty. The brand signifies the quality of the product and/or service. The customer's perception of quality becomes linked to the brand name so that the customer has a logical expectation of what the product or service will deliver. A BMW automobile carries with it the expectation of quality construction and performance coupled with exceptional after-sales service. If your BMW is repaired using substandard counterfeit parts, then your perception of quality may be forfeited when the car fails to perform up to your expectations. Brand loyalty and reputation are often time-consuming and expensive to establish, but they can be destroyed much more quickly. That is the real damage done by counterfeits; they destroy the customer's expectation of quality and performance. And once destroyed, it may be very difficult, if not impossible, to reestablish.

- *Such a Deal!* There may be times when customers do not care whether a product is authentic. They are attracted by the extremely low price. Nevertheless, when their $50 Rolex watch stops working after the first week, they realize they have paid a premium price for a piece of costume jewelry. While they may not have expected Gucci quality from their known fake Gucci handbag, they may nevertheless feel "ripped off" when it comes apart after a short time. What seemed a good deal at the time will now seem to be an excessive price for the product they actually received. The customer's disappointment may, or may not, be transferred to the legitimate brand.

- *Consumers May Hurt More than Their Pride.* The end user may actually suffer harm from ineffective (pharmaceuticals) or sub-standard (automobile or aircraft parts) forgeries.

  - *Faulty Medications and Pharmaceuticals.* An analysis of antimalarial drugs purchased from shops in Cambodia, Laos, Myanmar, Thailand, and Vietnam found that more than a third contained no drug at all.[13] Another study found fake and ineffective birth control pills in Brazil.[14]

    Some experts have estimated that half the medicines sold in subSaharan Africa are fakes. In 1995, Belgian doctors administering meningitis vaccine in Niger realized too late that it was fake, consisting mostly of salt water. Sixty thousand people were vaccinated with the fake vaccine. Later estimates suggested that at least 300 villagers who had taken the fake vaccine died of meningitis, while 60 others were handicapped for life.[15] Chapter 4 discussed the problem of counterfeit drugs in detail.

  - *Faulty Auto or Airplane Parts.* According to the Automotive Brand Protection Coalition Middle East (ACME), as many as 30 percent of the auto parts in the United Arab Emirates may be fakes. Many involve parts that could present great physical danger to drivers and occupants. A specific example that was mentioned were brake pads that burst into flames without warning.[16] Other critical parts that have been counterfeited have included engines, transmissions, steering and electrical systems.

    A recent scam was uncovered in Italy where old and faulty parts were being recovered from decommissioned and crashed aircraft and resold as new. Authorities speculated that as many as 10 recent air crashes may have involved some of these parts. The

Federal Aviation Administration (FAA) suspected that the multi-million dollar scam could have affected more than 1,000 aircraft and issued warnings to authorities in 167 countries.[17]

In 1989, 55 people died in a plane crash over the North Sea when the tail fin fell off the plane because of faulty parts. When most of the 36-year-old plane was recovered, investigators found bogus bolts, bushings, and brackets, though the origin of the parts was never determined.[18] Chapter 5 detailed the problem of counterfeit automobile and airplane parts.

○ *Faulty Liquor.* In a press release, the Anti-Counterfeiting Group (ACG) cited examples of large quantities of methylated industrial spirits, commonly used in paint thinner, showing up in counterfeit Scotch whiskey labeled as Scotch Blended Royal Crown. Similarly, officials in the United Kingdom seized 2,000 bottles of fake Stolichnaya vodka containing methanol, which can cause blindness. In fact, 22 people in Russia later died from drinking fake vodka. Referring to an illegal still in the Philippines, the ACG proclaimed, "The filthy, unhygienic conditions in which counterfeit alcohol is being produced and bottled will shock most people."[19]

In April 1998, *The Indian Express* reported that the police in Mumbai (Bombay) had arrested two men for peddling counterfeit liquor. The men had scavenged empty bottles of high-end liquor that had been disposed of at hotels and other locations. They then obtained fake labels, corks, and seals from a supplier in New Delhi, after which the bottles were refilled with IMFL (Indian Made Foreign Liquor) of a much lower cost and quality. The liquor was then sold to less reputable bars, but also to some of the high-class hotels from which the bottles had been recovered in the first place. A bottle of Johnnie Walker Blue Label fetched about 5,600 rupees, or roughly $115. Other popular brands of scotch included Chivas Regal Premier Scotch, Black & White, Glen Moray, and Laphroaig. Other liquor brands included Crown Royal Canadian Whiskey, Stolichnaya Russian Vodka, and cognacs by Remy Martin or Martell.[20] These are only illustrative examples of the widespread and growing problem, which was discussed in Chapter 3.

○ *Faulty Children's Toys.* Brand-name toy manufacturers are concerned about cheap knockoffs that could be extremely dangerous to children. Because they often use substandard materials, small parts could break off, thereby causing a choking hazard to small children. Other concerns are toys stuffed with unsafe materials or counterfeits containing lead-based paints.[21]

Governments

So far, we have seen that brand holders and consumers can be big losers in the counterfeiting game, but governments also are not immune. And actually, there is more than one government at risk. Both the national government of the country where fake goods originate, as well as the country where they are sold, may be harmed. Furthermore, within a single country, local and provincial governments may suffer, in addition to the national government.

First, consider the governments in the receiving state. They often lose substantial tax revenues; even state and local governments can feel the impact of counterfeit goods. In 1994, a NYC Consumer Affairs Commissioner said New York City lost $350 million a year in tax revenue from counterfeiting. Customs officials in the United Kingdom noted that more than £10,500 (over $15,000) in excise revenue had been evaded in a single busload of cigarettes and tobacco products about to board a ferry for the Isle of Wight. You can begin to see the potential of lost tax revenue from these seemingly minor examples.[22]

To be competitive in world markets, governments have a vested interest in seeing that their companies continue their investment in new products, industries, and markets. Indeed, governments often encourage such development through taxation schemes and other forms of subsidization. If a company can easily have its developmental efforts and investments negated by overseas counterfeiters, then there will be little incentive for them to continue to develop new products and markets. Governments will then have to increase their incentives to companies or risk falling behind in global competitiveness.

Likewise, a major concern for every national government is the level of unemployment in its economy. While governments may define unemployment differently, the loss of jobs, nevertheless, has considerable importance to any economy and therefore is often the focus of political attention. A 1998 Green Paper by the European Commission claimed the European Union lost more than 100,000 jobs per year to counterfeiting.[23] A 1999 study, commissioned by the *Business Software Alliance,* found there were over 100,000 jobs lost in the United States due to software piracy alone. The study further concluded, "If piracy were eliminated in the United States and reduced abroad, it is estimated that the industry would produce an additional 1 million jobs by 2005, and contribute $25 billion in tax revenue.[24]

There is also a government cost (as well as a private one) for increased surveillance and enforcement to protect the local economy from foreign (and domestic) counterfeiters. For example, U.S. Customs has had to increase its efforts, and therefore its expenses, in identifying foreign counterfeit goods coming into this country. The greater expense results from increased training and technology needed as the counterfeiters themselves become ever more proficient. In addition, the advent of the color copier and the computer scanner make the forgery or counterfeiting of documents—currencies, passports, driver's licenses, and the like— much easier than even five years ago.

There are also costs in apprehending, enforcing, and adjudicating cases that violate intellectual property rights. In 1998, the Republic of South Africa enacted a new law aimed at speedy and effective action against counterfeiters. This law requires customs authorities to seize and detain suspect goods entering the country upon receipt and acceptance of an application from any interested party (e.g., owners, licensees, distributors, importers, or exporters with an interest in protected goods.) There is an obvious cost to the government in increasing resources that can act quickly to apprehend counterfeit products.

Finally, to the extent that counterfeiting has a negative impact on overseas sales of American companies, it also negatively impacts the U.S. balance of payments. Likewise, the importation of counterfeit goods into the United States further exacerbates the balance of payments deficit (or reduces any surplus) in the merchandise trade portion of the current account. It is difficult to measure the true volume and value of counterfeit goods coming into the country. One indicator may be seizures by U.S. Customs; however, that is likely to be only a fraction of all counterfeits entering the country. For fiscal year 2001, the U.S. Customs

Service seized more than $57 million in counterfeit and pirated products, as follows:[25]

- Wearing Apparel ($7.8 million and 14 percent of total value seized).
- Media ($7.3 million; 13 percent).
- Watches and parts ($5.6 million; 10 percent).
- Batteries ($5.1 million; 9 percent).
- Cigarettes and rolling papers ($4.5 million; 8 percent).
- Toys and electronic games ($4.4 million; 8 percent).
- Computer Hardware ($4.1 million; 7 percent).
- Sunglasses and parts ($3.7 million; 6 percent).
- Handbags, wallets, and backpacks ($3.2 million; 6 percent).
- Footwear ($3.1 million; 5 percent).
- All other commodities ($8.6 million; 15 percent).

Thus, Customs made 3,586 seizures in 2001, with a "domestic" value of $57,438,680. However, it should be noted that "domestic value" is a significantly lower value than the retail value of genuine goods.

It should also be mentioned where these seized goods originated. Of the $57.4 million, 56 percent came from the People's Republic of China (including Hong Kong), and another 4 percent from the Republic of China (Taiwan). The other major originating countries (in order of value seized) were Korea, Singapore, United Arab Emirates, Netherlands, Honduras, Pakistan, and Thailand. At least 73 percent of the total goods seized (nearly three-quarters) originated in Asia, and that figure could be much higher as only the major originating countries were mentioned.

In contrast to U.S Customs, the European Union reported seizing 95 million counterfeit articles at the external borders of the community in 2001, with a legal market value of more than 2 billion euros. That is a substantially greater value than the U.S. seizures, and it represented a 900 percent increase over the number of articles seized in 1998. This was due, in part, to the greater diversity of articles now being counterfeited.[26]

We often think that the brunt of the damage from counterfeiting falls on the economy of the country where these goods are being sold. However, the country where they originate may also pay a price.

National governments lose if their countries develop a reputation for counterfeiting activity, because that will discourage foreign direct investment and imports of genuine quality goods from abroad. Conversely, many countries that have developed a good reputation for producing certain types of products (Japan for consumer electronics, Italy for shoes, Germany for luxury automobiles, or France for wine) can have that deserved reputation damaged by inferior imitations. An Associated Press article quotes Lauren Moriarty, a trade official with the U.S. Embassy in Beijing, as warning that the major reason cited by companies for not making new investment in China, is the concern over violations of intellectual property rights.[27] Likewise, the country manager for Microsoft in Mauritius has been quoted as warning, "Investors can't come to Mauritius if the authorities don't offer the guarantee that their products won't be pirated and sold at 200 or 300 rupees on the streets."[28]

◑ FOCUS 7.3 ◑

THE PEOPLE'S REPUBLIC OF CHINA

By just about any measure, China is a huge country. It is the most populous country in the world. The 2002 estimated population approached 1.3 billion people, making China roughly 5 times larger than the United States, which is the third largest country in the world. Likewise, in area China is the second largest country in the world, slightly smaller than Canada and slightly larger than the United States. However, whereas the United States shares a border with only two other countries, China shares a border with 14 other countries (not counting Hong Kong or Macau); they are Afghanistan, Bhutan, Burma, India, Kazakhstan, North Korea, Kyrgyzstan, Laos, Mongolia, Nepal, Pakistan, Russia, Tajikistan, and Vietnam. China currently has boundary or territorial disputes with 10 other countries. In terms of gross domestic product (standardized by purchasing power parity), China has the second largest economy in the world. It is slightly more than half the size of the U.S. economy, and more than 60 percent larger than the Japanese economy. Many think that the Chinese economy will be the largest in the world by 2020, as it has been the fastest growing of the major economies for several years running.

(continues)

FOCUS 7.3 *(Continued)*

China is still a one-party state, with the Communist Party firmly in control. In July 2001, President Jiang Zemin declared that capitalists should be allowed to join the party. And the government has gradually loosened restrictions and introduced some market reforms. China became a member of the World Trade Organization in 2002. (See Focus 13.3 in Chapter 13.) China is a very diverse country; while over 90 percent of the population is Han Chinese, there are at least 56 separate ethnic groups including Buyi, Hui, Korean, Manchu, Mongol, Miao, Tibetan, Uygur, Yi, and Zhuang. The International Olympic Committee has awarded the 2008 Summer Games to China.

Political relations between China and the United States have remained rocky even after the two countries announced full diplomatic relations in 1979. Many of the problems are related to the recognition and treatment of Taiwan, which China still considers one of its 23 provinces. In contrast, there was little international interference when Hong Kong was returned to Chinese sovereignty in 1997. Recent low points in U.S.-China relations were 1999, when the United States mistakenly bombed the Chinese Embassy in Yugoslavia, and 2001 when a U.S. spy surveillance plane collided with a Chinese fighter near the Chinese coast, killing the Chinese pilot.

Similarly, a spokesperson from Proctor and Gamble in China noted that the company has invested over $300 million in China since beginning its first joint venture in 1988. The company conservatively estimates that 15 to 20 percent of all P&G-labeled goods on Chinese shelves are fakes. Thus, counterfeiting may be costing the company as much as $150 million annually. The company's vice president of public affairs in Asia, William Dobson, has been quoted as warning that "counterfeiting is an issue that continually comes up as we think about new investment plans."[29]

The reduction in foreign direct investment from abroad is also likely to impact local employment. Companies rarely import unskilled or skilled labor from their home countries. In fact, one of the major reasons for making a direct foreign investment in a developing country is to take advantage of the relatively cheap labor, which in many cases is also highly educated, skilled, motivated, and hardworking. When foreign direct investment is reduced (or never made), the quantity of these local jobs will be reduced accordingly.

Other costs to the governments in countries where counterfeiting is epidemic include retaliatory measures from their trading partners. Many countries have laws supposedly protecting intellectual property. But in too many cases they are not adequately enforced. Such lack of enforcement can also bring retaliatory measures from trading partners. In extreme cases, retaliation may take the form of an embargo or refusal to trade. More likely, less severe penalties will be imposed, but the penalties may still be quite harmful to the economy.

In many cases, knowledge and technology is transferred from more-developed countries to less-developed countries through foreign direct investment by companies in those developed countries. The technology may be transferred through training of managers and skilled technicians, or it may be transferred through licensing agreements, compensatory trade agreements (e.g., buyback or coproduction), contract manufacturing agreements, or franchise arrangements. Whatever the mechanism for transferring technology to the developing host countries, that transfer will be reduced if foreign direct investment is reduced. This will surely be the case if companies from developed countries fear that their intellectual property will be jeopardized by counterfeiting operations in the host country.

Likewise, if inferior counterfeit products are originating from a particular country, it may taint the legitimate products being produced there. If consumers experience an abnormal amount of problems with products being produced in a particular country, they may begin to generalize their experience to any product being produced there. To some extent, this has been the recent experience with Russia. While Russia has long enjoyed a deservedly good reputation for producing many high-quality products, that general reputation is now being damaged by the increasing number of low-quality knockoffs being produced there for export.

If counterfeit goods are being produced in a particular country and also being sold illegally in that same market, then chances are the sales are not being reported and the government is losing tax revenue. This often happens with unauthorized overproduction by local contract manufacturers or licensees. If you are licensed to produce so many pairs of athletic shoes for export, it is a fairly low risk to simply overproduce and sell the excess at low prices in the local market. Some do not consider this to be counterfeiting, but it meets our definition because someone is trying to usurp the value of someone else's intellectual property without authorization.

Finally, it is probable in the future that retribution for violating intellectual property rights will be taken on a multilateral rather than a unilateral basis. A multilateral trade organization such as the World Trade Organization (WTO) has greater sanctioning power than the old General Agreements for Tariffs and Trade (GATT). Likewise, there are greater restraints on countries acting unilaterally until multilateral recourse has been exhausted. Furthermore, a reputation for not protecting intellectual property rights, or not vigorously enforcing laws already on the books, may hinder a country's application for membership in these same world trade organizations. Such was the case with China's recent application to join the WTO. In November 2000, a story in *The New York Times* reported that "Counterfeiting of products is 'out of control' in China and inadequate measures to stop it could complicate Beijing's efforts to join the World Trade Organization." The article reported that Washington and Beijing had been on the brink of a trade war in both 1995 and 1996 over the issue of intellectual property protection. However, while the Chinese have taken some corrective action, "fake brand name goods ranging from pharmaceuticals to car parts and sports wear remain readily available."[30]

Distributors and Retailers

Phony products (as well as gray market sales) can also create conflicts with distributors of legal product. In addition, retailers who are selling the brand may notice declining sales as their most popular brands decline in value, for whatever reason. In response, some retailers have increasingly created their own private labels which become well-known brands in their own right. Sears has done this for years with its Craftsman line of tools. In such cases, it does not matter so much who produces the product as who owns the brand.

Examples of the harm to authorized distributors include the loss of their revenues and market share. This is fairly obvious. However, it does assume that those who would purchase the counterfeit or unauthorized goods would also be part of the legitimate market, if the fakes didn't exist. It is conceivable that these purchasers represent a new market, in which case there would be less impact on revenue or market share. For example, maybe someone who buys an illegal copy of Microsoft Office for $50 would never buy the product for the legitimate price, which may be 10 times greater. If that purchaser would not have been part of the legitimate market, is it fair to say that the distributor has lost market share and therefore revenue, since it would not have made the sale in any case? The answer is yes, because down the road the real market will be hurt. Just because I would have bought the product for $500, does not mean I won't prefer the $50 price once I learn how many other people are buying it at the lower price.

Distributors are often approached to warrant or repair counterfeit goods that they never sold in the first place. This is a serious problem for authorized distributors. Assume I buy a counterfeit Streamlite flashlight, though I don't know that it is not the real thing. Though I was told it has a life-long guarantee, it soon breaks. So, I take it back to a local authorized Streamlite distributor to be repaired or replaced. Distributors (unlike the consumer) immediately recognize the product as a fake. They don't want to bear the expense of replacing the fraudulent product with the real product, and chances are they could not repair it if they wanted to. After all, they did not make the original sale nor can they return it to the original manufacturer for reimbursement of their expenses.

Continuing with the above example, if distributors refuse to service the product, as the warranty for legitimate product stipulates, then serious damage to the reputation of the product, its manufacturers, and its distributors may result. This is truly a no-win situation for overseas distributors. Even if the situation is explained to the consumer, he is still likely to hold the authorized distributors responsible for making good on his purchase. That is human nature. It is much easier to blame someone else than admit that you made a bad purchase because you were trying to save a buck. Remember, it isn't reality but the perception of reality that matters to the consumer.

It is possible that the distributors' damage is even greater. They could conceivably be held liable for damage or injury caused by the product, even if the product is not their own.

Counterfeiters

Are the bad guys ever losers? Sometimes! While it may seem strange to talk of potential damage or loss to the counterfeiters themselves, there is some. Though they may not get much sympathy, there are indeed some costs and losses that counterfeiters incur as a result of the business they have chosen.

The competitive arena has enlarged and changed. We are now in a global economy where products and production techniques are readily available worldwide. The technical ability to counterfeit products, brands and packaging enables some to realize the economic incentives that global brands present. From the counterfeiter's viewpoint, the rewards are quite high and the risks relatively low. However, as brand owners become more attentive to combatting counterfeiting, and the "authentication industry" provides better technology with which to do so, the cost of doing business as a counterfeiter increases.

In like manner, the counterfeiters bear the cost of continuous mobility. They often must relocate frequently in order to stay a step ahead of enforcement officials. For many illegal operations, this is not a significant expense as their operations are relatively low-tech and designed to be mobile. For others, the expense may be more significant. Some unauthorized producers may not require relocation at all. In the latter case, it is just a matter of disguising the unauthorized overproduction being carried out in the otherwise legitimate facility.

Legal penalties in most cases are woefully inadequate. Light penalties create a major incentive to counterfeiters in the first place. However, if they are caught and placed on the Denied Persons List (DPL) by the Bureau of Industry and Security, counterfeiters can lose their import privileges to the United States. This would be a serious blow to a party that also relied on the income from legitimate exports to the largest market in the world. For counterfeit operations that have the mobility to relocate and change their names, such punishment may represent more of an inconvenience than a serious cost.

Finally, if the counterfeiters are caught, the counterfeit goods will be seized by U.S. Customs, and the goods will probably be destroyed. They may also lose their production equipment, if the United States can elicit cooperation from enforcement officials in the host country where the goods were being produced.

We have seen that there are indeed many losers; counterfeiting is not a victimless crime. The losers include brand holders, manufacturers, licensees, distributors, customers, employees, taxpayers, and governments. We have even discussed the costs to the counterfeiters themselves. But, let's face it, those costs usually pale in comparison with the potential rewards. So who are the winners?

AND THE WINNERS ARE . . .

Counterfeiters

Our focus in this book is to bring attention to the significant losses experienced by many parties as a result of the explosion in global counterfeiting. However, there are certainly some who also benefit from counterfeiting operations. Foremost among them are obviously the counterfeiters themselves. It is this imbalance in the cost-benefit analysis on the part of counterfeiters that is the primary incentive driving this increasing problem.

By producing illegal and/or unauthorized products, the counterfeiters avoid many of the costs of doing business that legitimate producers incur:

- *Research and Development.* First among these is often the research and development costs. Take, for example, pharmaceuticals. Drugs are often so expensive, not because of the ingredients or the cost to produce them, but rather because of the extremely high costs to develop and test them before they get approval to be marketed. Even if the counterfeit product is identical in its composition, the counterfeiters have not had to recover any of this research and development expense. But in many cases, they do not even attempt to replicate the composition of ingredients, but rather the mere appearance of the product or packaging. In this case, their costs are even lower.

- *Marketing and Brand Development.* We have discussed the tremendous costs involved in developing brand recognition, reputation and therefore value. We also mentioned that building brand value is usually a slow and expensive process, whereas destroying brand value can be fast and cheap. Again, counterfeiters do not bear any of the costs of developing and marketing brand names. Rather they capture the value that legitimate sellers and right holders have already established.

- *Repair, Warranty, and After-Sale Services.* We also mentioned previously how counterfeiters do not bear the costs of repair, warranty, or after-sale service. Instead, they often rely on the fact that unknowing consumers will return to legitimate producers and distributors to remedy any complaints. In these cases, they not only avoid these costs themselves, but actually pass them on to others.

- *Distribution Costs.* Finally, while counterfeiters may have some distribution costs, they are certainly not of the same magnitude as those incurred by legitimate sellers. All of the factors previously discussed serve to drastically reduce the costs for counterfeiters, thereby allowing them to significantly undercut the price of the authentic product. In many industries, consumers do not understand the magnitude of the development costs described above (e.g., software, pharmaceuticals, pesticides, auto parts). Thus, they may understandably feel that the product is unjustifiably overpriced. In these cases, the lower price charged by counterfeiters gives them a significant advantage in the marketplace.

Besides facing a significantly lower cost structure, the other side of the very favorable cost-benefit equation for counterfeiters is a high profit margin. And, illegal production still provides jobs that benefit those who hold them. For example, it has been reported that at least 200,000 people are employed in producing counterfeit switchgear in Wenzhou, China—that is one product, in one city, in just one country. This explains why local communities are often quite supportive of some counterfeiting activity, and why they think of it as a victimless crime. Even if caught, the skilled and unskilled employees are not likely to suffer any severe consequences. Finally, profits from illegal counterfeit operations can often be invested in (laundered through) legitimate enterprises. Thus, even if the counterfeiters are caught, revenue can continue to pour in from these safe investments.

Customers

While we generally think of the customer as the one being hurt by counterfeiting, it is also possible to make the case that in many situations, they actually benefit. This might be particularly true where there is a significant price difference between the counterfeit product and the authentic product, yet functionality is affected very little. Another situation would be where the primary value to the customer comes from the brand itself (the snob factor), and not how the product actually performs.

Counterfeits may offer more value to the consumer. Value is really the ratio of benefits to cost. Assume a customer in China can buy a Microsoft software program for $30 that would normally cost $300. If it is a pirated copy, chances are that the software will perform fairly well. True, the customer won't have the benefits of after-sale service, cheaper upgrades, or technical support, but otherwise the functionality of the product is likely to be similar. Therefore, in calculating value, the customer is dividing a slightly lower "benefit" by a significantly lower "price," and the result is a substantially higher "value" for the pirated product.

Similarly, take the case where the customer buys a fake Gucci handbag for $10. The cost of the authentic Gucci product may be prohibitive for this customer, not that they would not like to have one. The primary benefit to this customer might not be the Gucci quality or functionality of the handbag, but rather the status afforded by the Gucci brand name. In this case, the benefit to the customer is roughly the same between the fake and authentic products. But, the significantly lower price results in a much higher value for this customer, when buying the fake product.

What kinds of products are most at risk of counterfeiting? First are products that are easy and inexpensive to copy or reverse-engineer. High on this list are computer software, videos, and CDs. It has been reported that Microsoft XP software with a list price of about $200 was selling in Malaysia for as little as $1.50. The same *Newsweek* article contends that in late 1999 when "Microsoft took over the National Theatre in Bucharest to launch Office 2000 Professional, which had gone on sale that day in Romanian stores for $300 to $400 . . . hawkers on the street . . . were already selling counterfeits of Office 2000 for $2 to $3."[31] Second are those products where the quality is not evident to the end user, but the price is. This would include automobile and aircraft replacement parts.

Finally, very high-priced items (Rolex) and those that have established strong brand-name recognition for quality or style (Gucci, Bolle, Sony) are at great risk of counterfeiting.

After all, if customers can satisfy some of their needs with cheaper fake or pirated products, then they will have more disposable income for other purchases. However, this assumes that they would have bought the authentic products at the higher prices, had the fakes not been available.

The Anticounterfeiters

Did you ever hear of the "authentication industry?" There is one entire industry that stands to benefit from the increasing trade in counterfeit and pirated goods. The emerging "authentication industry" has developed to deal with this problem. It is their "raison d'etre." As long as the problem persists, they are likely to experience continued growth.

A growing market niche? It is probably fair to say that before 1985 there was no product authentication industry at all, though authentication problems have been around for centuries. The seeds of the current industry were in the authentication of documents and currencies. However, in the last 15 years, a few companies have emerged to offer a variety of solutions to fake goods and documents. Some of these companies offer a variety of authentication tools and techniques that are applicable to a diverse set of industries. An example would be Applied Optical Technologies plc, one of the largest companies in this fast-growing industry. Another major player in this highly fragmented industry is 3M Corporation, which has a division competing directly in this area. There are also other small and more specialized companies that have developed solutions for particular market niches. Technology is the key success factor in this industry. Therefore, participants in the industry must continually enhance their technology in order to stay ahead of counterfeiters who increasingly are attempting to simulate the security devices themselves.

Like most new industries, this one is experiencing consolidation, which is likely to continue and even increase in the next few years. It is even possible that the industry will redefine itself by encompassing a broader range of international risks. In many ways, the demise of the Cold War has led to a less stable international economic environment, rather than the increased stability that many expected. Likewise, the exponential growth of the Internet has increased the ability of some to circumvent traditional distribution and regulatory systems, making it imperative that firms take action to protect their valuable brands. It is clear that the counterfeiting problem has tremendous international implications. It impacts, and is, in turn, impacted by the international economic, political, and even cultural environments that impinge upon international business. There is a rosy picture of growth for an industry aimed at solving problems in this complex arena.

The authentication industry has developed tools to protect against a wide variety of illegal activities like counterfeiting, forgery, copying, and misrepresentation. Certainly one of the most widely used and cost-effective tools available is a hologram. These are usually small labels or images (often 3-D) that are difficult and expensive to duplicate without sophisticated equipment and expertise. You have probably seen them used on credit cards and traveler's checks, if nothing else. Yet improved technology makes them quite inexpensive to produce in quantity (often pennies each), and they can be affixed directly to the product or package. In many cases, the end consumer will learn to recognize the hologram as representative of the official brand-name product; it may even be part of the trademark design. More likely, it will be those responsible for inspecting (Customs) or distributing the product that can be trained to recognize authentic products from the distinctive hologram. While holograms are not counterfeit-proof, they nevertheless represent one of the most effective, and least expensive, means to deter illegal activity and protect brand value.

The authentication industry has also developed numerous other means for authenticating products and documents, and for indicating tampering with legitimate products and their packaging. Chapter 12 discusses these new and emerging technologies in greater depth.

Finally, a new industry means new jobs, and the jobs provided by the authentication industry are often of the skilled high-tech variety. The authentication industry is part of a broader security industry, which also has an interest in the counterfeiting problem. This broader industry includes many other people whose jobs, in part, depend on the scourge of counterfeiting. They include intellectual property (IP) lawyers, investigators, consultants, corporate brand protection professionals, packaging and distribution experts, and even government workers. For example, Customs officials have taken a greater interest in IP-related issues.

Governments

Finally, there are some benefits to the country where illegal counterfeiting activities are taking place. It is perhaps such benefits that allow these countries to turn a blind eye to some of these activities. Though, as we previously discussed, the downside losses may actually outweigh the benefits.

Depending on the source, there are some differences of opinion as to which countries account for the most counterfeiting activity. China and Russia would probably make everyone's "Top 10" when it comes to illegal copies of entertainment software, CDs, cassettes, and videos. In these countries, pirated software makes up 96 percent and 95 percent respectively of the domestic markets. Other countries that have often been accused by the United States of substantial infringement on intellectual property rights (IPRs) include Iran, Bulgaria, Korea, Hong Kong, India, Mexico, Taiwan, Turkey, Indonesia, Thailand, Colombia, Peru, Italy, and Venezuela. In addition, it appears that organized crime syndicates in these and other countries are at the center of many large-scale, well-organized counterfeiting efforts. And, terrorist groups have been known to raise money through counterfeiting.

To the extent that they are developing their productive capacity, along with the distribution system, you could argue that there is some benefit to the host country. The same argument applies to the development of new technologies as counterfeiters and pirates attempt to stay ahead of the technological developments by the authentication industry.

To the extent that the counterfeiters increase exports from the country where the fakes originate, they are having a positive impact on that country's balance of payments, at least in the merchandise trade account. The reverse is also true. If they supply domestic demand with unauthorized overproduction from foreign licensing or contract manufacturing facilities, then they are favorably affecting the balance of payments by reducing what would otherwise be imports.

Just as we argued that the authentication industry provides jobs in its immediate economic environment, the same can be said for the counterfeiters. Counterfeiters create jobs whether lawful or not. And, if the job creation occurs in a country with an unemployment problem that is also tolerant of counterfeiting activity, then it may be welcome. Some have estimated that piracy in China accounts for as many as 3 to 5 million jobs, and revenues of $40 to $80 billion, at a time when unemployment is a growing problem.[32]

Finally, as mentioned previously, if one can supply the local consumers with unauthorized overproduction at a fraction of the legitimate cost, then the local consumer is indeed benefiting. This argument probably applies best to unauthorized overproduction of otherwise legitimate licensees.

SO THE BATTLE LINES ARE DRAWN

It is clear that there are a diverse variety of actors that stand to lose or gain from counterfeiting, or other illegitimate production activities. It is the on-going conflict between these competing interests that is the focus of this book.

There is some legal recourse; but that may mean litigating in a foreign country, under foreign laws, and at substantial expense. Furthermore, the validity of private property rights (including intellectual property) varies substantially from one culture to another. Some cultures believe that new developments should benefit the public good and not just those who have invented or developed a product or process. So, even if there are laws protecting intellectual property, they may not be enthusiastically enforced. Threats of retaliation and sanctions by your home country government, particularly if you are a U.S. company, can be effective. Likewise, soliciting the support of U.S. Customs in seizing and destroying counterfeit goods will help in the home market. Sometimes selling your product through local licensees helps. Since they are paying for the license, and counterfeiters in their country directly impact their revenues, you now have local partners with a vested interest in protecting your intellectual property. The above remedies, however, are mostly reactive. There are some proactive measures that companies can take as well.

From the point of view of the firm with the branded product, the competition for market share now includes legitimate competitors, as well as illegitimate producers of a firm's own branded products. Traditional competition is tough enough. Companies must not allow it to be exacerbated by illegal knock-offs of their products. First, effective internal organization is required, and adequate resources must be assigned to the task. There is a growing industry that can provide devices and technology to assure a company and its customers that the products are authentic.

The next chapter looks at some of the costs and consequences to society as a whole. Then, Part 4 of the book will examine some of the approaches available for protecting brand value from the threat of counterfeiting.

CHAPTER 8

The Social Consequences of Counterfeiting

DIFFUSE BUT SIGNIFICANT CONSEQUENCES

The social consequences of counterfeiting, as distinct from economic consequences, are perhaps more difficult to define and quantify. A company may very well estimate losses due to counterfeiting from a number of different sources—the relative availability of counterfeit products available in a particular market, a measurable decline in revenues due to the presence of counterfeits, the quantity of seizures, and harm to the company's reputation. A country may measure the loss of jobs or the loss of tax revenue due to counterfeiting. But, the social consequences tend to be more diffuse and more difficult to measure. What is the ultimate cost, for example, of the increased involvement by criminals and terrorists in counterfeiting? What are the social costs of not being able to enforce intellectual property rights?

While the social consequences of counterfeiting might be difficult to measure with precision, they can nonetheless, in many cases, be described as significant. This chapter describes some of the known social consequences of counterfeiting, and their side effects, in an attempt to further elucidate the costs of counterfeiting.

THE INVOLVEMENT OF ORGANIZED CRIME AND TERRORISTS IN COUNTERFEITING

The involvement of organized crime and terrorist organizations in large-scale counterfeiting is well-documented. As Peter Lowe of the

International Chamber of Commerce Counterfeiting Intelligence Bureau has written, the fact "that organized criminals should have been quick to perceive the attractions of counterfeiting is perhaps unsurprising since counterfeiting has come to be regarded as a high-profit, low-risk activity by such criminals. Indeed, the immense opportunities inherent in this field have encouraged more and more organized criminals and even terrorist groups to get involved in this field."[1]

Among the incidents Lowe and the Counterfeiting Intelligence Bureau cite in linking organized crime to counterfeiting are:

- The involvement of the Genovese crime gang in a conspiracy to market fake designer jeans in the United States in the early 1980s.

- The statement in 1991 by David Thai, the former leader of the Vietnamese crime gang Born to Kill, that he had earned over $13 million from the sale of counterfeit watches in New York.

- A two-year undercover operation in the early 1990s co-coordinated by the Asian Organized Crime Section of the U.S. Justice Department that uncovered the illegal importation of millions of dollars worth of fake designer goods by a Korean crime group. This led to 43 arrests and huge seizures throughout the United States in 1995.

- The repeated discoveries linking the Mafia in Italy with a number of different counterfeiting rackets, including illegal software and CDs. In 1995, the Mafia was also found to be linked with both the IRA and the Protestant Ulster Defense Association (UDA) in a huge illegal CD production and distribution operation based in Milan. The Mafia-backed production plant was producing 24 million illegal CDs each year that were exported throughout Europe.

- The linkages showing involvement by Chinese Triad groups with different counterfeiting operations. In 1995, police in Southern California raided the home of individuals connected with a U.S.-based Chinese gang called Wah Ching that was linked to Hong Kong Triads. The raid unearthed a huge quantity of counterfeit software manufactured in China.[2]

While it has not traditionally received a high level of public attention and press scrutiny, governments have certainly taken note of the increased linkages between criminal elements and counterfeiting. In late 2000, the White House issued a report on the international criminal threat to the United States. "If the stereotype of a typical criminal is a godfather-type who breaks bones, now you have a more sophisticated criminal figure who can hack your computer, who can influence financial markets around the world and can destabilize countries or regions of the world that are important to the United States,"[3] said P.J. Crowley, President Clinton's national security spokesman. These criminal cartels involve themselves in a wide range of activities, including "counterfeiting of money, counterfeiting of CDs and software, smuggling of people, smuggling of arms, smuggling of precious gems,"[4] said Richard A. Clarke, counterterrorism coordinator of the National Security Council.

The linkages between organized crime and counterfeiting are not the only disturbing trend noticed by governments around the world. Terrorists have also learned that counterfeiting can be a very profitable way to finance their activities. Again, the Counterfeiting Intelligence Bureau and others have been systematically cataloguing the growing linkage between terrorists and counterfeiting:

- Following the first bombing of the World Trade Center in New York, in 1993, the FBI examined links between 20 alleged counterfeiters and Sheikh Omar Abdul Rahman (who is currently serving a life sentence for organizing the 1993 attack). According to testimony before the Senate Judiciary Committee in 1995, the New York Joint Terrorist Task Force testified that it had reason "to believe that high-level players who controlled a counterfeit T-shirt ring were using the proceeds to support terrorist groups"[5] such as the one that carried out the attack. Then, in 1996, the FBI seized over 100,000 counterfeit T-shirts with fake Atlanta Olympic and Nike logos emblazoned on them. That operation was also run by followers of Rahman.[6]

- The Irish Republican Army's involvement in video copying rackets and the distribution of fake veterinary products has been documented. During 1995, the IRA is believed to have been involved in pirating of the "Lion King" video that netted about £4 million in illegal sales. Secret factories along the Irish Republic's border with Northern Ireland are believed to have produced thousands of pirated videos and music CDs, generating more than £200 million every year to fund IRA activities.[7]

- The charging in Chile of a naturalized Paraguayan citizen with selling millions of dollars of pirated software in Paraguay, the proceeds of which were allegedly funneled to the militant terrorist group Hezbollah. The individual, a man named Ali Khalil Mehri, fled to France to avoid trial.[8]

This linkage between terrorists and counterfeiting was thrown into stark relief following the 9/11 terrorist attacks on the World Trade Center and the Pentagon, when *The Washington Post* carried an editorial headlined "From T-shirts to Terrorism—That Fake Nike Swoosh May be Helping to Fund Bin Laden's Network."[9] In the article, Roslyn Mazer, a Washington lawyer and former associate deputy attorney general of the U.S. Justice Department, outlined the historical linkages between terrorists and counterfeiting and concluded that "the staggering economic losses to America's copyright and trademark industries—alarming unto themselves—now are compounded by the opportunistic trafficking in intellectual property (IP) products to finance terrorism and other organized criminal endeavors."[10]

Clearly, counterfeiting as an activity attracts unwanted individuals and groups for all the wrong reasons. It is a highly profitable activity; it operates at or beyond the margin of legality; it is difficult to detect, track, and enforce; penalties are often lax; and it is very rarely treated as criminal activity, but rather is often treated as a civil offense. Also, counterfeiting generally operates below the radar screen of "serious crimes" prosecuted by the police. That terrorists or organized criminals have found it a relatively safe and profitable way to finance their other activities is perhaps unremarkable. What is remarkable is that counterfeiting is not more vigorously prosecuted as a crime that not only causes grave economic harm to companies but also poses potentially larger risks to society.

THE IRONY OF COUNTERFEITING AS A CREATOR OF EMPLOYMENT

One of the ironies of counterfeiting is that while it reduces demand for authentic products—thus reducing employment that would otherwise be employed in making those products—it also *creates* jobs in the factories, sweatshops, and back-alley operations where counterfeits are made.

◑ FOCUS 8.1 ◐

COUNTERFEITING CONDITIONS

"In advanced Western economies, job creation is regarded as a vital imperative for all governments and politicians. This is because unemployment impacts on society in all sorts of ways, in lost tax revenue, unemployment pay, and attendant social costs. In developing countries where counterfeiting is rife, different considerations apply. Counterfeiters are able to tap a vast pool of low cost labor, which has no access to the sort of welfare benefits available in well developed industrialized countries. In addition, taxes are minimal or nonexistent, and counterfeiters can masquerade as Robin Hood figures providing a valuable service for the community at the expense of 'wealthy' rights owners . . . the message is that (while) counterfeiting does destroy the jobs of victim companies and their suppliers . . . it does create jobs for those in the counterfeiting industry. This of course may well be one reason why countries that have become well known as havens of counterfeiting have been reluctant to clamp down on this industry too hard."[11]

Peter Lowe, Counterfeiting Intelligence Bureau

In those economies where counterfeiting is an industry itself, jobs are created when counterfeiters employ people to make fake products. In one startling example described by the Counterfeiting Intelligence Bureau, an investigator in China visiting the city of Wenzhou, about 400 kilometers south of Shanghai, uncovered a vast industrial zone, with perhaps as many as a thousand companies engaged in the business of producing counterfeit low-voltage electrical switchgear. The investigator estimated that somewhere between 200,000 to 300,000 people were employed in these businesses.

Although this type of employment may appear as a benefit to those being employed, it often has other problems associated with it. The same investigator who described the switchgear counterfeiting industry in Wenzhou also described seeing child labor in the various establishments producing fake products. He described unsafe working conditions, with the assembly of finished goods often taking place on the street. Workers are paid by the piece, and unprotected by any insurance, benefits, union representation, or holidays.

Poor working conditions are endemic throughout much of the developing world—where much counterfeiting takes place. But one key difference between being employed by a counterfeiter and being employed by a legitimate industry is obvious: Counterfeiters have little long-term incentive to improve working conditions, and any legislation or change in government policy would not likely affect counterfeiters. When government interference or regulation becomes too onerous—or makes counterfeiting too risky an occupation in a certain location—the counterfeiters simply move to a more conducive locale.

It may not come as a surprise, though, to realize that support in local communities for counterfeiters can be quite high—these establishments, while illegal, create employment. Often this support can overwhelm government attempts to enforce crackdowns:

> A violent conflict erupted in Xintang Town, Zengchen City when 5,000 people who were involved in the manufacture of fake jeans and other imitation products confronted a team of government officials who had been sent to crack down on the trade in counterfeits. In what must have been a chilling experience for the enforcers, the local people surrounded the motorcade of more than 60 government officials, reporters and public security officers from Guangzhou who had come to maintain order. The situation turned critical when some of the local people threatened to disarm the public security officials. A "stand off" of more than three hours ensued after which negotiations were started which finally diffused the situation.[12]

The costs of hosting counterfeiting to a community are not simply those normally associated with low wages and child labor in unsafe conditions. More far-reaching consequences are being uncovered as the scope of counterfeiting throughout the globe has become more apparent. In the *McKinsey Quarterly* in the spring of 2000, a group of McKinsey consultants looked at the Russian economy's inability to generate growth throughout the 1990s. Among the factors cited as contributing to the poor labor productivity and the disincentive to invest in research and development was counterfeiting:

The software industry, one of the prime creators of jobs and value in healthy modern economies, employs a mere 8,000 workers in Russia, compared with 640,000 in the United States. Why is this important industry so small? For starters, 89% of all packaged software in Russia is produced illegally. Russian packaged-software firms, therefore, can't produce sufficient returns to justify investing in new products, or in research and development to improve existing ones. In addition, the software-consuming sectors, whose demand drives the emergence and growth of software firms, are both smaller and less interested in productivity-enhancing software tools than are their Western counterparts. In modern economies, for example, supermarkets—with their complex inventory management systems—are big consumers of software, but Russia has few of them. Similarly, modern banks use software to keep costs low and customer service high, but in Russia, where success in banking depends on relationships with the authorities, the demand for banking software is nearly nonexistent relative to demand in the United States. "[13]

EXHIBIT 8.1   Effects of Software Piracy on Productivity

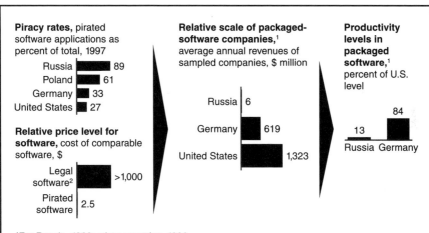

Piracy rates, pirated software applications as percent of total, 1997

Russia	89
Poland	61
Germany	33
United States	27

Relative price level for software, cost of comparable software, $

Legal software[2]	>1,000
Pirated software	2.5

Relative scale of packaged-software companies,[1] average annual revenues of sampled companies, $ million

Russia	6
Germany	619
United States	1,323

Productivity levels in packaged software,[1] percent of U.S. level

Russia	Germany
13	84

[1]For Russia, 1998; other countries, 1996.
[2]Indicative of total worth of software.
Source: Business Software Alliance; International Data Corporation; Russian Shield Association; financial reports; McKinsey analysis.

This excerpt is taken from Alexei Beltyukov, M. James Kondo, William W. Lewis, Michael M. Obermayer, Vincent Palmade, and Alex Reznikovitch, "Reflections on Russia," The McKinsey Quarterly, 2000 Number 1. The full article can be found on the publication's website, *www.mckinseyquarterly.com*. Copyright © 2000 McKinsey & Company. All rights reserved. Reprinted by permission.

This conclusion was echoed in the Counterfeiting Intelligence Bureau's book *Countering Counterfeiting*, which also concluded that "another national consequence resulting from the costs incurred by 'victim' companies is a general decline in R&D, since a company cannot expect the full return from its investment."[14]

In addition, the Organization for Economic Cooperation and Development (OECD) has highlighted the loss of direct foreign investment that can arise as a result of a country becoming known as a haven for counterfeiting. In the OECD's own report on the *Economic Impact of Counterfeiting* (1998), the organization writes that "such countries suffer both tangible and intangible losses . . . foreign producers of reputable products become reluctant to manufacture their products in countries where counterfeiting is rife as they cannot rely on the enforcement of their intellectual property rights. Hence, such countries not only *lose direct foreign investment but also miss out on foreign know-how.*"[15]

While counterfeiting can create jobs, it can also create a series of other problems that ultimately could lead to an economy being less competitive, less integrated into the stream of international commerce, and less productive than economies where governments choose to crack down on counterfeiters.

WHAT COMPANIES CAN DO ABOUT THE SOCIAL CONSEQUENCES OF COUNTERFEITING

A company confronted with many of the social ills that accompany counterfeiting has limited ability to address issues like international organized crime, terrorism, and employment-related ills among counterfeiters in developing countries. In most cases, companies will only be vaguely aware of these issues, focusing instead on the much narrower (and to a company) compelling problem of simply protecting the company's products. Nonetheless, actions that companies take can have a direct impact on the social consequences previously described.

These include:

- *Ensure control over a company supply chain.* Where a company understands and has control over its own supply chain, the lower the likelihood that suppliers or distributors will either produce or distribute unauthorized goods. The old adage fully applies here—"know your partners well." When your product, your brand, and your reputation are at stake, your company cannot afford to be sloppy or less than diligent. Know who the subcontractors are who produce components for your products and insist on a right to audit their operations—then carry out the audits!) Understand who your distributors are at every stage in the distribution chain of your products, and ensure that they are selling only authorized products. Rigorously enforce compliance at every step, and make it known that your company will "go the distance" to defend its product and its brand.

- *Ensure full cognizance of risks involved in outsourcing production to suppliers, particularly in countries where counterfeiting is known to occur.* One of the ironies of counterfeiting is that as production of goods throughout the world shifts to lower-cost countries, it is often shifting right into countries where counterfeiting is rife. As we have seen, subcontracted manufacturers often "moonlight" as counterfeiters themselves.

  While it is often rational to shift production of goods to locations where costs are lower, this should not occur without a full understanding of the implications of such a shift. Understand who your company is subcontracting or using to produce your product—and understand who *they* use to subcontract or supply their components. Audit them frequently and insist on transparency in their records. Police, and police again. Know with whom your company does business, and insist that they work to meet your company's standards. Without doing so, the full cost savings of moving to a lower-cost location may not be what you think.

- *Choose a cost-effective way to protect a product.* In Chapter 12, we outline ways in which companies protect their products with authentication technologies and track and trace systems. Find one that works for your product and use it—it will deter counterfeiters and provide your company with a wealth of information about the extent and nature of the counterfeiting problem it faces.

- *Use both public enforcement and private enforcement of your company's IP rights.* Insist wherever possible that the public authorities defend and protect your company's intellectual and trademark rights. This is not possible in many locations, though, due to corruption, inconsistent application of laws, or, in some cases, a complete absence of laws against counterfeiting (as we will explore in Chapter 11). Always safeguard against this by also having private company-led efforts to enforce your company's IP rights (which we explore in Chapter 10).

- *Lobby through trade associations for vigorous defense of the rights of IP holders.* Work with your competitors—who face the same challenges—to enforce laws that benefit all companies in a particular market (see Chapter 9). Many trade associations compile information and expertise in addressing the problems of counterfeiting at the company level. They also lobby governments and relevant international bodies to defend the interests of their members. Get involved.

While no single company can begin to address the myriad of social issues that are caused by counterfeiting, a vigorous awareness and defense of a company's interest can serve as an important starting point in addressing the conditions whereby counterfeiting is allowed to thrive.

PART FOUR

Protecting Your Brand and Customers

T he cost of counterfeiting to companies is high today and appears to be increasing. Counterfeiters are becoming more sophisticated. Company distribution channels are being corrupted, sometimes by the company's own suppliers or licensees. Against this backdrop, it may seem that legitimate producers face insurmountable obstacles in addressing this issue.

A range of tools exists, however, that allows legitimate suppliers of products to protect their brands and their customers, enforce their rights, and protect their distribution channels. These tools range from using private investigative services, to better understanding and monitoring of the problem, to using legal resources where possible. More recently, a host of new technological solutions have allowed companies to authenticate and track their products from production to sale. Governments and trade associations, along with other institutions, can also play a role. In many cases, these solutions have been tested and proven by companies under difficult conditions—and with considerable success in detecting and protecting their brands.

CHAPTER 9

Organizing to Address the Problem

FROM DENIAL TO STRATEGIC PROBLEM SOLVING

> Before you can organize to address the problem,
> you have to recognize that you have a problem.

Before organizing a plan or program to address a problem, a company or organization has to first recognize that it *has a problem*. This may seem to be a truism, but one of the distinctive features about counterfeiting is that its effect on company performance can be hidden from direct view. Lost or unrealized sales, diminished brand value, and damage from a loss in control over marketing are all costs that are difficult to quantify. At the outset, companies therefore often fail to realize that they have any problem. Or, if they do recognize the existence of a problem in a general sense, they often fail to realize that *they can do anything about it*.

In fact, Magali LeParc, a consultant to companies who suffer from counterfeiting problems, has written about the "culture of denial" found in many companies faced with a counterfeiting problem. Writing in particular about pharmaceutical companies, LeParc notes that "there is still a culture of denial among pharmaceutical companies . . . (about) publicly accepting there is a problem and subsequently, protecting their products and consumer safety."[1]

LeParc attributes this culture of denial to a number of factors:

- Counterfeit drugs are mainly seen as a developing country problem.

- To date, there have been relatively few incidents of counterfeit drugs appearing in distribution systems in developed countries.
- Pharmaceutical companies fear that publicizing the issue would result in revenue losses more significant than those associated with counterfeiting.
- There is a reluctance to report incidences of counterfeiting to authorities.
- There are potential liability issues.
- There is a reluctance to incur expense associated with introducing product security devices that are unproven.
- Counterfeiting is seen as a legal issue, not a business issue.[2]

This difficulty in recognizing the problem—so often found in many companies—is compounded even further by the fact that in most companies, no single person or group is charged with monitoring and understanding the extent of counterfeiting on the company's performance. Hence, what is already a diffuse problem is made even more difficult to recognize by the fact that no particular person or group is systematically charged with responsibility for the problem. The relatively recent rise of large-scale industrial counterfeiting has meant that very few companies have directors of brand protection or anticounterfeiting among their senior executives.

In fact, one of the major errors that most companies make at the outset, as noted by LeParc, is to look at the problem of counterfeiting and *consider it exclusively a legal issue.* While enforcement of a company's intellectual property rights—including copyright, trademark and design rights—is inherently important in any effort to combat counterfeiting and its consequences, very few, companies have successfully addressed the issue of counterfeiting through exclusively *legal* means.

The reasons for the lack of success in addressing the problem through strictly legal means are rooted in the fundamental nature of counterfeiting in today's global economy. First, counterfeiting of products today is a global endeavor, often involving manufacturing and distribution from and to diverse geographical locations. Attempts to stop large-scale counterfeiting via enforcement of legal rights in one particular jurisdiction are difficult enough. Enforcing legal rights across multiple jurisdictions can prove impossible.

Second, countries in the areas from which many counterfeiters operate—Southeast Asia, the Middle East, and former East bloc states—often do not have legal systems that allow outsiders to enforce their rights easily or effectively. In many countries, no laws exist that actually prevent or prohibit counterfeiting. In others, where laws do exist, poorly developed legal systems often make it impossible to actually enforce the laws. Corruption in many countries makes enforcement of rights virtually impossible—even with court orders and legal rights fully in place. The result is that much time and money can often be spent pursuing legal remedies in locations where there is little real prospect of any effect.

One real irony is that some counterfeiters operate within the legal system. For example, trademark theft—the registering of a trademark ahead of the registration of the mark by the legitimate holder—is a growing problem in many locations. In 1979, a Brazilian company registered the "All Star" brand held by Converse shoes throughout the world in Brazil. The Brazilian company, All Star Artigos Esportivos Ltda., now produces over a million pairs of All Star tennis shoes—virtually identical to those produced by Converse—every year. Converse doesn't benefit at all, as the brand (in Brazil) now belongs to another company. Recourse to a legal solution to this problem by Converse has yet to prove entirely successful.[3]

Third, even if legal remedies could hypothetically be pursued against counterfeiters with a high degree of effectiveness, a focus by companies on strictly legal remedies would still miss a central point about counterfeiting. *Counterfeiting is not simply the problem of someone coopting a company's property rights, it is a problem of that company not being in full control of its own supply chain.* Counterfeits which make their way into a market from a company's own suppliers or licensees are often indistinguishable from the authorized and authentic item. If a company is not in control of its own supply chain and does not fully understand where the problems arise, it is unlikely to be able to address the problem of counterfeiting in any effective manner—legal or otherwise.

Against this backdrop, it becomes important that a company realize it has a problem and that this realization takes place at the highest levels of management. A market manager for a specific country may appreciate that it has a problem with counterfeiting. A financial analyst may note that sales into a specific region are not at projected levels, for inexplicable reasons. A customer service agent in returns may notice poor quality packaging on returned defective products. But rarely are these strands put together so that the company appreciates that it must systematically address the problem. This requires a strategic focus from senior management in order that the various constituencies in the company who are affected by counterfeiting—and who will be affected by the fight against counterfeiting—are appropriately involved.

CREATE AN EFFECTIVE TASK FORCE

When organizing to address the problem, don't underestimate how many constituencies are involved throughout the company.

Once a company has realized that it has a problem, it is then charged with creating a strategy and organizing itself to address the issue. In our experience, the two most effective means we have seen companies adopt to address this issue are:

1. *Have the effort led by someone within the senior management who has real authority to make decisions across the company.*

2. *Create an intercompany task force to tailor a strategy and implement it. Have this intercompany task force report directly to the senior management person in charge of its implementation.*

The rationale for having a senior management person with real authority own the anticounterfeiting strategy is quite simple. Any effective implementation of a strategy will affect a large number of constituencies in a company, and without a single person driving the implementation— *and having authority to make changes*—the effort will founder.

For example, a packaging group may be called upon to make significant changes in the sourcing of its packaging. Purchasing may not be able to continue using certain suppliers, or new requirements may be required from suppliers and third-party manufacturing. Marketing may have to tailor the message it gives to consumers and specifically address the issue of counterfeiting directly with consumers. All of these can be painful decisions that in isolation may not make sense to any particular group within the company—particularly given the fact that it is unlikely that any one particular group will itself have seen the overall effects of counterfeiting on the company's overall performance.

The reason to create an intercompany task force is quite simple—to involve the various constituencies who are going to be involved in the solution and to give them ownership of the problem. In our experience, representatives from a number of groups in the company need to be involved:

- *Legal.* Even though it is unlikely that any solution is going to be purely legal, the legal department and the company's legal advisors will be involved in fashioning any solution to a counterfeiting problem. Issues of intellectual property, design rights, and trademark are inherently involved in any attempt to defend a company's rights against counterfeiters.

- *Brand Management.* Any effort to address issues of counterfeiting will involve an examination of the brand, its management, and any degradation to the brand arising from counterfeiting. Given that many solutions may involve changes in the way brands are presented, brand managers are critical to any process.

- *Marketing and Public Relations.* Many anticounterfeiting strategies will involve public relations and marketing campaigns to educate consumers about which products are authentic and which are not authentic. Similarly, the marketing and public relations groups will need to be involved, if any incidents of counterfeiting become public and need to be addressed in order to preserve a company's credibility in the market.

- *Manufacturing.* Manufacturing needs to be involved both in the definition of the problem (Are our products too easy to copy?) and in any solution that involves product marking and tracing. In addition, manufacturing is often involved in forensic examination of counterfeit products and in the design of anticounterfeiting features.

- *Purchasing/Outsourcing/Supply Chain Management.* Involvement from these groups is critical in addressing counterfeiting, particularly where such counterfeiting arises from a company's own supply chain. Issues of outsourcing of manufacturing, licensing to third parties, and security of distribution all require detailed analysis in any effort to combat counterfeiting

- *Packaging.* Many anticounterfeiting solutions require enhancements or additions to product packaging, particularly since counterfeiters often focus on duplication or simulation of packaging. As most companies tend to be very conservative about packaging costs, involvement by this group is important throughout the process.

- *Sales.* The sales organization often serves as an "early warning" system for counterfeiting—complaints about counterfeits (and about substandard counterfeits that are believed to be authentic) often are fed back through the sales organization. Additionally, the sales organization can often be involved in designing solutions to the problem that are then communicated back through the sales team.

- *Research and Development.* R&D is often involved, like manufacturing, in forensic analysis of counterfeit goods. In addition, the R&D group is often also involved in the design of new good that are more difficult to counterfeit.

- *Financial.* Any effort to organize an anticounterfeiting effort has to have very strong financial involvement, not only to track and understand the costs but, more importantly, to understand the benefits and gains accomplished by the program.

- *Security and Enforcement.* Corporate security is inherently involved in any supply chain issues, and possibly in any ongoing enforcement of company rights against counterfeiters.

- *Regional/National Operating Companies.* Large organizations, particularly those operating globally, need to involve their various regional and national operating divisions or companies. Many times, these divisions or companies operate with a high degree of autonomy, and they will need to be involved both to understand the global nature of the counterfeiting problem, and solutions to the problems. Solutions implemented in only one locale and not another may not be effective for the company.

- *Outside Constituencies.* Outside constituencies that may be involved in the process at various points could include outside counsel, private investigators, law enforcement, industry associations, authentication technology and service providers, and lobbyists.

Although not all of these constituencies need to be fully involved in any task force, it is critical at the outset to recognize that an effective strategy will affect them and may affect them in a significant manner.

CHALLENGES FOR THE TASK FORCE

We've got a task force, now what?

Several critical challenges present themselves to any task force at its inception:

- Has the problem been fully defined and scoped?
- What criteria should a company use in designing a program to combat counterfeiting?
- Against what standards is a successful program measured?
- What kind of ongoing follow-up and monitoring are necessary?

These questions provide a basic framework for any task force wishing to attack the issue of counterfeiting.

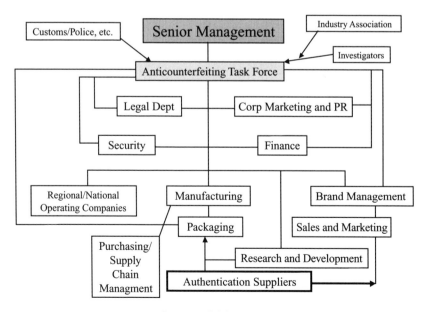

EXHIBIT 9.1 **Anticounterfeiting Task Force Constituencies**

Defining the Problem

As we have seen repeatedly throughout this book, counterfeiting takes a number of different forms and guises. The Harm Matrix again provides a basis for definition of the problem (see Exhibit 9.2).

Counterfeiting of products arising from a company's own suppliers or licensees is a pure supply-chain issue, most often resulting in products that are of very high quality, if not indistinguishable from the authorized item. This is most likely to result in sales of high-quality products to customers who either knowingly or unknowingly buy them—as shown on the right side of the Harm Matrix.

Where counterfeiting arises from third parties attempting to co-opt a company's brand, design, or IP, the quality of the products and the knowledge of the consumers in buying them can vary. Generally, the higher the quality the counterfeit that comes from a third party, the more deception is involved in selling it to a customer. But, the issues that arise from third party counterfeiting are inherently different in many respects than those involved in attacking counterfeiting that comes from within a company's own supply chain.

A related problem, mentioned throughout this book, has to do with diversion of products into distribution channels where they were not

		Low Quality	High Quality
Deception Level of deception inherent in the sale of the product	**High**	Cheap product purchased in belief that it is genuine.	High-quality counterfeits purchased by customers believing they are buying a genuine item.
	Low	Fake product purchased with knowledge it is fake.	Overruns or very high-quality counterfeits deliberately purchased with knowledge they are fake.

Low   High

Quality

Quality and functionality
of the counterfeit product

EXHIBIT 9.2 **Harm Matrix for Counterfeit Products**

intended. While this diversion, or gray marketing, is not covered by our definition of counterfeiting, it nonetheless does constitute a breach of the supply chain that often allows counterfeits to enter as well. Distribution channels that are porous enough to allow diverted goods to enter and be sold as fully legitimate can easily be used to sell counterfeit product also.

It is not often the case, however, that a company will have sufficient information at its disposal to be able to accurately and effectively answer all the questions about the nature of the problem it faces. More often, fragmentary evidence exists around the company that has never been centrally compiled and looked at in an organized fashion. A starting point, then, is to have the various members of the task force go back to their respective groups or departments and compile what information is available — what incidents of counterfeiting have been reported, what investigations (if any) have been made, what problem areas have arisen. Often, the concentration of this information in a single source — the task force — brings a focus to the problem that has been missing heretofore.

Another helpful step is to consult with outside parties who may be of assistance to the company. For example, outside counsel may have been involved in enforcement actions in specific locations or geographies. Private investigators may be called upon to conduct investigations of certain problem areas or specific problems. Embassies and government organizations who have confronted this problem in specific locales can be very useful allies in providing information and the means of addressing it.

Trade associations are also critically important in that they often have much expertise in addressing the issues and can also be an extremely important source of information. Trade associations often have direct experience in addressing these issues. Examples of trade associations that have taken a direct and effective role in addressing counterfeiting include the International Federation of the Phonographic Industries (IFPI), which has taken a leading role in addressing the duplication of CDs and music cassettes; The Business Software Alliance, which provides information for software companies in combating counterfeiting; the International Pharmaceutical Manufacturer's Association, and so on. Each industry faces its own unique set of problems, and by virtue of counterfeiting being a nondiscriminatory crime, each company in the industry often faces the same set of problems. Trade associations can effectively work on behalf of industries in attempting to define and address the problems.

In addition, several different trade associations exist that directly address the issue of counterfeiting. The Counterfeiting Intelligence Bureau of the International Chamber of Commerce compiles intelligence on counterfeiting and provides assistance to members in addressing the issue. The Anti-Counterfeiting Group and the International AntiCounterfeiting Coalition are composed of members from diverse industries that work together to address the issue of counterfeiting. Often these types of groups will exist in specific locations to address the unique issues associated with that locale, as with the Quality Brands Protection Committee in China.

The definition of the problem is often no small task, but is absolutely critical in designing any program. An incorrect definition of the problem can result quite easily in an ineffective approach with limited, if any, success.

Criteria for Design of a Program

Any successful anticounterfeiting program needs to address the following questions:

- What is the specific problem that needs to be addressed? For example, is it a supply chain issue, or third-party counterfeiting? Or is it diversion? As noted above, the definition and sizing of the problem is critical as a beginning step.

- Where is the problem most prevalent, and where does the company need to focus its resources? Often, incidents of counterfeiting of a company's products are concentrated in specific countries or regions where counterfeiters are particularly active at a given time, for example, Eastern Europe, the Middle East, and so forth. It is helpful to get a sense for where the problem is most critical and whether it makes sense to concentrate company resources there first (and whether it will be efficient to do so).

- What technologies and services are available to the company in designing a solution specific to its own needs? A host of technologies and solutions are now offered on the brand protection market, and these can often be tailored to meet a company's specific needs. We cover these solutions in more detail in later chapters, but matching the technologies and services available to the specific problem is critically important.

- How do the overall goals of the task force coincide with the financial and operating goals of the various groups within companies? How involved have the constituencies become in the definition and planning process?

- What level of involvement is necessary—and from whom—both in the company and from external suppliers? Options range from very heavy involvement on the part of the company staff to complete outsourcing of solutions.

- What follow-up services are needed after implementation of the program to ensure that the program is properly administered and the results are fully understood?

Success Indicators

No program should be implemented by any company without putting in place a set of measurements against which success or failure of the program—and the efficiency of the investment—can be gauged. In this respect, the investment decision to implement an anticounterfeiting program should face the same scrutiny as any other investment by the company. Criteria used by some companies are outlined in Chapter 12.

However, while the financial return from an anticounterfeiting program can often be compelling, it can also be fraught with difficulty. Financial losses in the form of "lost sales"—sales that would have been made had the consumers not bought counterfeit goods or even had them available—are often difficult to quantify as a base starting point. Increased sales after the implementation of a program can, and will, be attributed to "other factors"—better marketing, better product positioning, and so forth—as various constituencies in the company attempt to claim credit for such success.

It, therefore, becomes important, in addition to having a set of financial criteria, to have a set of measurements which are nonfinancial. These could include:

- *Brand Degradation and Recovery.* From the brand management side of the business, is there a sense that the brand is any less degraded or devalued in the market, as a result of the anticounterfeiting program? In one incident in the Middle East where a parts supplier suffered a serious problem due to widespread counterfeiting of its parts, the feedback from its distributors was that consumers were refusing to buy the brand because of the problem. The brand very rapidly fell from being the most desirable in the market and began to lose market share at an alarming rate to its competition. Concomitantly, positive feedback after implementation of an anticounterfeiting program was very rapid, in that the brand reacquired its previous luster, and consumers came back. And not coincidentally, the counterfeiters shifted their efforts to the competition who did not have a program.

- *Seizures.* Have seizures or detection of counterfeit products decreased since implementation of a program? Are counterfeit products more difficult to find? Are they less obvious in the market?

- *Public Relations.* Has the company received positive press about its efforts to combat counterfeiting? Has this raised the company's profile in a positive manner in its selected markets?

- *Government Cooperation.* Have the efforts by the company resulted in better cooperation from the governments involved? Often, high profile attempts to combat counterfeiting that are privately launched have the effect of forcing action by governments.

All of these "nonfinancial" measures play a role in deciding whether a program has been a success. Coupled with financial measures, they can tell a compelling story as to the effectiveness of any program.

Ongoing Follow-Up and Monitoring

No solution to any problem—and certainly not the problem of counterfeiting—can be static. Counterfeiters learn what their "competition"—the legitimate producers—are doing and react quickly. In many respects, counterfeiters are formidable in the skill and intelligence they use to adapt to changing market conditions.

The lesson for any company, then, is not to launch a program and disband the task force once it is launched. The task force needs to be an ongoing, adaptive body—ready to change the programs as counterfeiters react, target new problems as they arise, and evolve as the problems evolve. To do less would be to discredit the effort put in place to address the problem in the first place.

CHAPTER 10

Utilizing Private Investigators

I KNOW WHAT YOU DID LAST SHIPMENT

Counterfeiters generally don't report their sales to the Internal Revenue Service or local authorities. They don't issue press releases about how their latest scam has penetrated a company's distribution system and is fooling customers and law enforcement alike. Counterfeiting is a surreptitious business. To find it, you have to look for it.

Law enforcement and customs officials certainly play an important role in investigations, but the vast majority of work done to detect, characterize, and confront counterfeiting is done by private investigators. According to Bill Thompson, Senior Managing Director, China and Intellectual Property Services for Pinkerton: "The bulk of evidence collected in IP casework carried out worldwide is done by commercial investigations commissioned by IP rights holders. . . . [Yet it] is poorly understood and rarely well managed for maximum cost effectiveness."[1]

WHO IS MAKING THESE SOUTH PARK FAKES?

Stu Drobny received a call from Harvey Lewin, a partner in the New York law firm of Lewin and Keyton, in early 1999. "Stu, I need you to do some snooping for me. We are getting a lot of knockoff South Park (a cast of copyrighted and trademarked cartoon characters) shirts and caps." He went on to give Drobny, the head of Stumar Investigations, the details including the address of a shop where some of the fake merchandise seemed to be originating.[2]

Within days, Stumar's undercover investigators had visited the shop, purchased a variety of South Park goods and sent samples to Lewin to have them verified as fakes. While they were shopping, however, the investigators couldn't help but notice the range of Nike, Tommy Hilfiger, Nautica, Polo, Warner Brothers, Disney, and other goods also for sale. They contacted these brand holders and got approval to do some more investigating. On a second visit, they bought samples of these goods as well and began taking snapshots of the premises and personnel using their cleverly disguised "beeper cameras" (small digital cameras that look like an innocent beeper).[3]

Armed with a range of fakes, photos, and affidavits about what was clearly a counterfeit wholesale center, Drobny went to the Philadelphia Major Crimes office, laid out the evidence and obtained a search warrant. He and his men returned to the corner shop the next day with the Philadelphia Police Department and commenced a raid. They went immediately to the back room where they found large amounts of fakes, packaged and ready for sale, and also large quantities of "counterfeit blanks" (generic shirts, caps and other goods ready for the logos to be added).

But wait! As investigators probed further, they noticed electrical wires passing through the wall and into the adjoining building. They followed the wires and found yet another cache of fakes, and more wires leading to another building. This was clearly a bigger operation than anyone had initially realized. They assembled the evidence, sealed the building and returned to the District Attorney for an expanded warrant. When they returned the next day, they confirmed that the three-story corner shop, as well as the adjoining two buildings, were a major counterfeit distribution center. More than 1.5 million items were ultimately seized. It took four days of working around the clock and four tractor-trailers to empty the buildings.[4]

In the process, they also seized business and financial records. They also found a cease and desist order the owner had previously received for counterfeiting in a desk drawer.

Another lucky break! The records led investigators to a 150-person factory outside Philadelphia, owned by the wife of the storeowner. More goods, more equipment, and more records were seized. This time, the paper trail led to a second factory located in an industrial park. The trail was somewhat sketchy, however, and the investigators needed more evidence that this factory was also involved in counterfeiting. Stumar staked out the building and also talked to the security office at the park. Yes, the director of security said, he had been in the building a couple of weeks earlier and seen silk-screening and other equipment like he had seen described on the news of the first bust. It was a sultry summer day. As the Stumar investigators waited to make their move, the workers at the factory opened the bay doors in the back to get some ventilation. Presto! Investigators were able to see two 25-arm silk-screen machines and other equipment being used to make more fakes. Another raid, more seizures.[5]

Organized sleuthing, careful documentation, communication with the brand owner and police—these were the ingredients that led to the downfall of Mr. Poek and his eight codefendants. Analysis of the records showed that the gang was laundering the proceeds of the enterprise through casinos and travel agencies and was sending millions back to Korea. Technology played a role, too. High-tech equipment like the beeper camera and night vision recordings helped Stumar to gather the evidence to move forward on the investigation and ultimately was used in criminal proceedings to obtain convictions. Unfortunately, even though convicted under Pennsylvania's 1990 felony counterfeiting statute, the defendants only received suspended sentences and were ordered to pay restitution of $100,000 each. The seized fakes were destroyed and the Immigration and Naturalization Service (INS) has now begun deportation proceedings.

CAN YOU GET ME A DEAL ON THESE BATTERIES?

As discussed in Chapter 5, consumables and replacement parts make great counterfeiting targets. While purchasers tend to evaluate and examine new products, they are much less likely to exercise the same degree of care with replacement parts.

In the mid-1990s, a major international personal electronics company approached the London-based Counterfeiting Intelligence Bureau (CIB) with a problem. They were finding evidence of counterfeit batteries in various parts of the world. Could CIB help?[6]

The CIB is the anticounterfeiting arm of the International Chamber of Commerce (ICC) It operates as a part of the ICC Commercial Crime Services and, among other functions, performs counterfeiting investigations through its CounterSearch network of investigators.

Electronics supplies are global products moved through global distribution systems. Much of the manufacturing is done on contract by companies located in developing countries where labor is cheap. With these dynamics in mind, the CIB had to use a "sham business" investigative approach rather than the stakeout and surveillance approach that is suitable for localized counterfeit operations.

Careful groundwork was required. CIB had to create a sham import/export company with appropriate registrations, bank accounts, a business address, and so on that could be a credible tool for making contact with the counterfeiters. As Peter Lowe, director of the CIB, says, "As the stakes get higher, the criminals get more sophisticated. They often check the investigator's bona fides because they are concerned about the use of fake companies. The risks of violence also goes up."[7]

Having created the background, the CIB front company contacted Asian operators within the suspected counterfeiting rings by fax, indicating that they were interested in buying substantial quantities of batteries at the lowest possible price. According to the cover story, the group planned to establish distribution in the United States and Western Europe and believed that they could become major customers of the counterfeit ring.

Interestingly, at this point, the investigators were not Taiwanese or Chinese locals; rather, they were European. At first, this may appear to fly in the face of popular wisdom that investigators should be local and know the region they are working. On second thought, however, this is logical. If the sham company was organized in the West and was planning to sell in the West, then the contacts would most likely be Western as well. Of course, it is critical that the investigation team "knows its business." The CIB investigators had to spend significant time getting up to speed on the business and technical aspects of the electronic parts industry. They had to get to know details about some of the key players in the industry so that they could interact convincingly with their intended targets.

Trained, credentialed, and equipped with the front business, they took their next step. They intensified their correspondence, began a series of meetings and started to obtain samples. Interestingly, the samples generally were supplied free. The counterfeiters accepted that the samples would be used for evaluation purposes. How realistic did they look? How well did they perform (at least on initial use)? Were there obvious defects? Did they tend to break easily?

As the drama continued, investigators began to shift their inquiry to "quantity issues." Could the Taiwanese group supply the quantity that would be demanded? They began to move the inquiry from the group's "front office" and a few samples to the actual "manufacturing" site. "Yes," the criminals promised, they could supply quantities. They had multiple manufacturing sites. In fact, as investigators visited these sites, it became clear that there were several Taiwanese families working in an independent but cooperative manner. The assembly was being done by each family in its own little sweatshop but the injection molding dyes (the most expensive part of the whole operation) were jointly owned. Six families had each put up a share of the capital required to have the dyes made, and each used them "as required" for the production of their own fake product.

This was a critical piece of knowledge. Equipped with an understanding of how they functioned, CIB was able to describe the operation to state police and a series of raids were carried out. Because the dyes were seized as part of the effort, the counterfeiters were crippled and the perpetrators later received fines and prison sentences for their involvement in the racket.[8]

GET READY—HERE THEY COME!

A critical part of investigations should be, and sometimes is, using known and anticipated facts and intelligence to plan for the probable course of the counterfeiters' conduct.

The protection of licensed products at the 1996 Atlanta Olympic Games is an example of planning ahead to confront field challenges. Olympic merchandise is always copied. That is just a fact. Recognizing this inevitability, the U.S. Olympic Committee (USOC) and U.S. Customs Service began early to fight the coming flood of fakes.[9]

This precedent-setting effort employed two principal tactics: interdiction of counterfeit goods at the U.S. borders and enforcement of intellectual property rights at the Games. The interdiction program, dubbed

Operation Gold Medal, was organized by the U.S. Customs Service. On-site efforts were organized by the U.S. Olympic Committee (USOC) and its collaborators. The system was built around rapid, organized communication and was supplemented with holographic product authentication tags.

The USOC holds all U.S. legal rights to the use of the word "Olympics," the Olympic Rings, the Olympic Shield, and other terms and symbols related to the Olympics. It recruits financial sponsors and licensees who pay royalties in exchange for the right to use the Olympic symbols. In Atlanta, there were 150 sponsors and licensees, and payments totaled more than $100 million. Eighty-two percent of these payments went to support the training, housing, and transportation of U.S. athletes. In exchange for their payments, licensees and sponsors expect strong protection of their exclusive rights to use the Olympic name and symbols, according to their licenses and sponsorship agreements.

Experience showed that counterfeiters, often located outside the United States, would ship unlicensed products into the United States for sale. Some licensees also manufactured their products overseas and imported them for distribution in the United States. With jurisdiction over goods entering the country and with its experience in assisting the USOC at past Olympics, Customs took the lead in policing this importing activity. Customs adopted the name *Gold Medal* for the operation and assigned two special agents in its Atlanta Office of Investigation to coordinate Olympic anticounterfeit efforts at ports of entry nationwide.

Working with organizers, they built an enforcement program based on four principles: education of Customs officials; 24-hour licensee response to all Customs inquiries on detained products; supporting criminal investigations with affidavits and witnesses; and refusing to permit the entry of infringing products, even on the payment of royalties.

Jim Bikoff, attorney for the USOC, and others designed a detailed operations manual for use by Customs officers. Between 1994 and 1996, organizers put on 90 seminars in 48 different ports, training some 1,500 Customs inspectors. The training consisted largely of explaining the different trademarks, brands, and authenticating techniques to be used in border inspections, including showing examples of genuine and bogus products. They provided lists of known and suspected counterfeiters and their agents. The USOC also used a positive notice system, informing

Customs of each licensed shipment that was authorized to enter the country. With this approach, shipments of Olympic-branded products that had not been specifically identified by the USOC were presumed to be infringing product and not allowed to enter.

Customs, together with the organizers, sponsors, and licensees, also began building awareness of the coming counterfeit problem among other federal, state and local enforcement officials. Thousands of brochures were distributed describing the anticounterfeiting efforts and enlisting help. Among other things, the brochure used a bounty system—"Fraud Detection Pays," offering rewards of up to $250,000 for information on violations.

By March 1996, three months before the start of the Games, the system had resulted in 30 seizures valued at more than $400,000. By the end of the Games, Customs had made 125 seizures with property valued at nearly $2 million. Equally as important, the number of erroneously held shipments was minimal.

In an attempt to make field enforcement and subsequent criminal prosecution more efficient, organizers used an authentication device as part of their program. Four different holographic tags were used to identify different types of products—two hangtags and two pressure sensitive labels. Each tag displayed a printed, holographic Olympic torch, covert features and sequential numbering.

Different numerical sequences were made available for use by different licensees. The tag manufacturer maintained a database of issued serial numbers that could be accessed by enforcement personnel to determine to which licensee and product the tag had been assigned. All officially licensed merchandise was required to be tagged before it entered the country. Having this system in place reduced the need for investigators and officials to inspect the fabric, print, and other physical features of the product to determine its legitimacy.

As the Games approached, venue enforcement plans were put into motion in Atlanta. During 1995, organizers met with the U.S. District Attorney's office and the U.S. Marshal's office to build a working plan and communications. Local merchants were alerted to the existence of bogus goods (as well as the penalties for their sale), the local police were educated and pre-Games enforcement actions were used to generate local publicity.

A few days before the start of the Games, organizers filed a "John Doe" (unnamed) complaint in federal court for trademark infringement and obtained a temporary restraining order (TRO) and seizure order (to be executed by the U.S. marshals) for counterfeit goods within the greater Atlanta area. A counterfeit command center was established, staffed by organizing group attorneys. Once the games began, 16 enforcement teams, each consisting of two U.S. marshals and two experienced trademark investigators, covered each Olympic event, as well as the public transit system and outlying parking areas. When an infringer was identified, the teams requested that the products be voluntarily surrendered in lieu of service of the TRO and seizure of product. In all but four of the 469 total cases, the infringers complied voluntarily and were served with a cease and desist letter and a receipt for surrendered goods.

During the period from April 1 to August 5, 1996, approximately 166,000 counterfeit or infringing items, with a value of approximately $2.5 million, were confiscated at the Olympic venues. Customs seizures added another $3.5 million. In all, more than 400,000 items were confiscated, with a value of approximately $6 million, a record for this type of program.

WHO ARE THESE GUYS? WHAT DO THEY DO?

If investigators play such an important role in the anticounterfeiting fight, who are they? What do they do, what should they do? Who hires, pays, and directs them? How do they interface with law enforcement? And what about those gadgets?

In fact, the investigations field attracts a wide variety of individuals. As Bill Thompson of Pinkerton says: "We aren't police. Most of us aren't lawyers. We don't have judicial authority, and, these days, nearly none of us are armed. We have many people with ex-something backgrounds, former police, government, military, customs . . . but there are also many of us who began in our business with only backgrounds in commerce, journalism, law or other fields."[10]

Peter Lowe of the CIB echoes his observations: "Investigators are a diverse group. From Oxford philosophy majors to naturals that grew up in the business. There is no one path, although many do come from law enforcement, the military or police."[11]

There is actually some debate over the value of a law enforcement background. Certainly, coming from the FBI, Customs, or the Trading Standards Office (in the United Kingdom) gives investigators an understanding of the law and criminal analytical methods. It also helps them understand and relate to law enforcement contacts when their work involves raids, product seizures and litigation. However, some say that a law enforcement background can actually be detrimental because law enforcement is accustomed to "flashing a badge" and "leaning on suspects" rather than "using their wits" and "getting inside the scam." As Stu Drobny puts it, "you have to be an actor, you have to con the conmen."[12] In practice, both are probably true. The fact is that many, if not most, IP investigators have a law enforcement background, and there is definitely a law enforcement "old boy network" aspect to the profession.

There is no governing or overall licensing body for investigators in the United States. Forty-five states have laws requiring licensing; five do not. The laws governing investigators vary considerably and the statistics are quite sketchy.

California currently has approximately 10,000 registered private investigators. According to California law, to qualify for a license, an applicant must start with a clean criminal record. The applicant must then document at least three years (6,000 hours) of "compensated experience in investigative work; or a law or police science degree plus two years (4,000 hours) of experience," and then must pass a two-hour examination "covering laws and regulations, terminology, civil and criminal liability, evidence handling, undercover investigations, and surveillance." Investigators must take additional training and pass additional tests if they want to carry firearms or tear gas. And they must maintain at least $1 million in insurance if they carry weapons. Supervisors of investigators must meet most of the same requirements. California statutes make clear that "a private investigator may provide services to protect a person, but not property, which is incidental to an investigation for which the private investigator has been previously hired." That is, investigators are not authorized to fight to save or seize property.[13]

Florida, considered "an easier state," requires two years of demonstrated fulltime experience in "private investigative work or related fields of work that provided equivalent experience or training" but allows one year to be satisfied with certain educational experience.[14]

Colorado is one of the states that has no licensing provisions for investigators whatsoever.

The U.S. Bureau of Labor Statistics puts the number of private investigators at 39,000 nationwide.[15] With 10,000 in California alone, this may be low. Of these, a fraction specialize in intellectual property (IP) investigations and even fewer focus on anticounterfeiting. Ryan Beckwith, in the recent *Newsday* article "No Faking It: Investigators Track Counterfeiters," estimates that only 15 to 20 firms in the United States specialize in the field.[16]

Anticounterfeiting investigation is a specialized field. The underlying intellectual property law of trademarks, copyrights, fair use, and so on, is more complex than many other corporate security matters. Many cases are international, and some counterfeiters are quite sophisticated. Often, the issues involved in distinguishing high quality fakes from the real product take some training. Also, working effectively with the IP holder, police, and Customs requires knowledge and experience.

There are a few organizations, such as the American Society for Industrial Security (ASIS), the Association of Certified Fraud Examiners, and the National Association of Drug Diversion Investigators, that offer some relevant training and even certification programs that overlap the IP/anticounterfeiting area.[17] But none of them serve as an association for these specialized investigators. In many countries, there are loose networks of counterfeiting investigators often connected with the national anticounterfeiting associations. In the United States, this circle is tied somewhat to the International AntiCounterfeiting Coalition (IACC). Kris Buckner, the current chair of the IACC Investigators Committee, emphasizes the importance of these organizations for both investigators and clients. They give investigators a mechanism for sharing information and building skills. And clients can use the networks to check out a firm's reputation and get referrals. Indeed, the IACC Investigators Committee is exploring the development of more formal training and best practices approaches to counterfeit investigations.

Many firms conduct their own internal professional development training. This training can focus on investigative skill building, like field techniques and use of surveillance equipment, or analysis of financial documents and the use of the Internet in investigations. Buckner says his firm has weekly investigators' meetings where cases are discussed and client product-identification manuals are reviewed. His investigators are tested on their knowledge. It is also common for investigators to train others, such as Customs officials or local police, on how to spot fake goods.[18]

◑ FOCUS 10.1 ◑

CHINA: A WHOLE NEW WORLD

The scale of the problem in China is so fantastic that it is creating awareness in the international business press. The June 5, 2000 issue of *Business Week*[19] contained a detailed article, "China's Pirates," giving dozens of examples of companies and products being faked for the domestic and international markets. One of the best reports, however, appeared in the November 6, 2000 issue of *Fortune* magazine. This 11-page piece by Richard Behar entitled "Beijing's Phony War on Fakes," presents an insightful analysis of the problem.[20] Behar fills his report with specific examples that drive home the point that all types of products are counterfeited and distributed widely in China. Specifics include: Chinese officials put counterfeit losses at $16 billion per year, between 10 to 30 percent of the country's manufacturing base is devoted to fakes, 90 percent of videos and software are bogus, 35 percent of American Standard toilets sold in Shanghai during 1999 were fakes, and 99 percent of Suzuki motorcycles in Guangzhou are knockoffs. He cites examples of major consumer brands, including Unilever's Lux soap and Johnson & Johnson products, whose manufacturers have actually suspended sales because they were being taken over by fraudsters.

The private investigations field is equally as "other worldly." First, investigators are not really recognized or licensed in China. According to Bill Thompson of Pinkerton, "they are tolerated at best." There is only a thin line between corporate investigations and industrial espionage (a crime potentially punishable by death). So private investigation firms, as they exist in the United States and most of the rest of the world, are only beginning to develop in China. Interestingly, anticounterfeiting is one of the services that is opening the field there because the issue has such importance, both domestically and internationally.

Counterfeiting investigation services are being offered by a wide array of organizations. Major international companies like Pinkerton, Kroll, Hill, and Control Risk are active and are making cautious investments to build

(continues)

FOCUS 10.1 *(Continued)*

their presence. At the same time, several Hong Kong law offices, including Baker & McKinzey and Deacons assign their young Peoples Republic of China attorneys to investigative work. Likewise, some Chinese trademark agents, including Chung Lien, Shanghai Patent and Trademark Law Office, Wan Huida, and IntellectPro, are extending their activities into the investigative field. Then, there are hundreds of smaller local, one-city investigative offices, often headed by a retired police officer or other official. But that is not the end of the list of players. There are also thousands of professional informants, some specializing in specific products, others focused on particular geographic areas. They frequently sell their information based on a "rewards/recovery" basis; that is, compensation is based on on a per items-seized bounty formula.

Thompson doubts that any single player controls even 1 percent of the investigative market share at this point. He describes the investigative business as "a primordial soup, just beginning to come together." But it is a huge one. He and his colleagues sketched the size of the counterfeiting business in China as follows: tens of thousands of personnel employed by various governmental agencies at the national, provincial, state, city, and village levels; many thousands of attorneys and investigators serving the private sector; and millions of counterfeiters operating at different levels. In fact, China may have more people involved in the counterfeiting/anticounterfeiting area than the rest of the world combined.

One piece of good news is that there does appear to be some recent progress. Four years ago, the conviction rate for raids was approximately 0.25 percent. In 2001, it was 2.5 percent, with the number of raids having increased substantially. The overall conviction rate may have now increased 50 or 60 fold.

WHO DO I CALL, FAKE BUSTERS?

Without the equivalent of a "Counterfeiting Investigators Association," how do companies identify, evaluate, and manage investigators?

First, it is important to understand the demographics of the industry. Most service industries tend to follow a version of the 80:20 rule as far as company size distribution. That is, there are a few large firms, a number of medium-sized firms, and a lot of small companies. This is not the case with investigation companies. There are a few large, high-profile investigative firms, relatively few medium-sized firms, and a larger number of smaller firms and individual investigators.

Both Pinkerton and Kroll fall into the first category. Pinkerton was founded in 1850, to help the U.S. Secret Service pursue criminals across state and national boundaries. As part of the Securitas Group, the company boasts more than $6 billion in annual revenues, and has some 210,000 employees in 300 offices around the world. Kroll, founded in 1972, trades on the Nasdaq and employs more than 2,100 staff in its 60 offices worldwide.

Both firms offer significant IP/counterfeiting/brand protection practices. Pinkerton, for example, recommends a strategic approach, "focus[ing] on client manufacturing and distribution operations, mapping out all elements of the manufacturing process from the purchasing of raw product, through the distribution cycle, to waste scrap and product management."[21] This includes the use of authentication technologies, logistics monitoring, and Internet investigations, as well as investigative fieldwork. Among the relevant investigative capabilities are: surveillance, undercover activities, sightings, interviews and surveys, background investigations, computer forensics, field research, and product buys. Pinkerton's website[22] emphasizes that the company has extensive experience at finding the sources of counterfeit products, gathering appropriate evidence, working with authorities to conduct raids and take appropriate criminal and/or civil actions. Pinkerton can do this with its own agents in over 20 countries and can make use of agents in another 65 countries.

In other words, Pinkerton and a few other major firms offer a "global" reach, the ability to execute massive projects, and an *infrastructure* that can be useful in supporting certain types of investigations and litigation efforts.

Toward the other end of the spectrum, Stumar Investigations has 27 employees with offices in five states. The company is well-known in the anticounterfeiting field and has undertaken a number of important projects ranging from branded apparel to pharmaceuticals and consumer care products. And, yes, Stumar has even investigated counterfeit fighting cock spurs (the sharp knife-like attachments used outside the United States to make cock fights more exciting).

Solo investigators are also a common feature in the industry. The U.S. Bureau of Labor Statistics says that 40 percent of private investigators are self-employed.[23] In a 1999 article, "He Gets Paid to Chase Down Product Counterfeiters," the *Los Angeles Times* told the story of Ian Sitren, operating out of his house as Integrity Services International, Inc., conducting counterfeiting investigations for John Paul Mitchell Systems and other major companies.[24] In the Mitchell case, Sitren traced a lead that came from the hair care company's bottle manufacturer about a group wanting to buy bottles that replicated the Mitchell design. Sitren's efforts led to the identification of the perpetrator, Joseph Fredrick Thompson, who ultimately pleaded no contest to product counterfeiting and was sentenced to 16 months in prison and ordered to pay Sitren's costs of $41,500.

Because counterfeiting investigations tend to be so "down and dirty," they are hard to turn into "systems." Buckner says counterfeit investigations really resemble drug investigations—"usually you just have to dig in and get your fingernails dirty." This may help to explain the demographics and how they work. The big companies are set up to be full-service operations for large, multinational clients. They have the visibility and the advertising budgets. They also do a substantial amount of the actual investigation work. But clients, and sometimes the major investigative companies, depend on the small companies to do specific investigations or to cover specific markets.

Finding Pinkerton or Kroll is fairly easy. Look in the phone book or on the web. Finding the niche players is a bit tougher. This is where networks become important. Buckner points out that just because a company says it specializes in IP investigations doesn't necessarily mean that it does. It's a lucrative field and investigators, by their nature, are actors.

"Talk to other brand holders," says Buckner, "ask them who they use, who is good for the type of problem you need investigated."[25] Of course, meetings of groups like the IACC are ideal for having this sort of discussion. Go meet with the investigative company and meet them at their offices. "Remember, they may be your face where the investigation is being carried out," says Buckner. Customers, law enforcement officials, and attorneys may wind up meeting about your investigation in their offices. Check their license and state's record of complaints, and verify their insurance coverage. Talk to them and see if you can communicate and work effectively with them—you will have to.

Hiring the investigator is just the beginning. The client then has to define the enforcement philosophy of the project. What is the goal?

Criminal prosecution to the maximum extent possible, or civil seizures and destruction of fakes? Working back to the manufacturer, or discouraging street sales? Will there be a zero tolerance policy, or will only cases worth more than $10,000 (or some other number) be pursued? Over time, these issues affect not just the investigation but the effectiveness of the anticounterfeiting program and can shape the relationship between the brand holder and law enforcement—one of the most important relationships in the fight against counterfeiting.

Counterfeiters that focus on one brand within an industry almost certainly will attack other brands in the same industry too. It's just good business for the counterfeiters to diversify their product line. This has led to the formation of industry specific anticounterfeiting groups: the Business Software Alliance (BSA), the International Federation of Phonographic Industries (IFPI), the International Spirits Federation (ISF), and the Pharmaceutical Security Institute (PSI), to name a few. Increasingly, these groups are building their own sophisticated investigative operations.

The IFPI is an excellent example. It spearheads the music recording industry's antipiracy efforts worldwide through a team of 50 investigators and analysts. Most are ex-law-enforcement personnel, who assist governments, police forces and customs departments around the world. In 2001, IFPI completed formation of a worldwide antipiracy network with regional offices covering every continent. Resources in the network include a forensic laboratory to pinpoint the manufacturing source of pirate CDs, a Pirate Product Database to help trace pirated goods worldwide, and a training unit that worked with enforcement authorities and customs in more than 20 countries in 2001.[26]

Taking a global view, IFPI develops enforcement strategies at a continental level. The piracy rate for music recording is over 50 percent in Latin America. In 1999, this led to a problem involving the importation of finished products from replication plants in Southeast Asia. By 2002, the problem had been transformed. Ninety percent of the continent's pirate discs were being copied by small industrial pirate laboratories inside Latin America. Based on this, IFPI added a new enforcement prong designed to meet the changing criminal pattern: It began tracking and interdicting blank CDs destined for pirate producers. Investigators determined that the blanks were shipped from Taiwan to Montevideo, Uruguay, where they were transferred to river vessels and moved up the Parana River to

Paraguay, then smuggled across land to Brazil, where they were recorded, packaged and distributed. But, as Focus 10.2 illustrates, even this strategy requires constant monitoring and adjustment.

◐ FOCUS 10.2 ◑

TUNING MUSIC ANTIPIRACY ENFORCEMENT

One recent example of the constant refinement and tuning that must go on, based on the IFPI's investigations, took place in February 2002, when a Chinese syndicate in Paraguay imported 1.4 million blanks and sent them up the Parana on the ship Omar G. The syndicate became aware that the shipment had been identified and was going to be seized, so it directed the ship back down the river and told officials the blanks would be returned to Asia. When the ship reached Montevideo, IFPI investigators and Customs officials boarded and inspected the Omar G, only to discover it was empty. With good law enforcement relations, IFPI rapidly instituted a new policy. When ships containing blanks were discovered and told to leave the Parana, a Paraguay official would be posted on the ship to ensure that no more "in transit" unloading took place. In the year from July 2001 to July 2002, IFPI Latin America seized more than 40 million CD blanks.[27]

WORKING WITH LAW ENFORCEMENT

It is difficult to overestimate the importance for brand owners of building appropriate and strong relationships with law enforcement. In the case of IFPI, years of work have gone into building relationships with Customs and law enforcement around the world. Without the level of trust and respect born out of an extended relationship, Paraguay would not have readily adapted to the latest "in transit" unloading scam and the music industry would have a major new hole that it would have to plug as it attempted to preserve its legitimate market share in Latin America.

At the most basic level in the United States, private investigators have no authority to execute searches or seizures without official sanction and participation. They have no official powers of arrest and cannot secure wiretaps. In general, the brand holder and investigator will prepare information for police or a court to obtain a search and seizure order that will be executed by the police or the U.S. Marshals. Investigators will accompany the officials and, acting under color of their authority, may actually do the work finding, identifying, cataloging, and storing the contraband. Generally, the complainant will also have to post a bond against any possible wrongful seizure.

Given this need for official support, the relationship with law enforcement is an absolutely critical one. It can also be somewhat complex. Police (and other officials) are responsible for upholding the law, stopping crimes, and punishing criminals. Additionally, they have other more compelling criminal priorities, such as violent crime, sexual attacks, antiterrorism, and so forth. They are not responsible for, and may not be interested in, helping to repair the economic damage counterfeiters cause a brand or company. This can create a tension that good investigators and smart brand owners will treat with sensitivity. For example, if brand holders commit to criminal enforcement at the outset of the investigation but change their mind once the raids are complete, or if they fail to supply needed information promptly to police as a criminal case moves forward, officials will remember that they were let down and may downgrade any future requests coming from those groups.

U.K. law, and some other common law jurisdictions, are different with respect to private "self-help." Whereas U.S. brand owners must have their search and seizure orders served by law enforcement, in the United Kingdom, the courts can issue an *Anton Piller* order authorizing a named private party to enter a specified premises for the purpose of inspecting and removing goods. Similar provisions exist in Malaysia and Singapore.[28]

There are other differences, as well. In the United States, there are no domestic IP police that would naturally seize counterfeit goods on their own initiative. The U.S. Customs Service is charged with the responsibility of stopping infringing goods at the border. The FBI and Secret Service do become involved in some counterfeiting cases, especially where currency, bankcards, checks, and other financial documents are being faked. In the United Kingdom, the situation is different. The Trading Standards Officers (TSOs) are a part of over 200 local authorities in England, Wales, Scotland, and Northern Ireland. They are responsible for enforcing fair Trading Standards in the United Kingdom, including the detection and apprehension of counterfeit goods. TSOs routinely seize fake designer wear, computer games, private videos, DVDs, and CDs from sellers. Some of the seizures include potentially dangerous goods, such as toys, food, washing powder, automobile parts, and even medicines.[29]

It is important for investigators and brand holders to be creative in thinking about their potential relationships with law enforcement. There are a number of potentially interested officials, in addition to police, FBI, and Customs that may become allies. The Internal Revenue Service (IRS) has an interest in whether counterfeiters are properly reporting their income and paying taxes. The Federal Trade Commission, Consumer Products Safety Commission, Environmental Protection Agency, Food and Drug Administration, Child and Family Services, and others may have an interest in the counterfeit case, if offenses under their jurisdiction are taking place as part of the counterfeiting activity.

ARE WE ON THE SAME PAGE HERE?

Managing the investigation is a critical element for the success of the anticounterfeiting program itself. It can also be a potential source of liability and problems, if it is done poorly.

In the case of the TSOs and IFPI, investigators are a part of a significant management structure that maintains operating guidelines and supervises the conduct of investigations. The same is not true when brand holders first begin using investigators to understand the nature and extent of their own counterfeiting problem. Client control and oversight is crucial, however, because failure to establish meaningful guidelines and to monitor them can leave companies exposed to embarrassment, financial losses, and worse.

Recently, investigators for a U.S. scooter manufacturer uncovered a sizable counterfeiting operation. The information was taken first to one law enforcement agency, which as part of standard procedures requested proof of trademark registration. It was not supplied, and the agency demurred on pursuing the case. Investigators went to a second enforcement agency and convinced it that a large number of infringing scooters should be seized. More than 30,000 units were seized but later had to be released because the proper registrations were not in place.

Wrongful seizure actions against the brand holder are a real risk, if investigations are not properly conducted. For example, if the investigator and brand holder cannot demonstrate adequately that the products are, in fact, fake (as opposed to the actual products with manufacturing variations), or if they cannot prove that they own the trademark (as in the scooter example), they both run the risk of being sued. Of course, the seizure bond is at risk. The company whose products were seized would claim that they are due the cost of the seized products, but they may also claim that they are entitled to consequential loss for business disruption, damages for defamation and punitive damages to "teach the brand owner a lesson." If the investigative procedures were lax, a court could be sympathetic to the "poor small business" that was being unfairly beaten up by the careless brand holder.[30]

It can get worse. The award-winning *Fortune* article by Richard Behar, "Drug Spies Piracy—The Pharmaceutical Industry's Dirty Little Secret,"[31] describes just how out of control the process can get. According to Behar, in an attempt to thwart counterfeiting and piracy of their medicines, Bayer and other pharmaceutical companies retained investigators to go up to the line of deception, cross over it and keep on going. The article focuses on two outstanding ex-British policemen (Mick Flack and Paul Whybrow) who joined the investigative firm of Paul Carratu upon their retirement and took on a series of engagements for Bayer and others. In February 1997, the two found themselves breaking and entering a customs clearance house in Cyprus to steal documents related to the pirate production of Bayer products. The two were arrested by local police as they attempted to leave the country with 289 documents and subsequently spent 18 days in the most wretched solitary confinement Cypriot jails had to offer, followed by seven months of regular prison. The two were finally released in late September 1997, looking like they "had just come out of Belsen." Disputes still swirl around who did what, who should have done what, and who might sue whom. But, the story clearly illustrates how everyone involved in this uncontrolled investigation lost. Flack and Whybrow lost their good reputations and nearly a year of their lives in prison. Bayer lost its legal fees and possibly payoff money, management time, and focus. They also received a major dose of negative publicity in one of the world's leading business periodicals.

As Drobny says, with investigations "you have to con the conmen." One key question that will always exist in this field is—just where is the line? Buckner had some good comments, even if they are not a complete answer. "We can do anything any other person could legally do. We can lie, deceive, trick and fool. What we can't, or shouldn't, do is "create criminals." And, whatever we do in the field, we have to report it fully and accurately in court. As I see it, that is our obligation to the system—to be honest."

The line can get pretty vague in actual practice. We might agree that it would be wrong to keep offering more and more money in order to convince an innocent person to make a counterfeit. But is it equally wrong to use the same tactic with someone who has already admitted to counterfeiting in the past, but is reluctant to do it in this particular situation? Likewise, it may be all right to give targets blank T-shirts and pay them to embroider unauthorized logos on them. Yet, it is probably not defensible to give them the art work or embroidery programs to do the same job.

IS THAT YOUR SHOE RINGING?

Technology is clearly a part of the investigative world. Night vision systems, pager cameras, sensitive listening devices, geographic positioning systems, logistic tracking programs, overt and covert authentication devices, and a host of other technologies are increasingly a part of the investigator's equipment.

Probably the biggest technical change in the past few years has been on the information technology front. The Internet and the development of analytical databases have brought substantial change to the field.

The Internet has been a boon for the criminals and for investigators alike. Counterfeiters were quick to adapt to the promise of the web. They began registering domain names of famous brands, often long before many brand holders themselves focused on the issue. There are any number of stories of major brands having to buy or litigate to get their domain names from "cybersquatters." Fortunately, this has begun to change with some presumptions being given to famous brands with respect to the ownership of their brands on-line. Then came the use of brand names and other terms in the hypertext and other material used by search engines. Many crooks found that they could create a site, insert the brand names and other key words, sit back, and let the search engines bring them the traffic looking for the goods that they were counterfeiting.

A less well-recognized variant of this approach was the use of auction sites to sell counterfeits. Counterfeiters realized that they could post descriptions of their products on Ebay, Amazon, and Yahoo and again

---

◑ FOCUS 10.3 ◑

COUNTERFEITING ON THE AUCTION SITES

In the spring of 2000, the problem of counterfeits and pirated software on various auction sites had grown to become a major concern to the software industry. The Software & Information Industry Association (SIIA) undertook a four-day survey, between March 31 and April 3, 2000, to determine the extent of the problem. It found that 91 percent of the software being sold on four leading Internet auctions sites was illegitimate.

SIIA staff reviewed software auctions of Adobe, Corel, FileMaker, and Macromedia, products on Amazon.com Auctions, eBay Auctions, Excite Auctions, and Yahoo Auctions. SIIA studied the details of 1,588 auction offerings to see if there were indications that the products were illegitimate. They looked for such descriptions as: "backup copy," "academic version," OEM copies or other terms that indicated the copies could not be sold legitimately. Then the respective software producers reviewed the remaining auctions. The results showed that 1,366 offers (84.6 percent) were illegitimate, 138 (8.7 percent) were legal and 84 (6.5 percent) were "undetermined."

Based on these findings, the SIIA proposed a set of *Recommended Policies* that auction site operators should adopt to cut down on the trade in illegal software and urged site operators to adopt written policies, including corroboration of sellers' on-line identity; enforcement of the policy by terminating the membership of sellers that violate it; and giving buyers, as well as sellers, notice of the policy.

There seems to have been significant improvement in the policing of on-line auction sites more recently. eBay developed a very efficient "notice and take down" program that attempted to clear offending auctions within 24 hours of receiving notice of infringement. Amazon is credited for pioneering proactive screening of its auction sites.[32]

take advantage of the traffic looking for the real products. Someone looking for Microsoft Office, for example, would go on the auction sites and begin bidding for the product. The item being offered might be counterfeit, and the crooked auction holders would use the bidders' e-mail addresses as a basis for selling additional fakes by e-mail. In 2000, *Authentication News* summarized then current statistics of the rate of counterfeit sales from various auction sites.[33] The auction site companies began to realize what was taking place and instituted safeguards. In 2000, Amazon.com was recognized by a Global AntiCounterfeiting Award for its work in this area.

An equally important criminal application of the Web for counterfeiting is its ability to facilitate counterfeit "trade transactions." That is, the web gave counterfeiters and their colleagues around the world an instant business infrastructure. Chat rooms and bulletin boards serve as market places and professional training facilities. It gave suppliers, manufacturers and distributors of fakes a ready means for identifying each other and for

---

◑ FOCUS 10.4 ◑

CYBER COUNTERFEITING OF CREDIT CARDS

Credit card fraud and counterfeiting is one of the better-developed and more public areas of counterfeiting. Indeed, it was the attacks on credit cards in the 1970s and early 1980s that led MasterCard, and then Visa, to add holograms to authenticate real cards. The area appears to be maintaining its "trend-setting position" in the criminal world with an active network of fake card "business men" doing "business" through the Internet, and even potentially holding their own conventions.

The New York Times reported on cyberbazaars for payment card trading. Operated largely by residents of the former Soviet Union, these membership–only Internet groups traffic in tens of thousands of card numbers each week.[34] According to the May 13, 2002 article, the price of card details can vary from "40 cents to $5 depending on the level of authenticating information provided." Bulk purchasers receive discounts and some sellers even offer guarantees that the numbers are valid. Bulk numbers are usually obtained by professional hackers breaking into merchant systems and downloading by the thousands at a time.

doing business. Even the websites of brand holders were a treasure trove. Company websites created a ready source for logo art, product and label specifications for knockoffs, and even mailing lists and company executive signatures.

Of course, the Internet has also proved to be a great source of information to investigators as well. Anyone can go on the web, search for anything, and see the vast amount of "information" that is available, often free, 24/7, from anywhere in the world. "Information" because, of course, it's not all what it appears to be. Investigators who are professionals in sifting and using this sort of information took to it almost as readily as the crooks.

Some companies have developed specialized expertise in investigating counterfeiting with the web. Others tend to use it as one of the range of investigative tools available, and many brand holders have brought some or all of the web-sleuthing inhouse. Cyveillance and GenuOne are examples of companies that have developed a specialist offering. Cyveillance offers a web-based data collection technology and case management system that monitors for unauthorized uses of brand names and other corporate assets in Usenet Newsgroups, auction sites, networks, message boards, chats, and promotional "spam" email. The system gives customers the ability to selectively track offenders, automate and personalize cease and desist letters to site owners or ISPs, and track each incident through to point of resolution.[35]

GenuOne's service, called GenuNet, searches the web to find all suspected trademark and copyright infringement and unauthorized uses. Its system uses a proprietary crawler to automatically fill a database based on a list of key words and other indicators that describe the company. This information is then organized to make it useful to the brand holder and investigator. One example of the type of output is an analysis of website pricing information on a specific product (e.g., a specific model of a computer hard drive). Numerous websites are visited, and the system makes a comparison between the manufacturer's price and the website price. This frequently reveals a substantial number of sites priced well below the manufacturer's list. This, in turn, can be used to identify sites that may be dealing in fakes or stolen products.[36]

With information exploding, information management is becoming another big area of innovation for investigators. How is it possible to spot the important linkages between hundreds of people and companies, with tens of thousands of products traveling through myriad distribution channels around the world over a period of years? Traditional relational databases have been useful, but increasingly investigators and law enforcement are turning to specialized analytical tools. One of the up-and-coming analytical systems is the i2 connections and charting system. Originally created for logistical management and other business applications, a number of companies, law enforcement agencies, and trade associations have adopted i2 as an effective interoperable system. One company security officer said, "i2 gives us the ability to display relationships that we just couldn't visualize otherwise and we are able to just dump our data directly into the FBI system so we can combine information."[37]

Investigations are both one of the most "down and dirty" and one of the most high-tech areas related to the fight against counterfeiting.

CHAPTER 11

Legal Remedies

COUNTERFEITING IS ILLEGAL—ISN'T IT?

Perhaps the most frequently uttered comment when a corporate executive (for example, the president of a hypothetical company, Genuine Co.) first discovers his brands are being counterfeited is: "Counterfeiting's illegal. Isn't it? Let's stop the thieves!" A logical and understandable response. Counterfeiting is, generally speaking, illegal, and certainly it makes sense to want to stop the counterfeiters.

This sentiment points up a core issue in the field of counterfeiting: Counterfeiting is basically a legal conclusion. The legal analysis also sets up a dynamic that can lead to a mixed and incomplete response.

Using a common sense definition, a counterfeit product is one that is made to fool the customer into thinking they are receiving the products of the brand holders/manufacturers when they are not. The rights of the brand holders/manufacturers (for example, patents, trade secrets, logos, trade dress, trademarks, etc.) are basically intellectual property, created and defined by the law. Likewise, if there is a complaint, whether the customer was, in fact, or could reasonably have been fooled is also a legal question. And, of course, any remedies, arrests and convictions, seizures and destructions of the goods, fines, damages or injunctions are all within the purview of the law.

With this pervasive legal context, it is entirely logical for the president of Genuine Co. to call his general counsel and say, "Sally, we've got a counterfeiting problem and I want you to take the lead. Let's get rid of the problem!" Sally will naturally analyze the problem in terms of trademark (Lanham Act) infringement, copyright, trade secret, patent, breach of contract, and other legal issues. She will want the help of law enforcement in "catching the thieves and punishing them." It is likely that she, her staff, outside counsel, maybe security, and law enforcement will begin to focus on the pros and cons of pursuing criminal versus civil enforcement alternatives, and the need to hire investigators. So, our executive has set in motion a logical chain of events aimed at "catching the horses that have already left the barn." Not a wrong decision, but an incomplete one.

A LOOK AT THE LAW

Black's Law Dictionary defines counterfeiting as: "To forge, copy, or imitate (something) without a right to do so and with the purpose of deceiving or defrauding."[1] While the thrust is toward the counterfeiting of documents (and it uses as examples "money (or other security)," this is a good, apparently comprehensive definition. It sets just the elements we would intuitively consider—not the genuine manufacturer, imitation with intent to deceive, lack of authority, and distribution. However, considering previous chapters, this definition may be a bit narrow. For example, in the case of a brand holder that only uses contract manufacture, an increasingly common situation, the counterfeit good may be "made by the genuine manufacturer," but "without authority or right." Likewise, the real product could have been made with full authority by the genuine manufacturer, but the labeling, or merely the expiration date on the labels, could have been changed by the counterfeiters that bought shipments of expired baby formula from a disposal company. Certainly, we would want to include this in any legal definition as a basis for criminal and civil action.

Two important points emerge from this discussion. First, the actual legal definition of counterfeit is complex and not trivial to enunciate. Second, it is important because if a set of repugnant actions, like changing the expiration date on baby formula (which was actually done by funders of the first World Trade Center attack in 1993) is omitted from the definition, the perpetrators cannot be punished under the anticounterfeiting law.[2]

U.S. Anticounterfeiting Laws: Getting the Crooks

Until 1984, there was no federal criminal statute outlawing product counterfeiting. In 1982, a group of trademark holders banded together under the name of the International AntiCounterfeiting Coalition (IACC) to lobby Congress to enact such a statute, and it did. The Trademark Counterfeiting Act of 1984 criminalized the intentional counterfeiting of trademarks, authorized treble damages and attorneys' fees in civil cases, and established *ex parte* seizure of counterfeit goods.[3]

With the increase in the problem and the recognition of certain shortcomings in the law, there was soon pressure for changes to the law. And, in 1995, business and consumer groups again mobilized to campaign for the passage of tougher federal legislation. The International AntiCounterfeiting Coalition (IACC), and its president, John Bliss, were on the leading edge. In testimony before Congress, Bliss pointed out the need for stronger legislation: "The rapid growth in counterfeiting is directly related to the unlikelihood of prosecution. Counterfeiters have little chance of being arrested and prosecuted under current law, and even if their activities are discovered, the penalties are insignificant. The lure of easy money has drawn organized crime syndicates into the act. For example, David Thai, the former head of the Born to Kill gang in New York City, recently stated that he made an estimated $13 million a year selling counterfeit Rolex and Cartier watches."[4] (So that's where all the fake Rolexes are coming from.)

Congress passed, and President Clinton signed, the Anticounterfeiting Consumer Protection Act of 1996. It significantly strengthened both the criminal and civil provisions of the 1984 Trademark Counterfeiting Act and the Lanham Act. It attempted to focus federal enforcement attention on the growing problems of unlawful importation of counterfeit trademarked goods and violations tied to organized criminal enterprises. In line with this goal, it established the crime of counterfeiting as a predicate act for the invocation of the criminal Racketeer Influenced and Corrupt Organizations Act, or RICO statutes. It also established an annual anticounterfeiting enforcement reporting requirement for the U.S. Attorney General.

With the new federal legislation in place, the government and companies have a number of effective tools to fight counterfeiters. The crime of counterfeiting requires the government to prove beyond a reasonable doubt that: (1) the defendant intentionally (2) trafficked in goods or services, (3) with knowledge, (4) that the goods or services made use of a "counterfeit mark." In court, each of the elements of the crime requires more detailed analysis and proof. For example, in order to establish the "counterfeit mark" element, prosecutors must show: (1) the mark is "identical with, or substantially indistinguishable from" the "genuine trademark" (being counterfeited), (2) the genuine mark is registered on the U.S. Patent and Trademark Office principal register, and (3) the use of the counterfeit mark is "likely to cause confusion, to cause mistake, or to deceive" members of the buying public.[5]

If brand holders have registered their marks and the federal prosecutors can establish the other elements of the offense, harsh criminal penalties are possible. The 1996 Act provides for fines of up to $2 million and imprisonment of up to 10 years for individuals and fines of up to $5 million for companies for the first offense. For repeated violations, individuals may be fined up to $5 million and imprisoned for up to 20 years. Corporations may be fined up to $15 million. Additionally, operating on the lower preponderance of the evidence standard, the government may destroy any articles in the possession of a defendant that bear counterfeit marks.

The RICO statute gives law enforcement additional weapons. The IACC pointed out the need for this additional provision in testimony before the House Judiciary Committee. Referring to a criminal action in California, they told Congress: "In the recent seizure of over $10.5 million in counterfeit Microsoft products, the Los Angeles U.S. Attorney's Office declined to take part in the case, because the RICO laws traditionally used against criminal organizations do not apply to counterfeit activity."[6]

The 1996 Act made the crime of trademark counterfeiting a predicate offense under the RICO statute, meaning that the government can prosecute two or more parties if they conspire (through a pattern of two or more acts) to counterfeit, invest in the conspiracy, or own or operate a part of the conspiracy. The broad sweep of the statute gives prosecutors flexibility to attack perpetrators. The penalties are substantial: imprisonment of up to 20 years and/or fines of $250,000 (or twice the gross profits of the offense). RICO crimes also are treated harshly under the important federal sentencing guidelines.[7]

In 1996, the IACC and the copyright industries also successfully campaigned for a more specific anticounterfeiting law: Trafficking in Counterfeit Labels for Phonorecords.[8] This provision is a potentially powerful weapon for the music, motion picture, and software industries to use in fighting counterfeiters. It also points up shortcomings that are currently the subject of Congressional lobbying by other industries.

The counterfeit labeling law provides that "Whoever . . . knowingly traffics in a counterfeit label affixed, or designed to be affixed, to a phonorecord, or a copy of a computer program or documentation or packaging for a computer program, or a copy of a motion picture or other audiovisual work, and whoever . . . knowingly traffics in counterfeit documentation or packaging for a computer program, shall be fined $250,000 under this title or imprisoned for not more than five years, or both."[9] In other words, a counterfeiter who is making or selling fake packaging for a new music video can face a five-year prison sentence.

While these provisions should be quite helpful in attacking the counterfeiting of digital products, they do not cover such important goods as pharmaceuticals, neutraceuticals, foods and drinks, transportation parts, and medical equipment. That is, if the FBI or police find an organization engaged in the counterfeiting of these goods but do not have evidence of "trafficking in the goods" (i.e., manufacture or distribution of the complete product), they will have difficulty in applying the federal counterfeiting law. Likewise, if they uncover a diversion operation that is removing expiration dates or tracking numbers, as described in Focus 11.1, they may not be able to prosecute. Therefore, for several years, a coalition of personal care products makers, pharmaceutical companies, and others have been lobbying Congress to extend protections to all products, or to all products that could readily produce direct injury.

What about Diversion?

Under several different bills, including the U.S. Trademark Anticounterfeiting Act of 1998 and the Anti-Tampering Act of 1999, anticounterfeiting advocates have urged Congress to criminalize the removal or alteration of product codes.

It is common practice for diverters to buy products directly or indirectly from the manufacturers, to accumulate them from wholesalers and retailers that intentionally overstock, and even to buy products from criminal groups that hijack trucks or use gangs of shoplifters to steal off retail shelves. These products are then stripped of their coding and often recoded for sale through different retail outlets. There are also increasing reports of mixing decoded and counterfeit products. The proposed federal legislation would have significantly raised the stakes for decoders. Identification

◐ FOCUS 11.1 ◐

DIVERSION: ITS CAUSES AND CURES

Superficially, product diversion is quite distinct from product counterfeiting. While counterfeiting is a crime, diversion is often viewed as a contractual issue between the manufacturers and distributors/retailers of the products. Frequently, diversion is a by-product of a manufacturer's pricing policies and distribution limitations. However, a closer look suggests the presence of deeper criminal roots, closer ties to counterfeiting, and the basis for a legal battle over "antidecoding" legislation.

Diversion has become a major business in many industries. Frequently, the business is built around disguising the product's origins and often involves the distribution of counterfeit or stolen product. *Authentication News* provided the following revealing insights into this shady business:

"In interviews with officials from one company specializing in the diversion of over-the-counter drugs and personal care products, *Authentication News*™ learned that the company's annual sales had grown from $45M in 1996 to $75M in 1997 and could reach $120M in 1998. The company sourced its products from the excess purchases of retailers and wholesalers. It accumulated and processed the product at its repackaging plant. Processing included inspecting the product, often using ultraviolet lights and other techniques to find and eliminate distribution channel markings. Finally, it repackaged the products for sale and shipment to major discount chains. . . . [On an international level,] the basic scheme is for an offshore company to buy a quantity of high-demand U.S. goods, supposedly for sale into some other region of the world, to pay in the available currency through a series of wire transfers, to take delivery through a variety of sham techniques and to resell the products back into the U.S. diverter distribution system. This [is a money laundering scheme, it] gives the criminal clean dollars and maybe even a profit on top. It gives the diverter a supply of products. It also creates a ready distribution channel for criminally counterfeited products, opens the floodgates of discounted branded products, and defrauds the U.S. government out of millions of dollars of revenues.

"This is not a hypothetical situation. In one case prosecuted by Noel Hillman, Assistant U.S. Attorney for Newark, New Jersey, major pharmaceutical and other U.S. companies were defrauded and one death may have occurred as a result of such a diversion scheme. The case,

> U.S. v. Kotbey Mohamed Kotbey (Crim. No. 95-374 U.S. District Court, Dist. of NJ), involved a conspiracy to have Johnson & Johnson and Bayer/ Miles sell and ship over-the-counter diabetic test strips to a variety of off-shore organizations, including a supposed charity, the Anglo-American Foundation, serving the former Soviet Union. In fact, it was sold into U.S. distribution channels. According to Hillman, a manufacturing defect existed in one of the lots shipped to Anglo-American so the product was recalled. But because the distribution records for the recalled product had been disguised, the defective test kits could not be traced and withdrawn from the U.S. market. The result, according to Hillman, was that at least one customer may have died."[10]

and removal of codes would no longer be just a technical challenge (of finding and eliminating the marks). It would become a criminal offense punishable by fines or jail.

In its April 28, 2000 edition, *The Wall Street Journal*[11] pointed out the political complexities behind this legislation. "[W]holesalers, consumer groups and their Democratic champions on Capitol Hill warn that the measure will have the effect of crimping the flow of inexpensive name brand goods to discount giants such as Wal-Mart and the aggressive young E-tailers selling perfumes, shampoos and watches on the Internet." A great deal of opposition also came from the American Free Trade Association (AFTA).

The net result is that criminal "decoding" legislation has not passed at the federal level. It has, however, been adopted by a few states, including California. *Authentication News* reported on the application of this statute in October 2001. "Sebastian International, Inc. (Sebastian) won an important summary judgment in U.S. District Court that applies the state's criminal antidecoding statute to the removal of holographic security codes on hair care and other products by diverters (*Sebastian International v. Russolillo,* Case No. CV–00–03476 CM [JWJx], July 6, 2001). By clearly establishing the criminality of decoding most products for diversion, the decision sets the stage for more effective antidiversion programs in California and beyond. According to Mark Riedel, Vice President and General Counsel, Sebastian, the decision is 'the most important . . . for the professional hair care industry in many years. . . . It will help protect our channels of distribution in California and enable our industry to [fight diversion using] similar laws in other states.'"[12]

Federal Civil Remedies

The Anticounterfeiting Consumer Protection Act of 1996 gave private companies and brand holders stronger civil remedies as well. It provided for treble damages in most cases. According to the U.S. Department of Justice (DOJ) guidelines for application of the law, "it will be a rare case in which a defendant who has trafficked in goods or services using a mark that he or she knows to be counterfeit can show that he or she should not be assessed treble damages."[13]

The Act also created an easier mechanism for the *ex parte* seizure of goods. The purpose of the seizure provision is to give victims of trademark counterfeiting a means of ensuring that the courts are able to exercise their jurisdiction and avoid the increasingly common practice by counterfeiters of maintaining custody of the goods, only to destroy the merchandise as their day in court nears. In essence, the law permits the issuance of an *ex parte* seizure order if the applicant can show that the defendant would be unlikely to comply with a temporary restraining order and that there was no means of protecting the court's authority other than to seize the property in question.

Courts are required to have petitioners post a bond designed to ensure that the defendant's rights are adequately protected during seizure. According to the DOJ guidelines, judges are instructed to "err on the side of caution—that is, toward larger bonds—in light of the need to protect the unrepresented defendant, and to ensure that defendants will have an effective remedy if they are the victims of a wrongful seizure."

State Anticounterfeiting Statutes

While the Lanham Act, the federal trademark protection statute, is the primary vehicle for protecting trademarks, every state has its own statutory registration system and most provide criminal and civil statutes that afford some level of protection, as well. The exact protections vary significantly.[14]

Ironically, some states adopted criminal statutes applicable against counterfeiting in the 1800s, much earlier than the federal government. Until recently, many of these statutes were based on Model Penal Code provisions outlawing "simulating objects of antiquity, rarity, and so forth,"[15] or forgery. These laws were not drafted to be effective in prosecuting modern counterfeiting activities and were not used very extensively. More recently, the IACC has developed a State Model Trademark Counterfeiting Statute that has been adopted in various forms by several states. It streamlines prosecution by establishing mark registration as evidence of trademark ownership, creates a presumption of intent to sell from the possession of 25 or more counterfeit items and creates a felony crime for large scale and/or repeated offenses.[16]

The state of Massachusetts adopted a version of the Model Law in 1998.[17] It establishes three levels of crimes: (1) for 100 or fewer items with a value of less than $1,000, defendants face a sentence of not more than two and a half years in jail; (2) for 100 to 1,000 items, with a value of $1,000 to $10,000, up to five years in jail; and (3) for more than 1,000 counterfeit items with a value of $10,000 or more, a prison term of up to 10 years. Multiple offenses lead to increased penalties as well.

Kentucky, however, has an older simulation statute designed to punish a person who "with intent to defraud, makes or alters any object in such a manner that it appears to have an antiquity, rarity, source or authorship which it does not in fact possess."[18] The crime is a class A misdemeanor that carries a light sentence or fine.

Most states also have civil provisions that brand holders can use to sue counterfeiters. The federal provisions of the Lanham Act supercede any state law provisions. However, some states provide additional remedies. Again, the IACC has developed Model provisions that it urges the states to adopt.[19]

Other Anticounterfeiting Laws

The preceding laws are a part of the general federal and state criminal and civil statutes. There are a number of other sources of anticounterfeiting laws, as well. Many specialized agencies have their own legislation and enforcement systems.

The U.S. Food and Drug Administration is one case in point. Section 321 of the Food and Drug Laws defines a counterfeit drug to be "a drug which, or the container or labeling of which, without authorization, bears the trademark, trade name, or other identifying mark . . . of a drug manufacturer, processor, packer, or distributor other than the person or persons who in fact manufactured, processed, packed, or distributed such drug and which thereby falsely purports or is represented to be the product." The law specifically prohibits the counterfeiting or simulation of any label, tag, stamp, etc. and "the doing of any act which causes a drug to be a counterfeit drug, or the sale or dispensing, or the holding for sale or dispensing, of a counterfeit drug."[20]

It also establishes the FDA Office of Criminal Investigations (OCI) whose agents are authorized to act with the powers of federal law enforcement in the investigation of drug counterfeiting. Specifically, they are authorized to carry firearms, conduct searches, execute arrest warrants, and seize evidence. According to Commissioner Hubbard, the OCI opened 55 counterfeiting cases between 1998 and 2002 (16 in the first seven months of 2002) and made 26 arrests with 20 convictions during the same period (12 arrests and seven convictions in 2002).[21]

Likewise, the 2000 Federal Aviation Administration reauthorization bill[22] contained several sections devoted to counterfeit aviation parts. Section 505 provides that the FAA must deny professional certification to any person or company convicted of "the installation, production, repair, or sale of a counterfeit or fraudulently-represented aviation part or material." Section 506[23] goes on to establish harsh criminal and civil penalties for anyone who "exports from, imports or introduces into the United States, sells, trades, installs on, or in, any aircraft or space vehicle, any aircraft or space vehicle part using a fraudulent representation, document, record, certification, depiction, data plate, label, or electronic communication." Fines can range up to $1 million and prison terms can range up to 20 years. Violators whose actions lead to loss of life can be sentenced up to life in prison.

A number of other federal and state authorities have laws that directly or indirectly cover aspects of counterfeiting. Furthermore, other government agencies have authority to prosecute crimes that are likely to be a part of the counterfeiter's activities. For example, the Internal Revenue Service is likely to find unreported income. The U.S. Postal Inspection Service may well be able to establish a case of mail fraud or wire fraud. The Immigration and Naturalization Service might find that certain members of a counterfeiting group are illegal aliens and may take deportation or other actions.[24]

Counterfeiting Laws Abroad

Counterfeiting laws and enforcement vary widely around the world from country to country. The issue of IP protection, and counterfeiting in particular, have become increasingly important to governments, international businesses, and the international community both because of the increasing scope of the problem and due to the requirements of the World Trade Organization and Trade Related Aspects of Intellectual Property Rights Agreement.

Since adoption of the 1994 Trade Marks Act, the United Kingdom has provided criminal sanctions for the production, distribution, and sale of counterfeit goods, as well as the production of counterfeit labeling and packaging materials, and the manufacture of articles designed for use in producing counterfeit goods.[25] Under these provisions, those directly involved, as well as those supplying the tools of the trade, may both be subject to prosecution. And, under appropriate circumstances, the courts may order confiscation of the financial proceeds of the offender's counterfeit operations.

A further refinement of this legislation was adopted on July 24, 2002, with a threefold effect. First, it brought the penalties for the offense of copyright theft into line with counterfeiting (or trademark violation) from two to ten years. Second, it strengthened search warrant provisions allowing police to obtain warrants based on evidence that individuals were offering counterfeit articles for sale or hire and removing the need for evidence of actual distribution. Third, it gave owners greater powers to obtain forfeiture of counterfeit goods and materials.[26]

Laws in China and elsewhere in Asia are evolving as well, but generally beginning from a more rudimentary starting point. China amended its trademark law effective December 1, 2001, in order to comply with the requirements of the WTO's TRIPS agreement. The changes gave increased protection to famous foreign trademarks, where little existed before. The new law established statutory damages of RMB 500,000 (about $60,000 U.S.) for infringements where actual damages are difficult to prove, and it established penalties for government officials who are derelict in their duties to enforce the trademark laws. The Quality Brands Protection Committee (QBPC), the premier international brand-holder coalition fighting counterfeiting in China, observed that "over the past year [2002], the central government of the PRC has upgraded many laws and regulations relevant to anticounterfeiting, in large part to ensure China's compliance with relevant WTO standards. The QBPC is encouraged by these improvements in the law, and it is further encouraged to learn that new regulations and judicial standards are now being drafted to fill many of the remaining gaps in relevant laws. At the same time, some QBPC members have witnessed remarkable increases in criminal enforcement against counterfeiters of their brands, mainly due to increased willingness by local and national police to accept their cases and devote the required manpower." Notwithstanding these legal improvements, counterfeiting remains a persistent and very troublesome problem in China.

Over the past few years, China has refined its state apparatus for dealing with the issue. Focus 11.2 summarizes most of the structures that are relevant to fighting the problem today.

○ FOCUS 11.2 ○

CHINA'S ANTICOUNTERFEITING STRUCTURE

The following are the key organizations that play a key role in China's fight against product counterfeiting:

- State Intellectual Property Office (SIPO)—the restructured Chinese Patent office. The SIPO is responsible for China's patent regulations and laws, formulating policy on international IP rights issues, and coordinating foreign-related IPR affairs.

- State Bureau of Quality and Technical Supervision (TSB)—programs and activities in the fields of standardization, measures, quality control and safety surveillance. The TSB is responsible for quality standards, some of which are a basis for the control of counterfeits.

- The People's Procuratorates of the PRC—the highest procuratorial organ of the state. The People's Procurates supervise the lower courts and prisons, interpret the laws, and exercise jurisdiction over major criminal cases.

- Ministry of Public Security—the top organ for the people's police. The Ministry researches and formulates guidelines, policies, and regulations in public security.

There are also industry-specific regulatory bodies, such as the State Drug Administration that oversees medicines and the Tobacco Monopoly Bureau that regulates trade in tobacco. In addition to the Ministry of Public Security, the Administration for Industry and Commerce and the Administration for Quality Supervision and Quarantine (a part of the TSB) are available enforcement channels. According to QBPC data, as of June 2002, the SAIC reported that 1,084 "underground" factories producing counterfeits had been shut down and 53,296 other cases involving fakes had been dealt with by local AICs. Meanwhile from January to mid-June 2002, local TSBs conducted seizures against 2,535 factories and investigated a total of 65,020 cases.

HOW DO WE STOP THIS: CRIMINAL OR CIVIL REMEDIES?

A basic question that the president and general counsel of Genuine Co. will have to answer, whether their problem is taking place inside or outside the United States, is whether to proceed with primary emphasis on civil or criminal remedies. Both have advantages and both have disadvantages.

Using a civil attack, the company is basically in charge of the process. It is the company that initiates and directs the investigation, litigation, and sets the overall objectives of the effort. While the company will generally coordinate with law enforcement, it will have more control over the use of raids and product seizures. It initiates the litigation and manages the litigation process. If meaningful recovery is possible, it may well benefit, or be made partially whole, from the award.

While control over the process is a real benefit, ineffectiveness of remedies and the costs of litigation are significant downsides. In many instances, the individuals or companies sued may not have any financial substance. They may be small-time players or even "faces," stooges, or fronts put in place to take the fall and protect the real organizers of the counterfeiting operation. Even if defendants are key players in the scheme, there may be few assets to attach. Many of the defendants are completely judgment-proof, and the costs of litigation are substantial. *Trademark Counterfeiting* puts the minimum cost of embarking on a civil action at $50,000.[27] Thus, the brand holder is in a position to lose twice (a common problem in the

○ **FOCUS 11.3** ○

RETURNS FROM CIVIL ENFORCEMENT

Software companies Microsoft and Novell have both publicly described positive returns on their enforcement programs. Microsoft has always been one of the most active companies in fighting the problem of counterfeits and piracy. In 1997, at the Reconnaissance International Anti-Counterfeiting Conference, Nancy Anderson, senior corporate attorney for Microsoft Europe, explained that the company more than paid for its effort through its recoveries. In 1996 in Europe alone, Microsoft took $20 million of pirate product off the market; other actual income is derived from damages in civil litigation and out-of-court settlements. Against this were the expenses of in-house staff, costs of investigators and lawyers, plus the public relations expenses. Taking the direct value of the seized software and other income, Anderson said that the company was seeing a return of between $5 to $10 for each dollar spent.[28]

Utah-based Novell presented similar comments at a follow-on conference. Carolina Wuergler explained that Novell had been very successful in taking civil actions against counterfeit and pirate products. In one case, Novell took civil action against a network of 17 companies and was awarded a judgment of $17 million plus attorneys' fees. Overall, in 1996 the company opened over 1,200 cases and collected more than $45 million in cash and equipment seized in antipiracy/counterfeiting cases.[29]

counterfeiting field)—first by being victimized by the counterfeiter, second by spending time and resources in civil litigation, only to wind up with an empty judgment.

Opting to pursue the criminal route has advantages, as well. First, where prison is a likely remedy, the lack of assets becomes less important. The defendant is faced with jail time and loss of liberty, a much more serious consequence than having a meaningless judgment entered against him. Of course, the law enforcement and the criminal courts are still faced with the possibility of prosecuting a "face" or front. In several Asian countries, individuals are hired to play this role, and their criminal masters compensate them for their incarceration by taking care of their family.

Of course, law enforcement has the ability to seize property, bargain for testimony, and generally use the force of the state in a way that the private company cannot. From the brand holder's point of view, however, this may be of mixed value. Generally, brand holders cannot control the process and often do not benefit from it in their civil actions. Sometimes they are not even informed about developments. By opting for criminal enforcement, the company largely surrenders control and often loses even an ability to follow the process.

One particularly frustrating scenario can arise if law enforcement decides not to proceed with a case, even though initially it intended to prosecute. A variety of reasons can account for such a change, including politics, lack of resources, or a change in prosecutorial priorities.

Likewise criminal prosecution requires proof beyond a reasonable doubt, a much higher standard than the civil preponderance of the evidence. While the case may look "open and shut" to the company, prosecutors may not see it the same way, due to their evidentiary burden.

◑ FOCUS 11.4 ◑

THE REASONABLE DOUBT DILEMMA

A case involving the counterfeiting of certain Alfred Dunhill luxury leather goods illustrates the potential traps of the criminal evidentiary standard. During 1992, Alfred Dunhill became aware of high-end leather counterfeits in several countries. Test purchases were made in Hawaii, Hong Kong, Australia, Japan, and the United States. A product analysis determined that the leather goods were counterfeits of very high quality, almost indistinguishable from the genuine articles. Following investigations into a major distributor of the product, it was confirmed that the rogue business, eventually the defendant, was located in Los Angeles, California.

A series of meetings were arranged and a "sting" was set up. A pretext company had been established that subsequently placed and received an order of counterfeit leather goods from the defendant. The goods were accompanied by forged documents of authenticity. Following delivery, raids were conducted at the commercial premises and home of the defendant. The raids were carefully coordinated and involved 20 armed agents working for the U.S. Department of Justice, the IRS and Customs. From documents seized, it was estimated that the defendant

(continues)

FOCUS 11.4 *(Continued)*

was selling approximately $200,000 (in U.S. dollars) worth of the product per month in Japan and the United States. The U.S. attorney filed a criminal case based on trafficking of counterfeit goods.

The trial involved complex issues required to meet the criminal standard of proof. Specifically, it was necessary to prove the intent *(mens rea)* of the defendant and the counterfeit nature of the products. The defense argued that the defendant believed he was trafficking in genuine diverted products. Defense witnesses testified that the goods purchased by the defendants were of such high quality that it would be impossible to know whether the goods were genuine or counterfeit.

This led Dunhill to counter with extensive expert testimony concerning the manufacturing process of leather goods, including highly technical evidence about the manufacturing of the metal logo and how one could distinguish a genuine logo from a counterfeit. Explaining this to the jury was difficult and time-consuming. The jury became deadlocked, and the judge had to declare a mistrial. One of the problems in proving the case was the complexity of the evidence and the limited interest and understanding of the jury.

In a subsequent trial, the defendant was found guilty and sentenced to jail.[30]

Law enforcement and brand holders have similar, but sometimes divergent, goals. The brand-holder's goal is to minimize the counterfeiting activity and to control the problem. Hence, brand holders are usually more interested in deterring counterfeiting than punishing any individual. Law enforcement is focused on apprehending, convicting, and punishing individual criminals. This can lead to a curious Catch 22. While criminal prosecution and prisons are better potential deterrents than the entry of a civil judgment, law enforcement may act in a way that limits deterrence. For example, law enforcement may conclude that the case will end with prosecution of criminals operating within the United States, while the manufacturer may want to pursue the trail to a foreign country in order to attack the bigger fish. If the U.S. officials are not agreeable, the brand holder can be stymied. Necessary evidence and information that is a part of the criminal case may not be available for use in the larger effort of fighting the international counterfeiting operation.

Sally, our hypothetical general counsel, may well talk to her colleagues in other companies and to other lawyers while trying to make her decision about which way to proceed. She is likely to get varying opinions. Ralph Sutton of Kay and Boose would tell her: "Go civil! In almost all circumstances, at least in the United States, I believe proceeding with the control and tools of our current civil legal system is the way to go. You just lose control of the whole process if you depend on law enforcement. I'd only go the criminal route if you had a really serious criminal or terrorist involved, or if the facts were so outrageous that there would be strong political pressure to prosecute."[31]

Other longtime practitioners advocate the importance of criminal sanctions as the only true tool for dealing with criminal counterfeiters. They urge building strong working relationships with prosecutors and working with them to develop the evidence that they will need to get convictions.

The Law Is a Double-Edged Sword

While the law is the basis for most anticounterfeiting programs, it can also cause legitimate companies and their counsel real problems and even liability in certain situations.

Vicarious liability of the manufacturer for injuries caused by defective counterfeit products is one example. What does that mean? Can the innocent manufacturer of a legitimate product be held liable for damage done by a defective counterfeit it did not manufacture? Are we crazy?

Some scholars and plaintiff's attorneys don't think it's necessarily crazy. Professor Arthur Best of the University of Denver Law School wrote about this situation in his article "You only Lose Twice."

This is not an entirely academic issue. As discussed in Chapter 4, on April 20, 2001, attorneys for plaintiffs who used fake Serostim filed suit in California against Serono, Inc., various pharmaceutical distributors, and retail pharmacies involved in its distribution for injuries due to the fakes. The plaintiffs said that they purchased and used the counterfeits, causing "painful and adverse physical reactions while at the same time depriving them of the beneficial, antiwasting effect of true Serostim." The first claim in the suit was based on strict liability—that the counterfeit product that defendants distributed and sold was unreasonably dangerous when used as intended. The second claim was based on negligence,

◑ FOCUS 11.5 ◑

YOU ONLY LOSE TWICE

Everyone knows that a product counterfeiter hurts the authentic product manufacturer by stealing sales and hurting the product's reputation. But another risk of harm to the victimized company may be even greater. If a counterfeit product (like a drug or alcohol) injures a consumer, that consumer may be able to win large monetary damages from the company that produces and markets the legitimate product.

In general, a legitimate enterprise may have to pay for the consequences of a crime if the criminal conduct was foreseeable, the enterprise had a role in creating the risk of crime, and it failed to take reasonable steps to reduce that risk. If a manufacturer knew that counterfeiters were making bogus copies of its products, it would be very difficult, in a legal sense, for that manufacturer to explain why it failed to use low-cost authentication devices to identify its packages or its products. Those protections could have made it harder for the counterfeiters to commit their crimes, or could have made it easier for the consumers to make sure they were using a genuine product. While this legal analysis is entirely hypothetical, it could become real in an instant if a consumer suffers a serious injury from a counterfeit product.[32]

alleging that the defendants should have foreseen the possibility that counterfeits would be introduced into the distribution chain and should have taken better precautions to prevent this. The defendants settled the lawsuit for an undisclosed amount in 2002.

Also, as discussed in Chapter 5, Bell Helicopter has had to defend a number of lawsuits by plaintiffs who were injured in crashes of "fake" aircraft. Indeed, in some of the cases, the plaintiffs were the very counterfeiters themselves. Thus far, these suits have not prevailed but manufacturers may find themselves on the losing end of litigation if they are casual or intentionally ignore counterfeiting, particularly where defective fake products could cause human injury.

Counterclaims by alleged counterfeiters can also threaten brand holders and their counsel, as they implement their anticounterfeiting strategies. If private investigators become too aggressive in seizing alleged counterfeits, the investigator and his client may both face claims for wrongful seizure. The Lanham Act provides that a person suffering the wrongful seizure of goods may recover "damages for lost profits, cost of materials, loss of good will, and punitive damages in instances where the seizure was brought in bad faith." Other claims can be brought as well.[33]

A panel at the fall 1997 meeting of the IACC discussed this issue. The session panel began with a description of a real case. Lee Sporn, then Vice President for Intellectual Property for Polo Ralph Lauren Corporation, outlined a case in which Polo had been sued for the alleged wrongful seizure of goods and malicious prosecution. Polo's investigator had received an offer to supply counterfeit Polo goods. After working through a series of middlemen, the investigator identified a contact that offered to manufacture the counterfeit goods in China. Ultimately, the American contact was raided, records were seized, and Polo sued for damages. The defendant, who had no previous record of counterfeiting, filed a counterclaim alleging that Polo had fraudulently drawn him into the illicit deal and that he, not Polo, was the injured party. He demanded over $1 million in compensation. The defendant's attorney demanded a jury trial at which he attempted to confuse the issues, depicting Polo as the "greedy, big company" harassing and abusing a "poor, entrapped small businessman." Although the case resulted in victory for Polo, the defense counsel's impassioned rhetoric before a jury caused the company's trial team real concern. After reviewing the counterclaims that defendants have brought, or could bring, in civil and criminal actions, the IACC panel agreed that the costs to defend against counterclaims could be quite substantial.[34]

While no case has yet resulted in a judgment for a counterfeiter, counterclaims could divert resources and attention from the claim against the counterfeiter and could influence a company to compromise its settlement. In the worst case, by suing the company's legal staff personally, the counterclaim could potentially create a conflict of interest within the legal staff, requiring the hiring of separate counsel. Skilled defense counsel might also be able to create public/investor relations damage by forcing additional litigation disclosures in the filings of public companies. The risk of these claims can be minimized by having good coordination between the investigator and the company's representative, drafting narrow, specific seizure orders, and documenting carefully the counterfeit nature of the goods being seized.

Trademark the Bedrock

Trademark, the bedrock of product branding, has historic roots. As Europe emerged from the Dark Ages, swordmakers used marks to identify their products. In the 1200s, some craftsmen were required by law to mark their goods in England. In France, Charles V passed an edict in 1544 stating that the punishment for infringing upon the marks of Flemish tapestry makers was "the removal of the infringer's right hand."[35]

Early in U.S. history, there was a recognition of a need for trademark legislation. While the framers of the Constitution explicitly recognized patents and copyright, they made no provision for trademarks. Thomas Jefferson supported a petition to Congress in 1791 to recognize trademarks. But, despite attempts to pass a law in 1870, which was later invalidated by the U.S. Supreme Court, the United States did not have a federal trademark statute until the passage of the Lanham Act in 1946.[36]

With the passage of the Lanham Act, the common-law basis of federal trademark became established in statute. Product manufacturers may apply to the U.S. Patent and Trademark Office (PTO) for registration of their trademark. If the PTO approves the application on an initial basis, initial allowance is published in the Official Gazette of the Trademark Office to notify other parties of the pending approval, so that the approval may be opposed. Upon final allowance, the owner can maintain registration of the mark in perpetuity by continuing to use it and maintaining proper registration with the PTO.[37] The coverage of the act is broad and can include distinctive symbols, pictures, or words, but can also extend to packaging design, color combinations, product styles, and in some cases, even overall presentations. The trademark owner has the exclusive right to use the mark on the product with which it was identified and on related products. It is the infringement of this exclusive right to use of the mark that underlies counterfeiting claims.

But the Law Doesn't Apply Itself

Notwithstanding the strength of the Lanham Act, international treaties or criminal statutes, the law is only a collection of words, and words must be translated into actions to have effect. Some of the practical issues that might prevent law enforcement from acting were examined when Sally, the general counsel of Genuine Co., considered whether to use civil or criminal systems to attack the problem.

Examining the political priorities more closely illustrates the nature of the potential issue. The system of U.S. District Attorneys' offices is a major division within the U.S. Department of Justice (DOJ), consisting of 93 U.S. Attorneys supervising a staff of some 5,000 Assistant U.S. District Attorneys and a budget of just over $1.5 billion per year.[38] Different administrations set different priorities for this organization over time. Counterfeiting was not a priority crime in the 1980s but by the mid-1990s, the DOJ established the Computer Crime and Intellectual Property Section in the Criminal Section to prosecute IP crimes and to work with other federal investigative groups. In July 1999, the DOJ launched a domestic initiative committing DOJ, the FBI, and the U.S. Customs Service officers to work with the U.S. Attorneys in seven key port cities (increased to 10 cities in 2001) to ramp up investigation and enforcement. The U.S. Attorneys in these districts then created CHIP (Computer Hacking and Intellectual Property) units organized to prosecute IP related crimes, including counterfeiting and piracy offenses. While the DOJ's focus is now on increasing prosecution for IP, politics could also reverse this trend.

Even within the system, individual prosecutors respond to their own job performance and evaluation criteria differently. Part of their evaluation rests on their conviction rate for serious crimes. Sentences are a factor in this. In the mid and late 1990s, although there were strong criminal anticounterfeiting laws on the books, the Federal Sentencing Guidelines provided for relatively mild penalties. Under the current Guidelines, in order for a defendant to be sentenced to 10 years in prison, the counterfeiter would have to have been convicted of trafficking in more than $80 million of bogus goods. To receive just one year in prison, the counterfeiter would have to have been caught with more than $120,000 in pirate merchandise.[39]

These Guidelines act to discourage prosecutors from pursuing counterfeiting cases. In 2000, the U.S. Sentencing Commission toughened sentencing for digital piracy crimes, under the No Electronic Theft Act, but not for trademark counterfeiting. The IACC expressed its concern to the Commission that: "approaches that treat trademark counterfeiting cases as 'second class citizens' in the enforcement arena would send the wrong message to criminals and law enforcement officials. . . . Both trademark counterfeiting and copyright piracy pose serious problems for the American economy and consumers . . . criminals are attracted to the high profits and low risks that are currently possible. Penalties that result in actual jail time would have a significant deterrent effect."[40]

The technical and complex nature of counterfeiting cases can also be a barrier to bringing and winning counterfeiting cases, as illustrated by the Alfred Dunhill case. This can discourage prosecutors and civil plaintiffs alike. No one wants to mount a case that will confuse the jury and result in an expensive, embarrassing loss.

These nitty gritty issues become greatly amplified when a company attempts to enforce its rights internationally. Both the expense and management resource commitments grow tremendously as a company tries to pursue counterfeiters in foreign jurisdictions. Local investigators, counsel, and/or law enforcement must be brought in. Company management will have to commit time on the ground in the foreign country working with counsel, law enforcement and others, as well as potentially testifying at trial. There is also the cost, time, and disruption of having to travel, sometimes at short notice, to the foreign jurisdiction.

Courts in some countries are less than friendly to foreign companies attempting to litigate against their citizens. In many lesser developed countries, the IP laws may not be well-developed and the courts may be unfamiliar with, or dislike, IP and counterfeiting issues. If the case involves counterfeits being sold over the Internet, the problems can become even more vexing. Just finding the right jurisdiction and serving the defendants may be a nearly impossible task in itself.

The point is that even given strong laws, good evidence, and strong upper management commitment, other factors may affect whether prosecutors or brand holders will pursue their potential legal remedies. While the law is both the basis for most anticounterfeiting activities and is a necessary tool in the fight, treating the issue exclusively, or even primarily, as a legal issue can turn out to be incomplete, if not even unproductive. When the CEO and Sally, the general counsel of Genuine Co., our fictitious company, discuss their counterfeiting problem, they would be well-advised to consider the full range of options open to them. They should not end their discussion with the fact that "it's counterfeiting and that's illegal" and therefore proceed exclusively down a legal path.

The Developing Law—or Developing the Law

Of course the law is a living, changing thing. New statutes have been enacted to thwart counterfeiters, and new case law is constantly developing, some of which is proving to be quite important in the fight. Companies that take the protection of their products, consumers, and brands seriously will take advantage of the developing laws and work to develop the law as well.

Landlord liability for contributory infringement is one important example of this type of legal evolution. There is a body of developing U.S. case law that potentially exposes landlords, equipment leasing companies, and exhibit space providers to trademark and copyright liability based on their active support or willful ignorance of counterfeiting.[41]

The IACC held a panel discussion on this issue at its 1996 spring meeting. Lee Sporn again led this panel discussion. He pointed out that having landlords potentially "on the hook" was desirable because they are generally risk adverse, their real estate assets are hard to hide, and they are generally insured. The group discussed approaches that can make landlords allies. If, for example, the trademark owner notifies the property owner of the fact that the counterfeit activity is taking place on the property, explains the potential liability and outlines a positive course of action, the landlord may agree to work to clean up the problem. Likewise, lessors of production equipment and organizers of special exhibits face potential liability, as well as business disruption, and can often be encouraged to help.

The panel agreed that expanding the fight in this way could be helpful but also posed some risks. Brand holders could subject themselves to liability for interference in the commercial relations of a landlord and his tenants, or for defamation. Likewise, poor prosecution of a bad case in this area could lead to decisions that end this useful developing area of case law.[42]

The expansion of case law related to "decoding" of diverted products is another example. *Authentication News* ran an analysis of this issue in September 2001.

> *Federal courts in Florida, Massachusetts and California have recently made decisions that will make it much riskier for diverters to decode and resell products in the United States. This could give brand-holders more control over the distribution of their products and could provide an important legal basis for using*

product identity marking to protect brand integrity. . . . The U.S. Court of Appeals for the 11th Circuit affirmed a District court ruling that PDL International Corporation was infringing Davidoff & Cie's trademark when it etched batch codes off bottles of Cool Water fragrance products and distributed the product. . . . In a similar case, the U.S. District Court for the District of Massachusetts granted Montblanc a preliminary injunction against Staples' sale of Montblanc pens whose serial numbers and 'Pix' trademark had been obliterated. [And, i]n California, Sebastian International, Inc. (Sebastian) won an important summary judgement in U.S. District Court that applies the state's criminal anti-decoding statute to the removal of holographic security codes on hair care and other products by diverters.[43]

Both the Cool Water and Montblanc decisions were based on interpretations of the Lanham Act that typically extinguishes any control by the manufacturer/brand holder once the first sale has occurred. In these cases, however, the courts concluded that the "scarring" of the products, caused by the diverter's attempt to remove labeling and logos, created the likelihood of "consumer confusion," hence making the First Sale Doctrine inapplicable, and giving brand holders a right to prevent the sale of goods. Because diversion and counterfeiting are so closely related, this is a victory for opponents of counterfeiting as well. It also illustrates again how brand owners can "push the law" and develop new legal concepts and analyses that enhance their position.

An equally important method for promoting change in the law is for brand holders to work with organizations like the IACC to lobby Congress and state legislatures for the passage of stronger anticounterfeiting statutes.

There is growing activity at the international level, as well. Part III of the Agreement on Trade Related Aspects of Intellectual Property (TRIPS) establishes enforcement obligations for members of the World Trade Organization. Specifically, "Members shall ensure that enforcement procedures as specified in this Part are available under their laws so as to permit effective action against any act of infringement of intellectual property covered under this Agreement."[44] This, and the subsequent sections, are an important starting point for strengthening international IP enforcement. But as Tim Trainer, President of the IACC, points out in *International Intellectual Property Enforcement: SOP,*[45] "[a]fter looking at these provisions more closely, there seem to be a long list of weaknesses." He asks, for example, whether signatory countries are "required to do anything regarding the distribution of resources . . . [or] assign additional personnel to the courts, police [etc.]?" The answer is no. Failure to provide adequate resources for enforcement appears not to be a violation of the agreement. As another example, a decision on infringement need not be published in any official gazette; indeed, it may not even need to be written. To the extent that countries adopt these sorts of lax procedures, their TRIPS enforcement will be of questionable value.

Given this and other weaknesses in the international legal structure, Trainer and the IACC have decided to focus much of their efforts on engaging the United States and other governments to establish effective, sustainable IP enforcement systems. Through the United Nations IP Advisory Group, for example, officials and the private sector are actively reviewing the IP laws of various nations and describing areas of shortcoming. The group is also providing training to officials on their own laws and the requirements of international law.

Brand holders who are confronted by counterfeiting certainly must take advantage of the law to redress their problems. In order to be effective, however, they must look beyond legal remedies and to management and technological solutions. They should also understand the developing national and international frameworks and become active in supporting these activities.

CHAPTER 12

Anticounterfeiting
Technology Solutions

LIMITS OF LEGAL AND INVESTIGATIVE REMEDIES

Private investigators and legal remedies can be a strong weapon in the fight against counterfeiting of products. Often, the use of one or both of these weapons can be very effective in eliminating—or at least strongly decreasing—the incidence of counterfeiting of a company's products.

Limitations exist, however, to the effective use of these weapons in certain locations and under certain circumstances. As we have seen, even where private investigators or law enforcement agencies are able to locate a counterfeiter—itself no easy task—the effective use of legal remedies against that counterfeiter may be very limited. For example, legal remedies can be useless in countries where counterfeiting may not be illegal. Similarly, in many countries corrupt legal systems prevent effective enforcement of existing laws. Often, local political considerations may limit the effective use of legal remedies. And, as in the case of Dunhill, the quality of counterfeit products can be so high that *proving* counterfeiting in court can be very difficult—even where the counterfeiters have been uncovered and arrested.

WHY A "TECHNOLOGY SOLUTION"?

A plethora of *technological remedies* exist that address a core question about counterfeiting: How can someone "know" whether a product is genuine or counterfeit? Given the risks that are inherent in many counterfeit products, it is clearly in the consumers' own interest to know, for example, whether the pharmaceuticals they are taking are genuine. While some consumers may nonetheless choose to buy and use counterfeit goods (as described in the lower-right cell of the Harm Matrix), the vast majority of consumers will, when knowledgeable, choose to purchase authentic products—particularly where those products involve health and safety.

As we have seen, it is also in a company's own interest to know whether a product is counterfeit. As one company operating in the industry, Isotag, puts it: "Your brand attracted the customer, you should get the revenue." In addition to lost revenue, potential liabilities might be incurred by companies who become aware of counterfeiting and decline to do anything about it. In an era where very high-quality counterfeits exist, the ability to authenticate one's own products is the first step to understanding the nature and extent of a company's particular problem (see Exhibit 12.1).

A starting point for understanding what anticounterfeiting technologies do is that they are used by producers of products to deter, detect, and control counterfeiting. In their most basic form, anticounterfeiting technology solutions allow an individual consumer of goods—or a company—to examine a product and independently verify that the product is not a counterfeit. They do so by providing a feature on the product or its packaging that the counterfeiter cannot duplicate, or can only duplicate with great difficulty.

Deception		**Low Quality**	**High Quality**
Level of deception inherent in the sale of the product	**High**	Very high potential for harm to consumer and very high damage to the company.	High potential for harm to consumer and very high damage to company.
	Low	Very high potential for harm to consumer and damage to company.	Some potential for harm to consumer and high potential for damage to company.

Low   High

Quality

Quality and functionality
of the counterfeit product

EXHIBIT 12.1   The Harm Matrix

An example of this occurred in Greece. In the early 1990s, Nestle began to experience significant counterfeiting of coffee sold in catering packs for professional use in restaurants and cafeterias. Counterfeiters were duplicating the Nestle packs but using inferior coffee. The result was lost sales for Nestle.

Nestle responded to this counterfeiting, in part, by marking its catering packs with holograms that are difficult to simulate or duplicate. This allowed the users of the pack to verify their authenticity at the point of use. The users became familiar with the distinctive features of the holograms. Interestingly, it also provided Nestle with a way to track back through its distribution channels to find out where counterfeit packages were appearing. Working with authorities, Nestle was ultimately able to uncover and arrest the counterfeiters. After their arrest, Nestle continued the use of holograms on its catering packs as a deterrence against other would-be counterfeiters.[1]

In their most sophisticated form, anticounterfeiting technologies not only allow a consumer or company to authenticate products, but also allow companies to track the product through its distribution channel all the way to the point at which it is sold. These sophisticated technologies also provide forensic evidence of a product's authenticity for use by the company, Customs, private investigators, and ultimately the courts. In fact, the use of anticounterfeiting technologies can often detect problems in the supply chain that were previously unknown to the company.

◑ FOCUS 12.1 ◑

EXCERPTS FROM GLAXO WELLCOME'S PRIOR POLICY STATEMENT ON PHARMACEUTICAL COUNTERFEITING

Counterfeit medicines represent an unacceptable threat to patients' welfare. In addition, they can damage pharmaceutical companies, not simply through loss of sales, but also by involuntarily associating them with substandard or dangerous products. . . . Glaxo Wellcome is firmly committed to a program of action—involving a significant investment of resources—to reduce the threat of counterfeiting. In particular, Glaxo Wellcome products are designed to incorporate features that make them difficult to copy and that facilitate counterfeit detection.[2]

TYPES OF TECHNOLOGY SOLUTIONS

A very broad range of technologies exist that can authenticate products or packaging and provide information and control over a supply chain. The core premise in the use of these technologies is *the notion that by marking the product or its packaging with some feature that is itself difficult to replicate, counterfeiting can be detected and/or deterred.* Thus, while counterfeiters are today able to counterfeit products to an extremely high level of quality, they often will be unable to copy or simulate these marking technologies. This enables consumers and producers to distinguish between genuine and fake products by looking to the underlying marking technology.

It follows that any technology used to mark products must itself be difficult to simulate or replicate, and difficult to obtain. Otherwise, the counterfeiters will simply copy (or purchase the marking technology in the marketplace) along with actual product itself. The provision of these products therefore needs to come from a reputable, secure source.

The range of technologies that are available for these purposes can be categorized as follows:

Overt technologies are marking technologies that are visible to the naked eye and can be verified without the use of any reading device such as a lens, reader, or other equipment. Perhaps the most commonly recognized one of these technologies is the hologram—a three-dimensional representation of an object, logo or feature that can be transposed onto flat film. These films can then be converted into labels or thin films and then applied to products or packaging. Holograms and their many derivatives have two very key features. They can readily be recognized by any consumer taught to look for them, hence, they are "overt." And, they are not easily duplicated by counterfeiters.

When the Turkish tea industry was privatized in the late 1980s, the incidence of counterfeiting of branded tea bags—particularly those of the previous state monopoly ("Caykur")—grew at an alarming rate. Whereas previously Caykur had a monopoly on the supply of tea in the country, a number of counterfeiters entered the market, usurping the Caykur brand but using inferior tea now purchased on the open market.

Caykur began to use a holographic label as a means of identifying those packages of tea that were genuine. The public was educated to look for the holographic label, and the inability of the counterfeiters to replicate the label resulted in a significant increase in sales for Caykur.[3]

Another example of the use of overt technologies involved counterfeit printer ribbons. In the mid-1990s, NEC began receiving an unusually high rate of warranty returns on printers it sold to EDS. The printer motherboards were failing. Detailed product examination revealed that some of the printer ribbons were slightly different from the standard NEC product and were in fact counterfeit. Ultimately, it became clear that counterfeit printer ribbons were causing the electrical failures.

The company decided to use an overt authentication solution and to enlist the aid of its customers. It put a hologram on the ribbon cases and inserted a counterfeit alert in the packages telling users how to authenticate the hologram and the ribbon. Counterfeiting virtually disappeared, sales increased, and bogus warranty costs were largely eliminated.[4]

Another overt technology used to mark products or packaging is intaglio printing. This printing technique, which is identical to that used in currencies (where it is also used for anticounterfeiting purposes), is recognizable by its unique texture. It feels "rough" to the touch and is effectively a raised relief pattern or image on the paper or label. This technology is also difficult to counterfeit or simulate. When it is used as a marking device, it can be difficult for a counterfeiter to copy.

Still another family of overt technologies are "color-changing" or "color-shifting" technologies. These are films, coatings, or inks that change color when viewed from different angles. For example, when viewed from one angle, a label or package may appear to be green, but when tilted at another angle, the color may change to orange. The chemistry and physics of manufacturing these products is very complex. But they provide yet another type of overt technology which, when applied to genuine products or their packaging, makes it difficult for counterfeiters to duplicate with precision.

Holograms, intaglio printing, and color-shifting materials are just several of the overt technologies used in the market today to mark authentic products. Other types of overt technologies include a wide range of security inks, watermarks, and printed security features.

All overt technologies share a common attribute: They can easily be seen by an average consumer. If a company combines these technologies with a campaign to educate consumers, every consumer can be turned into an "investigator" who can verify the authenticity of a particular product. This can be an extremely powerful tool in combating the counterfeiters.

At the same time, the fact that overt technologies are readily visible also leads to one of their largest drawbacks—they are also visible to the counterfeiters. Where overt technologies are used, the risk to companies is that counterfeiters know immediately the type of authenticating technology that is used and can attempt to simulate or duplicate it. This compromises the very effort made by the company to protect its products. It becomes critical, therefore, for any company that utilizes overt technologies to choose technologies of a sufficiently high security level that are very difficult to duplicate.

Covert technologies are technologies that are not visible to the naked eye but require some sort of reading device or equipment. For example, printed features may be present on products, labels, or packaging that to the naked eye appear to be normal printed surfaces. When a small decoder or lens is held against the printed surface, a text message (e.g., the word "authentic") appears. A hidden message can only be revealed by someone with such a reader.

Another example of covert technologies are various types of "taggants," which are tailored chemical, biological, or other markers with unique characteristics. These taggants can often be applied via varnishes, inks, coatings, or films—or directly onto products themselves. The presence of these taggants is not apparent to the naked eye. But, by using any of a number of different "readers" (these range from reactive chemical pens to sophisticated handheld reading devices that can often not only detect the presence of a particular taggant, but also its dilution), a product can be verified as authentic.

The average consumer, however, would never know that this feature is found on the product or packaging. Unlike most overt technologies, which are designed specifically to be seen by anyone, these are designed not to be apparent. Their usefulness, therefore, is limited to company investigators, customs officials, or law enforcement officials who both know the taggants are present on the product and have access to the decoding device or other reading equipment.

This difference is not a subtle one, nor is it meant to be. Covert technologies are used specifically because companies do not wish to alert either customers or (more often) counterfeiters to the fact that there is any authenticating technology being used on the product. If counterfeiters knew such technology was being used, they would attempt to compromise and copy it, or at a minimum, attempt to simulate it.

A very successful use of the covert markers occurred in East Africa, where fuels were being sold under a number of brand names that were either not purchased from brand owners, or were adulterated or diluted versions of branded fuels. Often, petrol station owners would dilute or replace branded fuels with lesser-quality versions, then sell branded fuels to the consumers at a higher price, pocketing the difference themselves.

Working with brand owners in the region, a company called Biocode began tagging fuels sold in the region with their proprietary covert marking process, which is based on detection of minute amounts of specific antibodies introduced into the fuels in minute, measured quantities. These markers can be detected at very high levels of dilution—50 parts per billion—by a simple portable reading device, thus establishing whether any particular fuel is authentic or not. This test can be carried out on-site at a fuel station or other retail site. In addition, a lab test can also detect dilution quantities of the markers in any particular batch of fuel. Where a branded fuel has been diluted, the markers not only indicate this, but show by how much they have been diluted.

These markers cannot be seen with the naked eye and cannot be detected without a very specific test and measurement kit that recognizes only the particular Biocode technologies. An average consumer looking for these technologies would never know they are present. A sophisticated counterfeiter or reseller looking for a way to subvert the system would need a sophisticated laboratory and a profound knowledge of biology and chemistry to even begin to attempt to replicate the markers.

Since the program was introduced in East Africa in 1998, the incidence of counterfeiting and dilution of branded fuels has been cut dramatically. Tests were carried out at a wide number of locations throughout the region. This was accompanied by a concerted effort to arrest and prosecute those found selling fake or diluted fuels. As word spread that the fuel companies were undertaking this effort (and the test could not be beaten), more and more sellers of fuel began to do what they were supposed to be doing—selling the branded fuel instead of a substandard version. Confidence among consumers also grew. As one quality manager for Total

Kenya put it, "this is working very well. Since this was implemented, there has been increased customer confidence in our products."[5]

A combination of overt and covert technologies is often used today. This combination provides overt authentication to the customer but also includes a covert invisible element that counterfeiters will not know is present—and thus will have difficulty in attempting to replicate or simulate. These "layered" technologies provide redundant authentication of a product.

An example of layered technologies might be the use of a hologram in combination with covert taggants or other authentication technologies. Thus, the consumer can authenticate a product by looking to the overt authentication technology—in this case, the hologram. The producers, or law enforcement, investigative, or customs officials the company chooses to educate can also look to the covert technology as a secondary check.

This example again points up a critical difference between overt and covert technologies: They are fundamentally directed to different audiences. Overt technologies are meant to be seen and "used" by the average consumer, and often are the center of educational campaigns to enlist consumers in the fight against counterfeiters. This strength is also their potential Achilles heel—their very visibility makes them a target for counterfeiters too.

By contrast, covert technologies are *not* meant to be seen by anyone other than the producers or any customs or other law enforcement agencies they choose to inform. The purpose of covert technologies is not to prevent the consumer from buying a product—they won't even know it is present—but to provide the producer with the ability to quietly authenticate a product and not alert the counterfeiters to the fact that the product is marked.

An example of a "layered solution" using both overt and covert technologies involved a high-end French apparel label manufacturer, Montagut, which experienced counterfeiting of its high-end warm climate apparel in several countries in Asia. This apparel was extremely popular, but as counterfeits began to appear, the brand image began to be tarnished. Consumers often did not have confidence that they were buying legitimate items.

After some early experimentation, and working with a reputable security printer, Montagut devised a label that was sewn onto the garment buttons (and self-destructed when removed, thus preventing reuse of the labels). The labels contained overt elements (intaglio printing, a fluorescent silver logo image, visible fibers in the paper, and an optically variable or color-shifting ink) and covert elements (a latent image, invisible fibers in the paper, and a micro-printed embedded thread). The resulting label not only gave consumers confidence that the product was legitimate, it also provided a covert means for Montagut to check any attempted simulations of the authentication label by counterfeiters.

Interestingly, the fact that the company took the effort to authenticate its own products had an unintended side effect. The authenticating label became so associated with the brand that some customers actually began to wear the labels with the apparel, as if to show the world that the product they were wearing was genuine. The authentication became associated with, and part of, the brand itself.

Montagut has since introduced new versions of its authentication labels and has deliberately set out to educate its consumers about the overt features on the labels. The new labels also contain covert features, known only to the company and law enforcement. And the brand continues to be associated with the authentication features themselves.[6]

Machine-readable technologies are technologies—either overt or covert—where authentication can be verified by machines (very often at high speeds) and may not require human presence or interaction with the product. Most covert technologies do, in fact, require some sort of "reading device" (some as simple as a pen with a reactive ink, some as sophisticated as handheld spectrometers or other types of readers). "Machine-readable technologies" normally refers to technologies where the entire authentication process does not rely on an individual's judgment, but the precision of a tailored "reader." Originally, many of these technologies were developed for applications where very high quantities of items need to be authenticated—for example, tickets for subways, or currency that is being counted in a high-speed counting and sorting machine in a bank. The pressing need for brand authentication technologies to address *product authentication* has resulted in many of these technologies making their way into products.

For example, using machine-readable technologies, an investigator can enter a shop selling suspected counterfeit goods and from a distance "interrogate" products with a reader, possibly without even picking them up, and discern whether they are real or fake. Similarly, products in containers might be interrogated and their authenticity verified. Radio-frequency chips can accomplish this and store information about the product, as well.

Using magnetic and other readable technologies, labels on packages on an assembly or wholesale distribution line can be authenticated. This can prove very useful if products are, in fact, distributed through one or a few central "choke" points.

However, the drawbacks to machine-readable technologies for product authentication remain significant. By virtue of their sophistication, the cost of these products can be much higher than the alternative, nonmachine-readable technologies. The cost of the readers may also be a factor. Control and distribution of these readers presents its own logistical questions. If only one were to make its way into the wrong hands, the entire program and technology might be compromised. And finally, the cost-benefit calculation to the use of these technologies may not work out. For most products, some combination of lower-priced overt and/or covert technologies may provide a sufficient deterrent to counterfeiters, without incurring the extra cost of a machine-readable technology.

Track and trace technologies refer to technologies or systems that, in addition to providing authentication services, also allow producers to track the product in its distribution channels. Again, these technologies can be overt, covert, or both, but they also provide numerical or other data which, in combination with a database, can be used to track products and trace their movements.

An example of this technology would be an overt hologram where every discrete hologram was individually "personalized" with a printed or laser-engraved number or bar code. When these numbers are entered by producers into a database that tracks to production and distribution records, a company can tell not only that a product is authentic but also track the product from a discrete production site to the point of sale. A company might, therefore, be able to tell that a product manufactured at its plant in Spain has been authenticated and sold at four different locations in Latin America.

More often than not, these track and trace products are used not only to deter and detect counterfeiting but also to detect diversion of a company's products. As we have noted, companies will often ship products for sale only into specific geographical locations in order to take advantage of pricing differentials, or to accommodate local regulatory, packaging, language content, or other regimes. Diverters often find it profitable to take these products and ship them for sale to other locations. An identical perfume might, for example, be offered for sale in Argentina at a price substantially reduced from the price in New York. A diverter would buy the lower-priced perfume in bulk in Argentina, ship it to New York (often in violation of contractual distribution contracts), sell it for the higher price, and pocket the difference.

Track and trace systems and technologies would allow a company to detect that products are being diverted. By individually numbering, coding, and tracking products, the company could tell that very large quantities which *should have been sold* in Argentina are, in fact, showing up in shops in New York.

Exhibit 12.2 shows a brief overview of some of the technologies that are used today in authenticating and tracking products in the marketplace.

EXHIBIT 12.2   **Examples of Authenticating Technologies**

Overt Technologies	Covert Technologies	Machine-Readable Technologies

• Holograms/optically variable devices (OVDs)
 • Color-shifting films
 • Color-shifting/optically variable inks
 • Fluorescent inks
 • Intaglio printing
 • Security papers
 • Watermarks
	• Taggants (biological, chemical, spectroscopic)
	 • Security inks/coatings
	   • Reactive inks
	   • UV inks
	   • IR inks
	   • Thermochromic inks
	 • Hidden printed messages
	 • Digital watermarks
		• Radio frequency ID
		 • Magnetic-based systems
		 • Barcodes (2D or 3D)
		 • Laser marking
		 • Optically-stored marks

RETURN ON INVESTMENT OF AUTHENTICATING TECHNOLOGIES

While not much publicly available information exists about the cost effectiveness of using authentication technologies, anecdotal evidence in the

◐ FOCUS 12.2 ◐

ESTIMATING COST/BENEFITS FROM USING PRODUCT SECURITY SYSTEMS

One of the key questions asked as companies evaluate the possible use of product security systems is: "What do they cost and what will I get out of it?" Here is a method of estimating the answers.

The Security System

Today, most security systems are as much a service as a product. One example would be using a product security labeling program supplied by a secure and reputable authentication provider. In this type of program, the brand owner is supplied with authenticating security labels, bearing serial numbers, which are recorded in a distribution database. At the brand-owner's option, investigators are also provided to inspect the products in the field. A "typical" U.S.-based, security labeling program for a widely distributed brand good might cost between 1–3¢ per label. The cost of applying the stickers might be an additional 1–1.5¢ each. This price would include cataloging the serial numbers in a database. A very modest (10-city), quarterly field inspection program within the United States could add $20,000–$30,000 per year to the price of a product. This would give the brand owner information about distribution of the products and an alert if counterfeiting or diversion problems were found.

Assuming the brand-owner's program involved tagging 10 million items annually, the cost of the security authentication program would be approximately $325,000 per year (10 million pieces × (2¢ per label + 1¢ per application) + $25,000 field program), depending of course on the quantity of items labeled, the complexity of the labels, the geographic coverage of the program, and the sophistication of the data base system.

Estimating the Cost/Benefit

Now assume that the brand-owner's products sell at an average wholesale price of $15, and it operates its business on a 60 percent gross margin. In this case, the brand owner would be realizing gross revenues of $90 million per year. Before the brand owner implements its security authentication program, let us assume further that it is suffering a 25 percent counterfeit problem: That is, another 2.5 million fake items are being sold illegally each year, or the equivalent of $37.5 million in bogus sales.

If the brand owner is able to reduce counterfeit sales, by 40 percent, through an anticounterfeiting program and capture half of the displaced revenue, its sales will increase by $7.5 million, or 5 percent. Its gross profits will rise by $4.5 million to $94.5 million, or an increase of 3 percent of its prior sales. The following table illustrates how using the assumptions above a company's gross profits are improved by different levels of counterfeit conversion (i.e., percentage of counterfeits converted into sales of genuine products) and product margin.

TABLE 1   **Improvement in Gross Profit by Introduction of Anticounterfeiting Program**

Gross Margin	30%	40%	50%	60%	70%
% Counterfeits Converted					
5%	1.5%	2.0%	2.5%	3.0%	3.5%
10%	3.0%	4.0%	5.0%	6.0%	7.0%
15%	4.5%	6.0%	7.5%	9.0%	10.5%
20%	6.0%	8.0%	10%	12%	14%

With some further assumptions, it is now possible to estimate the cost/benefit of implementing the program. Assume that the company's fixed operating costs are $5 million per year and that its variable costs run at 35 percent of sales. Using these data, Table 2 calculates the customer's net profits before and after implementation of the anticounterfeiting program.

TABLE 2   **Financial Summary Pre- and Post-Anticounterfeiting Program**

($ million)	Pre-Program	Post-Program
Sales	$150	$157.5
— Cost of Goods	60	63
Gross Profit	90	94.5
— Oper. Exp. Fixed	5	5
— Oper. Exp. Var.	52.5	55.1
— Cost of Program	0.00	0.33
Net Profit	$32.5	$34.07

A 5:1 Return

In this case, the company's net profits would increase by $1.57 million or 4.8 percent (including the cost of the authentication program). Dividing

(continues)

FOCUS 12.2 *(Continued)*

this increase in net profits by the cost of the program gives a cost/benefit ratio of 0.210 or a return of approximately $4.78 for each dollar spent on the program.

It is significant that this example does not assume that counterfeiting must be totally eliminated or that 100 percent of the counterfeit sales are converted to genuine sales.

Obviously, other benefits can accrue from the use of security systems: product liability avoidance, decreased return/warrantee repair costs, and decreased brand damage.[7]

---

industry and among brand owners suggests that the return on investment in using these technologies is quite high. As a starting point, their use by brand owners clearly raises a new and higher barrier to counterfeiters, who in addition to actually counterfeiting a product must also deal with the presence of authentication technologies. Even then, the scale of the counterfeiting problem is often so large that even incremental improvements in combating it can result in very large financial returns, justifying any investment by brand owners in authentication technologies.

In a somewhat backhanded affirmation that authentication technologies can be a significant barrier to counterfeiters, in November 1997, armed robbers broke into a factory in the United Kingdom, tied up three employees, and made off with 200,000 Microsoft Certificates of Authenticity. These Certificates of Authenticity were designed to accompany all Microsoft software supplied to computer makers, and they provided an assurance to customers that the software was not counterfeit.

In June 1998, some of the stolen certificates surfaced in the United Arab Emirates alongside pirated software. The armed raid in the United Kingdom was obviously well planned and shows the extent to which counterfeiters will go to secure authentication technologies. It also shows that the presence of these technologies is a valuable part of a brand protection program.[8]

CHAPTER 13

What Governments and Multilateral Institutions Can (and Can't) Do

INTRODUCTION

This chapter discusses some of the many legal and political developments and remedies that have been developed at both the national and international levels to assist in the protection of intellectual property rights. We will start with international developments.

THE NATURE OF INTERNATIONAL LAW

One is always tempted to compare international law with national legal systems. When doing this, international law always seems to come off second-best, even in contrast to a weak national law system.

What Is International Law?

First, international law itself seems to grant primacy to national law. That is because the cornerstone upon which international law rests is the notion of state sovereignty. A decentralized system based on the sovereignty of each part means that each part is equal. No problem there, but sovereignty means that every state (read country) has the right to establish its own laws and legal system. This means that there is no higher authority in the world system than the individual country, unless the state chooses to cede some of its legal authority to another organization. This is a voluntary act on the part of the state. Some of the European countries have done this as they have created European institutions under the umbrella of the European Union. For example, the European Court of Justice does take priority on certain topics over the individual legal systems of the member states, but only because the latter have agreed that that should be the case. Likewise, states have subordinated their national laws to a variety of specialized organizations within the United Nations system. They have done this because the common expectations and practices that have resulted have been perceived to outweigh the importance of the state's right to act arbitrarily and independently—the more recent unilateral posturing of the United States notwithstanding. Sovereignty guarantees the state autonomy in internal affairs and also in its external relations with other states. This principle is enshrined in the current international system.

The Statute of the International Court of Justice (ICJ) best summarizes the sources of international law. Most relevant to the topic at hand are international treaties (particularly multilateral ones), or laws that groups of states have agreed to amongst themselves. Other sources of international law include customary practices, national and international court decisions, the writings of legal authorities and specialists, and other "general principles" of law recognized as part of any legal system since early times. The reason that international law falls short in comparison with national law is the absence of the institutions necessary to make, interpret, execute, and enforce the laws. Most sovereign states have such institutions, but at the international level they are either weak or nonexistent. Perhaps the best example of this is the International Court of Justice itself. The name would imply that this is an institution charged with independently and objectively adjudicating international laws. However, the ICJ cannot even hear a case unless all the states party to the conflict agree to let the court hear the case. Furthermore, states are not obligated to use the World Court, nor are they required to comply with its verdicts if not in their best interests. As such, the ICJ is not involved in the settlement of really critical issues. Similarly, the legislative and executive institutional functions are also lacking at the international level. The result is a rather undefined set of rules that are enforced only by the strength of the individual sovereign members.

Other factors that tend to constrain international law, thus making it less effective, are discussed by Kegley and Wittkopf:[1] (1) The international system is culturally very diverse and, therefore, there is no common set of values upon which to base international law. (2) In justifying the pursuit of national advantage, international law concedes to power differences rather than constraining them. (3) Because of the voluntary consent system, international law advantages the strong states over the weak. (4) Being based on existing practices, international law is reactive rather than proactive in shaping the behavior of states. (5) The lack of concrete institutions and the ambiguity of the mostly uncodified law allow states to interpret the law as serves their purposes.

These criticisms are perhaps less constraining when the sources of the "laws" are international treaties and agreements to which sovereign states have voluntarily acceded. These treaties tend to be rather specific, and therefore it is more obvious when a signatory state is not abiding by the rules to which it has agreed.

Recourse under International Law

International law is normally divided into public and private international law. The first governs relations between sovereign states, while the latter refers to the rules that govern the actions and interactions of private parties when acting internationally. Both have some relevance to the topic of protecting intellectual property. Public law is codified in the multilateral treaties dealing with the topic. However, it is up to the states themselves, as we saw in the previous section, to seek compliance with the terms of those treaties from other member states.

If you wish to rely on international law to enforce your intellectual property rights (IPRs), then you are in the realm of private law, or what is sometimes called "conflict of laws." Here three factors are very important to the resolution of private international conflicts: the choice of law, the choice of forum, and the recognition and enforcement of judgments.

Consider the following example. Assume that Nike signs a licensing agreement with a Korean firm that allows the latter to produce a certain quantity of Nike shoes and to sell them in the Korean market. The Korean firm will pay royalties to Nike based on the number of shoes produced.

However, what if the Korean firm decides to produce a few extra shoes and to sell them through black market or gray market channels? It does not report the extra production and, therefore, they will not pay royalties. Furthermore, if it exports the shoes to other markets through unauthorized channels, then the authorized Nike distributors in those markets will be undercut, and Nike itself will lose market share. This extra production does not constitute counterfeit goods in the common usage of that term. But it is an attempt to usurp the value of the brand and therefore consistent with our definition of counterfeiting. It is unauthorized production according to the licensing agreement and, therefore, a violation of Nike's intellectual property. Since it is a violation of a signed international contract, it ought to be enforceable by legal recourse.

The first question that must be answered is what law applies to this dispute. This is the "choice of law" question posed above. It will be helpful if the two parties specified the laws to be used in case of dispute in the contract itself. They may have agreed that U.S. law, or California law, or Korean law would be used. If they failed to specify which laws were applicable, then there must first be a legal determination to decide this question. This is where private international law comes in.

Second is the "choice of forum" question. It concerns where the case will be heard. The parties could agree that California law will govern, but also agree that the case will be litigated in Korea. In this case, Korean courts would have to agree to base their decision on California law and not Korean law. The choice of law and choice of forum are separate issues. Again, it will be helpful if the parties to the contract have already specified the forum to be used. If they have not, then this is another legal determination that must be decided. This will increase the time and the costs of a legal remedy to this dispute.

Finally, if a Korean court hears a case based on California law and determines that the Korean firm is entitled to damages, will the California or U.S. courts be willing to enforce this judgment on the American firm? You can begin to see how confusing this may be, even when the dispute seems rather straight-forward. And, we haven't talked money yet. Consider the expense of flying a few international lawyers back and forth to Korea at $500 per billable hour and you can see that the cost of the legal remedy will add up very quickly. Also, depending on the answers to the questions discussed above, you may get a judgment (win the case) but never receive any monetary damages.

Alternative Dispute Resolution Mechanisms

Because of the cost and uncertainty associated with legal remedies to international disputes, we are going to discuss some alternative approaches in this chapter. The four approaches to dispute resolution that involve third parties are (in increasing order of third-party involvement) conciliation, mediation, arbitration, and litigation. We discussed some of the pitfalls of litigation above. At the other extreme is *conciliation,* which is a fairly weak form of third-party assistance. Nevertheless, it may be appropriate and effective in some situations, particularly when the other party to the dispute comes from a culture that sees litigation as proof that the relationship has failed. Conciliation is often referred to as providing "good offices." Basically, the job of an outside conciliator is to facilitate the opportunity for the disputants to resolve their problem themselves. The conciliator keeps them talking, often by providing a neutral venue where they can resolve their conflict.

A step up from conciliation is *mediation.* Mediators become a bit more involved. They serve as a go-between in an attempt to enhance communication between the disputants. As such, they will not only convey each party's position to the other but they may incorporate their own opinions and suggestions. In this way, the reasonableness of each disputant's position is continually moderated by a supposedly objective third party. However, with mediation, it is important to remember that the mediator's opinions and suggestions are just that. They carry no obligation for the parties to accept them, or even to consider them. Nevertheless, if a resolution is in each party's best interest, then the mediator can serve an important role in reaching an outcome acceptable to each party.

The alternative dispute resolution (ADR) approach that has gained the most popularity in international business disputes is *arbitration.* Unlike the case with conciliation and mediation, an arbitrator makes a binding decision thus bringing resolution to the dispute. The arbitrator is charged with hearing the position of each party and then making a decision. That decision may be totally in favor of one disputant or the other, or it may split the difference in a way that gives each party a partial victory. Thus, it is a much faster and cheaper alternative than international *litigation*.

It is quite common for international contracts to include an arbitration clause in them. In this way, the parties to the agreement decide in advance that disputes will be settled through arbitration. They may actually select the arbitrator or arbitrators. More likely, they will specify a particular arbitration group that will then select the actual arbitrator(s). Such services are provided by the International Chamber of Commerce (ICC), the American Arbitration Association, the London Court of International Arbitration, the Arbitration Institute of the Stockholm Chamber of Commerce, or at the regional level by a group like the North American Trade Dispute Resolution Center. For example, if both parties agree to settle any disputes through arbitration under the auspices of the ICC, the following clause should be stated in the contract:

> *All disputes arising out of, or in connection with, the present contract shall be finally settled under the Rules of Arbitration of the International Chamber of Commerce by one or more arbitrators appointed in accordance with the said Rules.*

There is also an international convention (the United Nations Convention on the Recognition and Enforcement of Foreign Arbitral Awards) that requires signatory states to enforce arbitral awards that have been made outside the country by one of these arbitration bodies. When signing the convention, a state can restrict their enforcement. For example, the United States acceded to the convention in 1970 but has limited its enforcement to arbitral awards made in another "contracting state" and "only to differences arising out of legal relationships . . . that are considered as commercial under the national laws of the United States."

INTERNATIONAL LAW AND INTELLECTUAL PROPERTY

International law as it applies to intellectual property has developed primarily from multilateral agreements between sovereign countries or states. Thus, while a country may be a signatory to a particular agreement, all right holders trying to enforce their intellectual property rights will be dependent on the institutions within those countries to enforce those rights. If law enforcement will not vigorously investigate and apprehend violators, nor will the courts punish them, then utilizing international law may be both expensive and ineffective in this field. Many of the major multilateral agreements are now administered by The World Intellectual Property Organization (WIPO), a specialized organization of the United Nations.

World Intellectual Property Organization

At least 175 countries (roughly 90 percent) are now members of the World Intellectual Property Organization (WIPO). The international organization has a distinguished history (see Focus 13.1) and is now the primary organization dealing with intellectual property at the international level. The organization's primary purpose is to continue to promote creativity by protecting works of the mind. The world community now seems agreed that such protection spurs human creativity, thus expanding the boundaries of science and technology, as well as the arts and literature. This is the result of recognizing and rewarding creators and protecting the ultimate owners of their creations from outside infringement. Following is a brief discussion of the various forms of intellectual property and the related international treaties.

International Protection of Patents. It was in the area of patents that the international protection of intellectual property got its start. The need became obvious in 1873 when several creators refused to participate in the International Exhibition of Inventions in Vienna for fear that their creations would be copied or stolen and someone in another country would be the commercial beneficiary.

In 1883, at about the time Johannes Brahms was composing his third symphony, the Paris Convention for the Protection of Industrial Property was born. In addition to patents on inventions, the Paris Convention (as it was commonly referred to) also covered trademarks and industrial designs. It officially came into force a year later when 14 member states ratified the agreement.

According to WIPO, "A patent is an exclusive right granted for an invention, which is a product or a process that provides a new way of doing something, or offers a new technical solution to a problem."[2] The patent provides protection to the inventor, normally for a period of about

---

○ **FOCUS 13.1** ○

WIPO

WIPO was established in 1970 after the 1967 convention that officially created the organization. In 1974, it became a specialized agency within the United Nations system. Its predecessor was the United International Bureau for the Protection of Intellectual Property, known by the French acronym of BIRPI. This organization itself came into existence back in 1893 when the bureaus of two previous conventions were combined. They were the Paris Convention for the Protection of Industrial Property (1883) and the Berne Convention for the Protection of Literary and Artistic Works (1886). The former was the first international attempt to protect inventions (patents), trademarks, and industrial designs in other countries, while the latter was the first international attempt to protect creative works through copyrights. While the Paris Convention had only 14 sovereign members, WIPO (at the start of the new millennium) has 175 member countries. Likewise, it has 760 staff members from 83 countries in its Secretariat, and a budget of 410 million Swiss francs. It administers 21 international treaties—15 on industrial property and 6 dealing with copyrights. In 1996, WIPO entered into a cooperative agreement with the WTO. Its headquarters are in Geneva, Switzerland.

---

20 years. This means that someone else is prevented from making, using, distributing, or selling a product or process without the inventor's (or owner's) permission. The owner and inventor are not always the same, since the inventor can decide to lease or sell the patent rights to another party. Sometimes when an invention results from one's regular paid job, it is understood that the patent for same belongs to the organization, not the inventor. An inventor can also give permission for another to use their patent, or they can lease it to someone else for a fee.

In order to be granted a patent, it is expected that the product must be of practical use and be novel in some aspect from what currently exists. That said, WIPO also cautions, "In many countries, scientific theories, mathematical methods, plant or animal varieties, discoveries of natural substances, commercial methods, or methods for medical treatment (as opposed to medical products) are generally not patentable."

These restrictions contain significant concerns for those working today in the hot new biochemical industries. Nevertheless, the product can be as basic as a ballpoint pen or as sophisticated as a microprocessor and still receive patent protection.

To protect your patents from infringement, it is usually necessary to seek protection from the courts. There is no universal patent that provides protection in all countries. Rather, you must file for a patent in each country where protection is sought. However, in 1978 the Patent Cooperation Treaty (PCT) was adopted. This permits the use of a single international patent application, which saves time and money. However, you must still consider in which countries you wish to continue the application process, and it can become quite costly to file a patent in several countries. There are now over 100 members of the PCT. Since its beginning more than 75,000 applications have been recorded (which, in reality, represents more than 5.8 million national applications).

International Protection of Copyrights.   Two years after the Paris Convention was created to deal with patents, the Berne Convention for the Protection of Literary and Artistic Works brought copyright protection to different forms of intellectual property. Copyrights offer protection to the creators of literary and artistic works. Included in this broad category are novels, short stories, poems, plays, songs, operas, musicals, sonatas, drawings, paintings, sculptures, architectural works, photographs, reference works, newspapers, computer programs, databases, films, choreography, advertisements, maps, and technical drawings. Note that ideas cannot be copyrighted; only their expression can be copyrighted. Thus, one cannot obtain a copyright for the idea of making a film about the sinking of the Titanic. The actual film *(Titanic)* can be copyright protected, once it has been created.

Similar to a patent, the copyright gives the original creator "the exclusive right to use or authorize others to use the work on agreed terms."[3] The copyrighted work cannot be reproduced, performed, recorded, broadcast, translated, or adapted without permission of the copyright holder. The Napster issue seems more understandable when you realize the kind of protection that copyrights afford. A few years back, it was fairly common for academics to put together a packet of articles copied from various publications for one of their classes. In fact, Kinkos would do it for you.

No more—at least not without following a rather laborious procedure of obtaining copyright approvals.

Normally, the creator has economic rights for a period of 50 years under WIPO treaties. However, some countries may extend this protection period. These rights accrue to one's heirs as with other property rights. There are also moral rights that prevent others from claiming authorship and allow the right holders to prohibit changes to the work that they feel may damage their reputation.

In addition to the rights of the original creator, there are some "related rights" or "neighboring rights" accruing to other parties. These other parties are those that serve as links between the creator and the communication of their works to the broader public. These related right holders include performers, recording companies, and broadcasters. For example, an actor performs a part in a play written by someone else; the recording industry produces songs written by others; and, broadcasters play music written and produced by others. An international convention was signed in 1961 to protect these related rights. It is the International Convention for the Protection of Performers, Producers of Phonograms, and Broadcasting Organizations, more conveniently known as the Rome Convention. Many holders of copyrights and related rights become members of "collective management organizations." These organizations serve as intermediaries between the creators and the users in order to assure that the former receive proper remuneration for the use of their works. You can imagine how impossible it would be for songwriters to monitor every radio station playing their songs. The reverse is also true. How would a radio station be able to contact songwriters in order to get permission to play their songs and to remunerate them. The collective management organization facilitates these complex interactions by serving as the one-stop shop between these two groups. Specifically, the organizations negotiate the rates and the terms of use, issue the appropriate licenses, and collect the royalties from users and distribute them to the right holders. Most collective management organizations are constrained by the national laws of the country where they reside. However, through reciprocal representation agreements and allegiance to the principle of national treatment, foreign artists are protected in like fashion to domestic ones.

Unlike patents, there is no requisite copyright application. Rather, a creative work is considered to be protected as soon as it exists. However, many countries do have offices where works can be registered. Nevertheless, it would be nearly impossible for individual creators to monitor the use of their work everywhere around the world. Plus the cost of enforcing the copyright would be prohibitive, except in the most grievous cases. Here again, the collective management organizations provide a valuable service to their members through their greater administrative and legal expertise and resources.[4]

International Protection of Trademarks.   In ancient times, craftsmen would often affix their signatures or signs to their works. This allowed consumers to identify the source of the work and to begin to associate a particular level of quality or style with the product. Today's trademarks accomplish the same purpose. So that consumers are not confused, trademarks can be registered, thereby preventing their use by someone else. Most countries now have provisions for the registration of trademarks. Of course, some trademarks can lose value as well as gain value. Witness the recent troubles of Firestone, for which counterfeiters are not to blame.

More than other kinds of intellectual property, the trademark is the one most associated with the brand itself. As such, trademarks are most relevant to the focus of this book. We saw in Chapter 2 just how valuable a brand can become. Thus, if someone could use the same trademark or one that is deceptively similar, great damage could be done to the brand's value.

What can be used as a trademark? A trademark can be composed of one or a combination of any of the following elements: a letter or letters, words, pictures, symbols, three-dimensional signs or figures, colors, sounds, or even fragrances.[5] Try to think of trademarks that utilize these elements individually or in combination. How about the "golden arches" of McDonald's (a word, a symbol, a color)? Or what about the Olympic Rings (symbol and colors)? Actually there is a whole separate international treaty for the protection of the Olympic symbol (the Nairobi Treaty). Did you know that the colors of the interlocking rings were chosen because they contain the colors found in all the national flags of the world? There is also that little tune you associate with the friendly skies of United. Can you think of any trademarks that use smells?

In addition to marks for individual products and companies, there are also "collective marks" that can be used by members of an association, like a cooperative. There are also "certification marks," such as the mark used by the European Union for products in compliance with environmental standards. Thus, trademark protection is enforced through national or regional court systems.

Unlike patents and copyrights, trademarks do not necessarily expire, though they may have to be periodically renewed, usually for a fee. It was noted above that the Paris Convention also covered trademarks. However, as with some other forms of intellectual property, trademarks had to be registered in each country where protection was sought. Today, there are some regional arrangements where marks can be registered for a group of countries. In addition, the WIPO administers an international registry of trademarks under the Madrid Agreement Concerning the International Registration of Marks and the Madrid Protocol. At present, more than 60 countries are signatories to one or the other. If a person or organization has a link to one of the member countries through nationality, domicile, or establishment, then by registering with that national office, they can receive protection in some or all other members of the Madrid Union.

In the United States, trademark infringement hinges on deception to the consumer. Thus counterfeiting is a form of infringement. However, courts have held that the consumer does not necessarily have to be confused at the time of purchase; if there is the likelihood of post-sales confusion, then goods may still be considered counterfeits.[6] Similarly, the courts have even held that unauthorized overruns may be counterfeits, if they have not been subject to the approval and quality control of the authentic brand holder. This is because the consumer is still being deceived by relying on the trademarked goods to represent a certain level of quality.[7] Even genuine goods that are deceptive in their packaging can be considered counterfeits.[8] Offers to sell counterfeit goods can also be considered infringement, as can facilitating the sale of counterfeits by others. Trademark infringement was originally covered by the Lanham Act. More recently, the Trademark Counterfeiting Act of 1984 made the counterfeiting of trademarks a federal crime, and the Anticounterfeiting Consumer Protection Act of 1996 increased the criminal penalties for infringement. Remedy today can include seizure of the counterfeit goods, as well as other property and equipment. In addition, treble damages and criminal prosecution can result. Intentionally trafficking in counterfeit goods could result in a $2 million fine for a first-time offender ($5 million for a corporation) and 10 years in prison.[9]

International Protection of Geographical Indications. A type of geographical indication called an appellation of origin is protected by international agreement. These refer to a geographical location where something is produced. The location designated may be a village, town, region, or country. The assumption is that some products exhibit certain characteristics or quality because of where they are made. It is important that the product and location are specifically linked, that is to say that the product derives its characteristics and reputation because of the location. Perhaps one of the most obvious examples is Bordeaux wine, from the Bordeaux region of France. Others would include Habana tobacco (Cuba), Colombian Coffee, Tequila (from a particular part of Mexico), Gruyere cheese (Switzerland), Scotch whiskey (Scotland), and so forth. While the above examples imply that it is only agricultural products that can be protected, that is not necessarily the case. Sometimes the unique and valued characteristics result from human factors in a particular region. Examples would be Isfahan rugs (Iran), Venetian glass (Italy), or perhaps Swiss watches (Switzerland).

However, sometimes the geographic designation becomes so generic that it really refers to a type of product rather than the place where it is produced. When that happens, the geographical designation is not protected as an appellation of origin. An example of such a generic designation is Dijon mustard. While originally referring only to mustard produced in the town of Dijon in France, it is now used more commonly to refer to a particular style of mustard regardless of where it is produced. The same can probably be said for Swiss cheese or Cheddar cheese.

Appellations of origin are closely associated with trademarks. However, while a trademark can be used by a single producer, appellations of origin can be used by any producer within the designated area.

Geographical indications are most often protected under various national laws. These may be laws against unfair competition, laws protecting marks of certification, or consumer protection laws. Courts can usually impose injunctions, fines, or both. However, geographical indications were also protected under the early Paris Convention for the Protection of Industrial Property (1883). International protection is also provided by the Lisbon Agreement for the Protection of Appellations of Origin and Their International Registration. They are also included in the more recent TRIPS agreement discussed on the following pages.[10]

International Protection of Industrial Designs. Industrial designs refer to the ornamental or aesthetic aspects of an item. Products are designed to appeal to the eye. It is not the technical features of the article that are being protected under the category of industrial design, but rather the appearance. Industrial design may refer to two-dimensional features such as lines, patterns, and colors, or it may include three-dimensional features such as shape. Industrial design may apply to a variety of products, including clothing, appliances, vehicles, architectural structures, jewelry or other luxury items.

To be protected as an industrial design, the design must be "new" or "original." However, how new is defined may differ substantially between countries. Generally, protection is limited to the country where protection is granted. Even then, protection is often for a period of only five years. However, this can often be renewed for up to 15 years. Sometimes the design can also be protected as a work of art under copyright law. But, in some countries, you must choose between industrial design protection and copyright protection. You are precluded from having both kinds of protection.

Internationally, protection has been made somewhat more efficient by the Hague Agreement Concerning the International Deposit of Industrial Designs. This treaty is also administered by WIPO. By depositing the design with WIPO or one of the member countries to the agreement, it can then be protected in other member countries without further application.[11]

International Protection of Internet Domain Names. Responsibility for the assignment and recording of international domain names rests with the Internet Corporation for Assigned Names and Numbers (ICANN). Domain names represent a new form of intellectual property that some feel is just as important to protect as trademarks. Domain names are tied closely to the company name and often the trademark and brand name as well. ICANN assigns domain names within what are called the generic top-level domains (gTLDs). Until quite recently these included ".com," ".net," ".org," ".edu," and ".gov." Several new gTLDs have been approved and came into effect during 2001. The new ones are ".aero," ".biz," ".coop," ".info," ".museum," ".name," and ".pro."[12] This proliferation of domain extensions may make it even more difficult for a company and brand to distinguish itself. Rather, the resulting dilution of identity may harm many of the more well-known brand names. Would you know if you had reached the desired location if you had to choose among "virgin.com," "virgin.aero," "virgin.org," and "virgin.biz"?

The reason that domain names have the same import as other forms of intellectual property is that they identify a company and product to the customer. There is value that has already been established for particular corporate names and/or brands and, therefore, there is residual value associated with certain domain names. This is increasingly true as the Internet becomes the primary means of communicating with customers and selling one's products and services. If I am McDonald's (of Ronald McDonald fame), and someone else comes along and registers the domain name "mcdonalds.com" before I do, I believe I have a valid concern and complaint. This is particularly true if the registrant has no particular connection to the McDonald's name and is simply trying to benefit from the value I have created in the name. This is every much as unfair as registering a popular trademark in another country before the legitimate trademark-holder has done so. However, according to common law, a company can sometimes own a trademark through use, even if it has not registered it. The same is not true for domain names, which instead are allocated on a first-come basis.

Previously, we mentioned various approaches to international dispute resolution. These included mediation and arbitration. Appropriately, at the end of 1999, WIPO started an Arbitration and Mediation Center for resolving disputes involving the registration and use of domain names. The service adheres to the ICANN policy of preventing the bad-faith registration and use of domain names associated with legitimate holders of trademark rights. The process begins when a complaint is filed. The respondent then has 20 days to file a response. At the end of that period, the WIPO Center appoints a panel (which might be a single arbitrator)

◑ FOCUS 13.2 ◑

THE TRADE-RELATED ASPECTS OF
INTELLECTUAL PROPERTY (TRIPS) AGREEMENT

The TRIPS Agreement was negotiated in the Uruguay Round of negotiations under the old GATT. These negotiations were finally concluded in 1994. GATT has now been replaced by the WTO. TRIPS has attempted to bring some standardization to the way in which intellectual property is protected around the world. Perhaps more importantly, when there are disputes involving intellectual property, the dispute settlement system of the WTO is available. The dispute settlement system is one of the major differences (and improvements) between the former GATT and the new WTO. The TRIPS Agreement covers all the types of intellectual property that have been discussed above.

The basic principle underlying TRIPS is that of nondiscrimination, which is also true of the WTO as an organization. The principle of nondiscrimination takes two forms. The first is what is usually referred to as "national treatment." This means that a country will treat foreign nationals the same way it treats its own citizens. The second form of nondiscrimination was originally called "most favored nation treatment," or MFN. It means that each WTO member must be treated in the same manner. In other words, more favorable treatment cannot be given to one member country than to another. Currently the more popular term for this is "normal trade relations." Therefore, national treatment assures nondiscriminatory behavior internally among nationals and nonnationals, while most favored nation treatment provides external nondiscrimination among nationals of all other member countries. The latter does not automatically apply to nonmember countries, though a country can still choose to provide MFN status to a non-member country (as the United States did annually with China before China became a WTO member).

The TRIPS Agreement establishes some minimum standards that all signatories agree to provide in the way of protecting IPRs. In many cases, they used the standards under the existing Paris and Berne Conventions. In other cases, they created new or higher standards. For example, in the area of copyrights, TRIPS specifically includes software as a literary work. Databases are also covered. The agreement also deals with rental rights, prohibiting someone from commercially renting someone else's works to the public without approval; this applies to computer programs, recordings, and films. Furthermore, the rights of performers of copyrighted works are also protected. Thus, the unauthorized recording, reproduction, or broadcast of someone's live performance is prohibited.

In the area of trademarks, service marks are protected as well as those for goods. Well-known marks (in a particular country) have even greater protection under TRIPS.

TRIPS also includes geographical indications under its protective wing, particularly for those related to wines and spirits. Industrial designs, including integrated circuit designs, must be protected for at least 10 years. Patent protection (for both products and processes) must be protected for at least 20 years. However, if someone has a patent for a product but is not using it or making it available to particular markets, then TRIPS allows governments to issue "compulsory licenses" to competitors so that the health and/or welfare of the society is benefited.

The TRIPS Agreement also covers the enforcement of rights at length. It requires governments to assure that the rights can be protected under their national laws. Penalties should be tough enough to deter infringement. The process should be fair and equitable but not costly or complicated. Willful counterfeiting or piracy is to be considered a felony, and the government has the right to seize, and destroy or dispose of, counterfeit goods. It also stipulates that right holders should be able to obtain assistance from national customs authorities to prevent the importation of counterfeit or pirated goods.

The TRIPS Agreement came into force at the beginning of 1995. Developed countries had only a year to assure that their laws and practices were in conformance with the agreement. Developing countries generally were given five years, and the least developed countries 11 years, to accomplish compliance. This multilateral agreement should have increasing effectiveness in protecting intellectual property in the international trading arena. Violation of IPRs had become a major obstacle to freer trade and therefore TRIPS is a very important development for the further growth of international trade and the resolution of international conflicts.

to decide the case. The registrar under the auspices of ICANN is then obligated to support the decision by canceling the domain name for the loser and/or transferring the domain name to the winner. The whole process is complete within two months. In its first year (2000), the WIPO Arbitration and Mediation Center received 1,841 cases dealing with 3,200 domain names. Cases were filed at the rate of about one per day at the beginning of the year. By the end of the year, that had increased six-fold. About 70 percent of the cases were resolved, 80 percent in favor of the complainant. The complaints came from 46 countries and the respondents from 72. The WIPO Center is now expanding its services to the area of country code registrations, which is the two-digit alpha code following the gTLD in the Internet address. For example, ".ve" stands for Venezuela and ".ch" for Switzerland.[13] Your "Who Wants to Be a Millionaire" question is "What does the 'ch' stand for?

International Nongovernmental Organizations

In addition to multilateral intergovernmental organizations (IGOs) such as WIPO and WTO, there is also some help from international nongovernmental organizations (INGOs).

One such organization is the Counterfeiting Intelligence Bureau (CIB) that is part of the Commercial Crime Services division of the International Chamber of Commerce (ICC). The CIB was formed in 1985 and was the first private business initiative at the international level to provide real prevention and enforcement support to law enforcement and customs authorities. The Bureau has three component groups:

- *Counterforce* is a link between law firms specializing in issues of intellectual property.
- *Countertech* similarly brings together providers of anticounterfeiting technologies.
- *Countersearch* serves as a focal point for investigators of counterfeit product manufacturing and distribution.

Information provided by specialized investigators is provided to member companies and to local law enforcement officials, thus enabling the arrest of fraudulent producers and distributors. The CIB also provides expert advice and training and operates a Hologram Image Register, thus thwarting attempts to circumvent one of the most popular and effective anticounterfeiting tools. Holograms were discussed in greater detail in Chapter 12.[14]

NATIONAL LAW AND INTELLECTUAL PROPERTY

Currently, there are no international patents or trademarks, and the multilateral agreements previously discussed are often only partially effective. As a result, right holders are often dependent on national laws to enforce their intellectual property rights. Also, some national legal systems are more effective than others.

Responses by the U.S. Government

National governments have taken some steps to counter the illegal activity within their borders. Often this comes as a result of sustained pressure from some of the international institutions previously mentioned, or by particularly influential governments such as the United States. As a major market and trade partner for many countries around the world, the United States has a good deal of clout when it comes to fighting counterfeiting and intellectual property violations in general. Its influence is enhanced by a number of trade-related weapons at its disposal. These include a variety of trade restrictions such as higher tariffs, lower quotas, and the much more punitive option of an economic embargo. Many of these options are written into U.S. law and therefore are taken seriously by countries targeted by the United States. Thus, lobbying the U.S. government, directly or through trade associations, can be an effective tool for protecting oneself from counterfeiters.

Foremost among U.S. statutory trade weapons are the Special 301 provisions of the Trade Act of 1974. Under this statute, the United States Trade Representative (USTR) is charged with annually reviewing the compliance of foreign governments in protecting U.S. intellectual property rights. A country is generally categorized as a "priority foreign country" if the United States has major concerns about its IPR protection. In the 2002 report, Ukraine remained the only country so designated, though China and Paraguay were listed under Section 306. Specifically, the USTR stated in the report:

> USTR notes with disappointment the continued designation of Ukraine as a Priority Foreign Country due to its persistent failure to take action against significant levels of optical media piracy and to implement intellectual property laws that provide adequate and effective protection. As a result, the $75 million worth of sanctions imposed on Ukrainian products on January 23, 2002, remain in place. This continued failure to adequately protect intellectual property rights could also jeopardize Ukraine's efforts to join the World Trade Organization (WTO) and seriously undermine its efforts to attract trade and investment. The U.S. Government continues to remain actively engaged with Ukraine in encouraging the nation to combat piracy and to enact the necessary intellectual property rights legislation and regulations.[15]

This statement indicates a number of very significant sanctions that give credence to threats made by the U.S. government regarding IPR protections.

The Special 301 report also lists countries on the Priority Watch List and the less serious Watch List. Countries so designated know that they must improve their performance in the area of IPR protection or face the real possibility of being designated a priority foreign country. In the 2002 Report, the countries on the Priority Watch List included Argentina, Brazil, Colombia, Dominican Republic, Egypt, the European Union (EU), Hungary, India, Indonesia, Israel, Lebanon, Philippines, Russia, Taiwan, and Uruguay. Those on the Watch List were Armenia, Azerbaijan, Bahamas, Belarus, Bolivia, Canada, Chile, Costa Rica, Greece, Guatemala, Italy, Jamaica, Kazakhstan, Korea, Kuwait, Latvia, Lithuania, Malaysia, New Zealand, Pakistan, Peru, Poland, Qatar, Romania, Saudi Arabia, Slovak Republic, Tajikistan, Thailand, Turkey, Turkmenistan, Uzbekistan, Venezuela, and Vietnam. The sheer length of the list suggests how pervasive the problem is. What is not as clear is the role that political considerations played in categorizing certain countries (e.g., cooperation in the war on terrorism in the aftermath of 9/11).

Recently, a multiagency center called the *National Intellectual Property Rights Coordination Center* was formulated. Core staffing is provided by U.S. Customs and the Federal Bureau of Investigation. It is intended to provide a unified government response to IPR issues and violations. The center will serve as a clearinghouse for collecting and disseminating both domestic and international information related to IPRs. It is also charged with "developing enhanced investigative, intelligence and interdiction capabilities."[16]

In a common law country like the United States, previous court decisions are also important in determining how the courts will deal with intellectual property cases such as trademark infringement. One such case that helps to explain what the courts are looking for in any trademark infringement complaint is *Brookfield Communications vs. West Coast Entertainment Corp.* In this case, an entertainment-industry information provider brought action against a video-rental store chain claiming that the latter had infringed on the trademark "MovieBuff." The United States District Court for the Central District of California denied that there was any trademark infringement. However, the Court of Appeals reversed that decision. The court found that the plaintiff had, in fact, registered the trademark MovieBuff with the Patent and Trademark Office. According to the court, this constituted *prima facie* evidence that the mark was valid and that the plaintiff had the exclusive right to use the mark. What the video-rental chain tried to do was to extend their trademark "The Movie Buff's Movie Store" by creating a domain name called "moviebuff.com."

However, the appeals court found that the plaintiff was indeed the senior user of the mark and that this inclusion in the defendant's website would create the likelihood of confusion to consumers. Furthermore, the appeals court found that a plaintiff is entitled to a preliminary injunction, when it establishes the likelihood of success on its claims. A fundamental principle of trademark law is that "prior use" governs ownership of the mark. The first to use a trademark is considered to be the "senior user." However, being the senior user of a mark in one product line does not automatically mean that one is the senior user when that mark is expanded to a second product line. It depends on whether that expansion is a natural one, for example, in expanding from jewelry to watches or from clothing to shoes. Remember that a major function of a trademark is to help consumers identify the source of a product. Therefore, a determining factor in trademark infringement cases is whether there is the likelihood of confusion for the consumer. That is why we have incorporated this into our Harm Matrix for analyzing various types of piracy and counterfeiting.

In determining whether there has been an infringement of a trademark, the courts will look at a number of different factors. First is the similarity of the marks in question. In this case, the court found that the mark "MovieBuff" was indeed similar to the domain name "moviebuff.com." Second, the court will look at the similarity of the products and services of the companies in question. Also, are the companies involved in the same industry? In this particular case, both companies were seen as being involved in the entertainment industry. The third factor is the strength of the plaintiff's mark. A strong trademark is more likely to be associated with the mark's owner in the mind of the consumer. Thus, strong marks are afforded greater protection so that the consumer will not be deceived. Some trademarks are so strong that they have become generic terms for describing a particular product rather than a particular brand. Examples include "Cellophane," "Scotch tape," and "Kleenex." In this case, the term Movie Buff would probably be classified as a "suggestive" mark since it generally conveys some impression of the related product or service. A fourth factor that might be considered in trademark infringement cases would be the marketing channels used by the disputants. In this case, both companies used the Internet as a marketing channel, and the defendant had incorporated the trademark name into its website. Fifth, it is important to consider the care that will be exercised by the consumer when purchasing goods. In trademark infringement cases, it is not necessary that there be an intent to confuse consumers. It is assumed that the consumers will be more discerning when purchasing expensive items that are marketed to savvy consumers. A sixth factor is the defendant's intent when selecting its mark. Was it intended to more clearly describe the product or service, or was there an apparent attempt to confuse the consumer by way of reference to a similar mark? The seventh factor is whether there is, in fact, confusion on the part of the consumer. And finally, the eighth factor looks at the likelihood of expansion in product lines. Not all these factors will be considered equally in deciding any particular trademark infringement case. Rather, it is the totality of information related to these factors that should lead the courts in their decision.

Steps Taken by Other Governments

Thailand has long been a haven for piracy in Southeast Asia. The U.S. Assistant Secretary of Commerce noted that Thailand alone accounted for $200 million in lost revenue to the U.S. economy.[17] Much of this was in the piracy of U.S. software, videos, and CDs. The Thai government has created an intellectual property court and has also increased raids on violators of intellectual property rights. The European Union even funded a program to help the Association of Southeast Asian Nations (ASEAN) draft laws and improve its members' infrastructures in order to fight counterfeiting and comply with WTO standards.

Probably no country in the world has been more vilified for counterfeiting and piracy than China. Trade groups in the United States have claimed that Western businesses lose $16 billion in sales each year because of these illegal activities in China. Now that China is a member of the WTO, it has vowed to uphold the regulations against these illegal activities. Many feel that China already has sufficient laws on the books but that enforcement of those laws is lacking.

The products being counterfeited are wide ranging. They include Budweiser beer, Gillette razor blades, Marlboro cigarettes, Yamaha motorcycles, Skippy peanut butter, Microsoft software, Rejoice shampoo, Nike shoes, Prada handbags, Kotex feminine products, and many more. Many are true counterfeits, and many are unauthorized products from otherwise legal licensees. No doubt part of the problem has arisen from sharing information with Chinese joint venture partners. For years the only way that companies could enter the market in China was by taking on Chinese joint-venture partners, and Beijing usually required the transfer of production technology to those local partners. Despite the tremendous lure of a market as big as China, some multinationals are now reassessing future investments because of the counterfeiting problem.[18] The fakes have traditionally sold for a fraction of the authentic products. However, as counterfeiters have become more proficient duplicating the packaging, they have been able to blend the fakes with the real products in the normal channels of distribution. In this way, they have been able to capture a much higher proportion of the brand premium for themselves.

Numerous other countries are also starting to respond to pressure and self-interest by getting tougher on counterfeiting. Under new laws in Hungary, counterfeiters can be subject to both criminal and civil sanctions. Jail sentences of up to three years are possible, though the courts favor fines. Counterfeit goods can be destroyed, and the courts can require the defendant to reimburse any profits gained to the plaintiff. Hungarian law is being harmonized with the TRIPS Agreement and with EU regulations as they prepare for entry into the European Union.[19]

In 1998, a group measuring political and economic risk ranked Singapore as the top Asian country in protecting intellectual property rights. This was particularly true for copyright infringements, which tend to be the most infringed IPR worldwide. In 1998, police seized $5.4 million worth of pirated software CDs, which was the largest seizure at that time. In Singapore, courts are not reluctant to impose both fines and jail time. In 1998, a record fine of $1.5 million was imposed on a software pirate. Singapore has a "self-help" system where warrants for seizure are issued after a complaint is initiated by the IPR owner. However, there is a special IPR Warrant Unit for coordination and execution of those search warrants. Singapore is a good example that strong laws and penalties, coupled with efficient enforcement, can make a difference in preventing counterfeiting.[20]

◗ FOCUS 13.3 ◗

WILL WTO MEMBERSHIP IMPROVE CHINA'S PERFORMANCE?

When any country seeks membership in the WTO, its performance in protecting intellectual property will be scrutinized in some detail. When that country is China, it will be "scrutiny squared." This is becoming one of the primary criteria for determining whether a country is capable of becoming a member of the modern global trading system. Since China is so big and its record in protecting IPRs has been so poor, this became a major hurdle in considering its application for membership.

Some have even speculated why the Chinese leadership considered WTO membership to be so important. It wasn't because the economy was stagnating. Chinese foreign trade increased from roughly $20 billion in the late 1970s to $475 billion by 2000. Simultaneously, the country became a major target for foreign investment—now second only to the United States—as well as a major overseas investor in its own right. There will certainly be costs in opening its markets to trade and investment, and yet the Chinese apparently consider the benefits of membership worth the costs (see Focus 7.3 in Chapter 7).

China seems committed to playing by the new rules. Hong Kong, which became the more globally integrated part of China's "one country, two systems" approach in 1997, was already more accustomed to the rules of international trade. Also, many did not realize that days after China's ascension to the WTO was complete, Taiwan (referred to as Chinese Taipei) also became a member. This is interesting since China maintains that Taiwan is part of China, and yet the WTO (with China's concurrence) is treating it as a separate member. This may be beneficial for a couple of reasons. First, by lowering trade barriers between the mainland and Taiwan, cross–strait trade should increase even further. By 1999, Taiwan already sent a quarter of its exports to the mainland, as well as over 40 percent of its foreign investment. Further integration of the two economies can only be positive for them and for the world economy. Second, mainland China will not want to come off looking like a less reliable global partner than Taiwan. The cross–strait competition should be a plus.

Before, there were no rules that applied to China; now there are. China is on record as accepting new responsibilities under those rules. That includes full compliance with the TRIPS Agreement. China is also subject to the WTO sanctions that could result from unfavorable WTO findings. Compliance will not be immediate (nothing in China ever is), but gradually China will develop the legal and enforcement infrastructure that should drastically improve its IPR record. As China develops more of its own brands and intellectual property, it will have an even greater incentive to play by the rules. Economic development also will reduce the importance of counterfeiting to depressed rural areas. Finally, the threat of declining foreign investment and lost tax revenues to the government (estimated to be over $2 billion) will be further incentives to reduce the counterfeiting problem. The outlook is hopeful that WTO membership will help China improve its performance in the protection of intellectual property rights!

That said, the IACC, which speaks for roughly 150 corporations and trade associations, contends that the criminal enforcement system in China is still failing to provide effective protection of intellectual property. The group notes that China remains the primary source of counterfeit goods. Seizure of Chinese counterfeits by U.S. Customs has been greater than from any other country in five of the last six years. This demonstrates that the harm is not within the Chinese market alone, though that is substantial, but rather from the exports of counterfeits to markets all over the world. Can China become a responsible participant in the global trading community? Only time will tell.

Latvia passed a new trademark law in 1999, also in an attempt to begin harmonizing their laws with those of the European Union, which it hopes to join soon. Not many counterfeit goods are actually produced in Latvia, though the country is becoming a distribution center by importing counterfeit goods and then exporting them to other countries. There is also a substantial gray market problem in Latvia, where legitimate goods and counterfeit goods get commingled. There are fairly rigorous procedures for seizing suspected counterfeits upon complaint from the legitimate trade mark holder. However, if the seized shipment does not contain any illegal products, then the trademark owner must pay storage costs for the detained shipment and also pay compensatory damages to other parties who were damaged by the detention of the goods. This is a valid provision that makes it more important for the mark owner to have accurate information so as to prevent a volley of frivolous detentions.[21]

Mexican law has a similar provision where the complainant must post a bond in order to compensate for damages where no illegal goods are found. In 1994, Mexico created the Mexican Institute of Industrial Property (IMPI) to address the counterfeiting problem and to comply with NAFTA regulations. The jurisdiction of IMPI is broad, covering violations of trademarks, trade names, slogans, industrial and circuit layout designs, copyrighted goods, patents, and appellations of origin. The law regarding copyright violations includes several steps that take advantage of alternative dispute resolution procedures such as mediation and arbitration, that were discussed earlier in this chapter.[22] Nevertheless, a 1998 expose in *Authentication News* described Mexico as one of the largest pirate markets in the world. While IMPI was making efforts at control, Mexico had evolved from "counterfeit importer, to counterfeit producer for domestic consumption, to counterfeit exporter, over the past ten years."[23] The abuse was widespread, encompassing clothing, digital media, pharmaceuticals, beverages, personal care products, software, footwear, and books.

A 1999 article in *Managing Intellectual Property* was quite blunt in describing the situation in Romania at that time:

> *We believe Romania is among the top of the central and eastern European countries regarding trade in counterfeit products. From wheat and maize hybrids to alcoholic beverages, cosmetics or medicines, counterfeit products have the dominant sales figures. It is practically impossible for the Romanian consumer to be certain that the product he purchases is original and will satisfy his demands.*[24]

The Romanian situation is instructive by demonstrating the importance of effective legislation and enforcement capabilities. These do make a difference. Organized networks of counterfeiters and other organized criminal elements are quick to find countries where these critical elements are missing or ineffectual. Because of Romania's weak customs code, counterfeit products are easily imported into the country. Trademark counterfeiting and product counterfeiting are distinctly separate violations. The intention of the violator of a trademark must be proven and criminal proceedings are slow and ineffectual. However, there are laws on the books, and Romania is in need of training as to how to make them more effective.

In Japan, it is sometimes difficult to get Customs to even begin verification of suspect goods unless they are quite confident that the goods are actually infringing upon the rights of legitimate producers. Therefore, it is critical that right holders maintain current information, and that they be prepared to document for customs officials exactly how to tell real products from fake ones. Customs officials are reluctant to determine that a mark is "similar" to an authentic one; for example, variations in fonts or spelling of names may be enough to make Customs indecisive. Furthermore, Japanese law does not block "parallel imports" from authorized licensees, even when they are in violation of the licensing agreement.[25]

The Republic of South Africa affirmed a new Counterfeit Goods Act in 1997. Like many other countries we have discussed, the infringed party must make an application to the Commissioner for Customs and Excise, along with providing an example of the protected good and information about the protected right. Again, the party claiming infringement must guarantee to bear the costs of detentions that do not find infringing goods. However, when illegal goods are found, then the party bringing the complaint can obtain the counterfeit goods and get reimbursed for related costs of bringing the complaint.[26]

There is a thriving pharmaceutical industry in India that specializes in producing generic equivalents of some of the most popular drugs in the world. One company, Cipla Ltd., produces over 400 different drugs, many of them knockoffs of more well-known brands. These include Erecto, a knockoff of Viagra, and Nuzac, a knockoff of the popular drug Prozac. These drugs are sold by the Indian company for anywhere from one-twentieth to one-fiftieth of the selling price for the well-known brand in the United States. Needless to say, the big pharmaceutical companies like Pfizer and GlaxoSmithKline consider the Indian companies to be pirating their intellectual property for profit. It is true that the Indian companies are profitable. The annual turnover for Cipla is about $200 million. However, if the Indian companies sold their generic drugs for the price that the brands sell for in the United States, their turnover would be $4 billion (20 times more).

This certainly seems like a blatant example of piracy, and yet what the Indian companies are doing is perfectly within the law—Indian law, that is. Frederick Scherer, an emeritus professor of public policy at Harvard's Kennedy School, is on record stating that "what they're doing is perfectly legitimate, until 2005, under the Paris Convention and the Uruguay Round of trade talks" that set up the World Trade Organization. The new WTO Treaty recognizes 20-year patents for most inventions, but countries have until 2005 to bring national law into conformance with the multilateral treaty. Furthermore, the Indian Patents Act of 1970 does not recognize Western-style intellectual property rights on chemicals for medicine or agriculture. That same law recognizes "process patents" rather than "product patents" for pharmaceuticals. This means if someone can find a different process for combining ingredients into an identical molecule, then the resulting product can be legitimately sold.

Some Western pharmaceutical manufacturers contend that as much as 10 percent of the $400 billion worldwide pharmaceutical market is being lost to this kind of piracy. However, others suggest that few sales would be made in many of the poorer developing markets at the prices being charged in developed countries. Noting that some Western drug companies had cut the prices of AIDS medicines by 80 percent, the Indian Minister of Health said, "If they can offer an 80 percent discount, there was something wrong with the price they started off with." The prices of drugs in India have gone from among the highest in the world to the lowest, a fact that some have said explains the significant increase in the average life expectancy in that country. The President of Research for Ranbaxy (another Indian generic drug manufacturer) notes that it makes generic Zantac for $50 per kilo. Under the GlaxoSmithKline patent, the price was $9,000 per kilo. Understandably, it is hard for the average consumer to believe that such large mark-ups are necessary to recoup past R&D expenditures and stimulate ongoing research and development.

There are more than 20,000 drug companies in India, and not all of them are making safe generic equivalents. Some low-quality fakes indeed present a threat to those who consume them. Nevertheless, not all producers should be painted with the same brush. As a signatory to TRIPS, India has committed to bringing national law into conformance with the international agreement by 2005. However, even under TRIPS, there are circumstances for legitimately voiding product patents. One such circumstance is failure of the patent holder to work the patent. This may include failure to make or import the product, or even failure to sell it at a price that the average citizen can afford. This may help to keep drug prices low. Generic manufacturers in India have already demonstrated that they can produce an equivalent product at a fraction of the cost in a country where the average expenditure per year on drugs is $3.50.[27]

These various examples suggest that many countries are becoming aware of the counterfeiting problem and are enacting more effective legislation and enforcement capabilities. We started this chapter with a discussion of multilateral institutions. The examples discussed also suggest that various multilateral arrangements have been instrumental in bringing pressure for reform. Countries that either have become or are hoping to become members of regional organizations (e.g., NAFTA or the EU) or international organizations (e.g., WTO) find that they must make legislative and enforcement changes in order to be in compliance with the regulations of these communities. As both regional and international arrangements continue to increase, we can be optimistic that they will bring increasing effectiveness in the war on counterfeits.

PART FIVE

Conclusion

T his book has endeavored to show that the counterfeiting of products is a real and growing problem for brand owners and consumers worldwide. The problem transcends the generally held views that counterfeiting is a victimless crime or that only high-priced luxury goods are involved. Modern industrial-product counterfeiting is a threat not only to companies wishing to preserve brand equity but also to consumers and users of products as well as investors, employees, distributors, governments, and law enforcement authorities. In their most pernicious form, counterfeits have caused deaths. The linkage of counterfeiting with terrorists and organized criminals provides companies and consumers with an additional reason to take the threat seriously.

There are means and methods by which companies can protect themselves, their products, and their customers from product counterfeiting. For any company to avail itself of these solutions, it will have to commit senior management time and attention to the issue, and understand the complexity, cost, and nature of the solutions. Many companies have found these solutions to be extremely cost-effective and have minimized the cost of counterfeiting by using them. As counterfeiting continues to grow as a problem, companies that care about their brands and their customers will have to address this issue or face the consequences in the open market.

Notes

CHAPTER 1

1. Editorial Staff Report. "Bogus Parts—Detecting the Hidden Threat." *Flight Safety Foundation Flight Safety Digest,* Jan.–Feb. 1994, pp. 1–30. See also Willy Stern. "Warning! Bogus Parts Have Turned Up in Commercial Jets. Where's the FAA?" *Business Week,* June 10, 1996. See also "Father and Son Plead Guilty in Scheme to Fabricate Helicopter Rotor Blades That Were Not Airworthy; One Set of Blades Led to Crash That Killed Two," USAO/CDCA Press Release dated October 30, 2000, available at *www.usdoj.gov/usao/cac/pr/pr2000/192.htm.*

2. World Health Organization. "Prevention of Counterfeit Drugs: Working Together for Safe Drugs." Counterfeit Drugs Action Sheet, November 14, 2002. See *www.who. int/medicines/organization/gsm/activities/qualityassurance/counterfeit/counterfeit_info_ facts.shtml.*

3. Andy Newman. "DVD Counterfeiting Arrests Called Largest Case." *The New York Times,* January 12, 2002. Available at *www.nytimes.com.*

4. Michael Dorgan. "China Leads in Counterfeiting." *Knight Ridder News Service,* January 11, 2001.

5. International Chamber of Commerce, Counterfeiting Intelligence Bureau. *Countering Counterfeiting.* Paris, France: ICC Publishing SA, 1997. See also The Organization for Economic Co-operation and Development, *The Economic Impact of Counterfeiting.* Paris, France: OECD, 1998.

6. International Trademark Association. "The Economic Impact of Trademark Counterfeiting and Infringement on Worldwide Sales of Apparel and Footwear," April 1998; Confidential Bulletin to Members, International Chamber of Commerce Counterfeiting Intelligence Bureau, November 2000, no. 11, p. 7.

7. "GM's Strategic Enforcement to Fight Counterfeiters." *Authentication News,* vol. 2, no. 6, Dec. 1996, pp. 3–4. See also Peter Lowe. "Criminal Attacks—Anatomy of Crime." International Chamber of Commerce Counterfeiting Intelligence Bureau.

8. "Pharmaceutical Counterfeiting: Fears into Facts." *Authentication News,* vol. 8, no. 7, Oct. 2002, p. 1.

9. IFPI. IFPI Music Piracy Report, June 2002. Available at *www.ifpi.org.* Seventh Annual Business Software Alliance Global Software Piracy Study, June 2002, p. 2. Available at *www.bsa.org.*

10. World Trade Organization 2001 Annual Report.

11. International Monetary Fund Staff. "Globalization: Threat or Opportunity?" April 12, 2002, Available at *www.imf.org/external/np/ib/2000/041200htm*.

12. Peter Lowe. "Criminal Attacks—Anatomy of Crime." International Chamber of Commerce Counterfeiting Intelligence Bureau.

13. Ibid. See also discussion in Chapter 8.

14. Ibid.

CHAPTER 2

1. "Cooking Martha's Goose." *The Economist,* September 12, 2002.

2. Thorsten H. Nilson. *Competitive Branding.* Hoboken, NJ: John Wiley & Sons, 1996, p. 57.

3. "The World's Most Valuable Brands 2000." See Interbrand website: *www.brand channel.com/interbrand/test/html/event/mvb_99_and_00.pdf* (accessed January 8, 2001).

4. Nilson, "Competitive Branding," p. 63.

5. Nilson, "Competitive Branding," p. 52.

6. Vauhini Vara. "Samsonite Hopes to Bag More Sales with Point A." *The Denver Post,* July 16, 2002, p. C1.

7. Naomi Klein. *No Logo.* New York: Picador, 1999, p. 24

8. "Who's Wearing the Trousers?" *The Economist,* September 6, 2001. See also *www. strangelove.com/articles/Who's%20wearing%20the%20trousers.html*.

9. Ron Irwin. "Can Branding Save the World?" April 8, 2002; *www.brandchannel.com*.

10. Ibid.

11. "Oprah Talks to Ralph Lauren." *The Oprah Magazine,* October 2002, p. 221.

12. "Biography: Ralph Lauren." *www.askmen.com/men/business_politics/30c_ralph_lauren. html* (accessed September 18, 2002).

13. "Polo Ralph Lauren Outfits OneWorld Challenge America's Cup Team." *PR Newswire,* May 2, 2002.

14. "Valuing Intellectual Property and Calculating Infringement Damages." *Consulting Services Practice Aid 99-2,* American Institute of Certified Public Accountants, 1999.

15. James P. O'Shaughnessy and Patrick H. Sullivan. "The Role of Intellectual Capital in Valuing Knowledge Companies," Article 21 in *Profiting from Intellectual Capital.* Hoboken, NJ: John Wiley & Sons, 1998.

16. Neil Gross. "Commentary: Valuing 'Intangibles' Is a Tough Job, but It Has To Be Done." Cover Story, *Business Week,* August 6, 2001, pp. 54−55.

17. "The 100 Top Brands." *BusinessWeek Online,* August 6, 2001. See *www.businessweek. com/magazine/content/01_32/b3744010.htm*.

18. "The 100 Top Brands." *BusinessWeek Online,* August 5, 2002. See *www.businessweek. com/magazine/content/02_31/b3794037.htm*.

19. Nicholas Kochan (editor). *The World's Greatest Brands.* New York: New York University Press, 1997.

20. Tracie Rozhon. "Dropping Logos That Shout, Luxury Sellers Try Whispers." *www. nytimes.com,* September 15, 2002.

CHAPTER 3

1. Robin Fields. "He Gets Paid to Chase Down the Product Counterfeiters." *Los Angeles Times,* Orange County Record Edition, June 9, 1999, p. 1.

2. Lynn Smith. "Faking It in the Fashion World." *Los Angeles Times,* March 19, 2000, p. E1.

3. Karl Greenfeld and Aixa Pascual. "Battle Deluxe." *Time,* vol. 155, no. 18, May 1, 2000, p. 48.

4. Mark Johnson. "And the Winner Is . . . ." *Global Finance,* vol. 15, no. 11, October 2001, p. 12.

5. "Facing the Music." *The Economist,* vol. 362, no. 8261, February 23, 2002, p. 69.

6. Sara Gay Forden. "Unmask Late Gucci Head's Mystery Financier." *Daily News Record,* vol. 25, no. 217, November 14, 1995, p. 4 (1).

7. "Gucci Fined $162K for Copying LVMH." *Women's Wear Daily,* January 31, 2001, p. 13.

8. Loretta Prencipe. "ISP's Trademark Liability." *InfoWorld,* vol. 23, no. 23, June 4, 2001, p. 62.

9. Smith, "Faking It," p. E1.

10. Ruth La Ferla. "NOTICED; Fakes Now Dangle on Arms That Once Sported Brand Names." *The New York Times* on the Web, July 9, 2000, *www.nytimes.com.*

11. *Why You Should Care About Counterfeiting: The Costs and Dangers of Buying Fake Products.* Market Opinion and Research International, 1997.

12. Ibid.

13. Rebecca Quick and Ken Bensinger. "Sleaze E-Commerce: The Internet Has Become Designer Labels' Worst Enemy." *The Wall Street Journal,* May 14, 1999, p. W1.

14. Ibid.

15. Richard Boudreaux. "In Italy, It's Survival of the Fakest." *Los Angeles Times,* October 6, 2000, p. E1.

16. The Anti-Counterfeiting Group (ACG). *The Menace of Counterfeiting.* Reprinted 1999.

17. Benjamin Jones. "Winemakers in Spain Take Protective Steps." *The New York Times* on the Web, November 24, 2000, *www.nytimes.com.*

18. Jason Vest. "Psst! Want Cheap Cubans?" *U.S. News & World Report,* vol. 122, April 14, 1997, pp. 63–64.

19. "A Churchill, or Factory-floor Sweepings." *The Economist,* March 13, 1997; *www.classified.economist.com/PrinterFriendly.cfm?Story_ID=145521* (accessed August 9, 2002).

20. Jeff Barnard. "Branding Beef—For Profit." *The Denver Post,* November 5, 2000, p. L8.

21. Manuel Ramos. "Counterfeit Coffee Scheme Lands Man Behind Bars." *The 5 Pix Page,* CBS Worldwide, Inc., December 5, 2001.

22. "Paul Mitchell Wages War on Makers of Fake Products." *The Chicago Tribune,* Chicagoland Final Edition, June 13, 1999, p. 12.

23. Presentation by Walter N. Clemens, Associate Director, Global Security Services, Procter & Gamble, Inc., International Anti-Counterfeiting Coalition Conference, Napa, California, May 2–4, 2001.

24. Ibid.

25. Mike Eisenbath. "Fake Sports Memorabilia Is a Sign of the Times." *St. Louis Post-Dispatch,* April 30, 2000, p. F11.

26. Toni Jones. "CeleBritney: Can This Brand Last?" *Forbes.com,* July 3, 2002.

27. "Customs Officers Seize Counterfeit Designer Sports and Leisurewear." Irish Revenue Department website, December 21, 1999. *www.revenue.ie/wnew/press/cfeit.htm* (accessed January 29, 2003).

28. Gerry Khermouch. "The Best Global Brands." *Business Week Online,* August 6, 2001.

29. Leslie Gevirtz. "Gillette Says Counterfeiting, Currencies Cut Bottom Line." *Reuters Limited,* December 18, 2000.

30. William Green and Katherine Bruce. "Riskless Crime?" *Forbes,* August 11, 1997, pp. 101–102.

31. Peter G. Chronis. "Store's Luggage Nice—But Fake." *The Denver Post,* January 4, 1990.

32. Greene and Bruce, "Riskless Crime," pp. 100–102.

33. Calum MacLeod. "A Powerful Faux: China's Drowning in Pool of Counterfeits." *China Online,* July 13, 2000.

34. Ibid.

35. Dexter Roberts in Yiwu, with Frederik Balfour in Hong Kong, Paul Magnusson in Washington, Pete Engardio in New York, Jennifer Lee in Los Angeles. "China's Pirates." *Business Week,* June 5, 2000, p. 26.

36. Steve Berry. "Probes of False Designer Labels Raise Questions." *Los Angeles Times,* May 6, 1999, p. 1.

37. Ibid.

38. Paul Paradise. "Trademark Counterfeiting in the Garment Industry." *Authentication News,* vol. 6, no. 3, May 2000, p. 1.

39. Boudreaux, "In Italy," p. E1.

40. Beth Frerking. "Samsonite Loses Luggage Copycat Case." *The Denver Post,* November 26, 1987, p. D1.

CHAPTER 4

1. 21 U.S.C. § 321(g)(2).

2. "Biotech Fakes in USA as Congressional Hearings Resume." *Authentication News,* vol. 7, no. 3, May 2001, pp. 1, 5.

3. "Pharmaceutical Anticounterfeiting: Legal Developments." *Authentication News,* vol. 8, no. 1, February 2002, p. 6. See *www.AuthenticationNews.Info.*

4. *Lynn v. Serono,* San Diego Superior Ct. (Case No. 761598).

5. Testimony of William Hubbard, Sr. Associate Commissioner, U.S. Food and Drug Administration before the House Committee on Energy and Commerce,

Examining Prescription Drug Reimportation, July 25, 2002, p. 11. See *www. pharma-anticounterfeiting.info; updates; hearings.*

6. "Pharmaceutical Counterfeiting Issues Come to the Fore." *Authentication News,* vol. 7, no. 5, July 2001, pp. 1, 3.

7. *The Lancet,* no. 9272, June 16, 2001, p. 357.

8. Ibid.

9. "Counterfeit Drugs Issue Emerges in the U.S." *Authentication News,* vol. 6, no. 5, July 2000, pp. 1–2.

10. Ibid.

11. Ibid.

12. "WHO Identifies Counterfeit Pharmaceuticals as a Growing and Dangerous Problem." *Authentication News,* vol. 3, no. 8, Dec. 1997, pp. 7–8.

13. World Health Organization Press Release. See *www.who.int/inf-pr2000/en/pr2000-WHA02.html,* May 17, 2000.

14. "U.S. Food & Drug Administration Anticounterfeiting Project Begins." *Authentication News,* vol. 8, no. 7, Oct. 2002, p. 3. See *www.productsurety.org.*

15. "Pharmaceutical Diversion in the U.S." *Authentication News,* vol. 7, no. 7, Oct. 2001, pp. 8, 10.

16. "Significant Amounts of Procrit Counterfeited in U.S." *Authentication News,* vol. 8, no. 5, June 2000, p. 10.

17. "FDA Issues Four Counterfeit Drug Alerts." *Authentication News,* vol. 8, no. 4, May 2002, p. 6.

18. Ibid.

19. Ibid.

20. *United States v. Bindley Western,* U.S. Dist. Ct. Nevada (Case no. CRS00268-kdj).

21. Hubbard, "Testimony," p. 11.

22 Ibid.

23. U.S. International Trade Commission. *Pricing of Prescription Drugs* (Investigation No. 332-419, Pub. No. 3333).

24. "Pharmaceutical Pricing and Distribution Drive Debate." *Authentication News,* vol. 8, no. 6, Aug. 2002, p. 5.

25. Ibid.

26. UNAIDS in the "Report on the Global HIV/AIDS Epidemic June 2000." See *www.unaids.org.*

27. Ibid.

28. Ibid.

29. "Pharmaceutical Counterfeiting: Fears into Fact." *Authentication News,* vol. 8, no. 7, Oct. 2002, pp. 1, 3.

30. "HIV Drugs for Africa Diverted to Europe: Probe Targets Wholesalers." *The Washington Post,* October 2, 2002, p. A10; *www.washingtonpost.com/wp-dyn/articles/A35216-2002Oct2.html.*

31. "Terrorist Links to Diversion and Counterfeiting." *Authentication News,* vol. 7, no. 7, Oct, 2001, p. 9.

32. "Hologram Successes Reported at IACC." *Holography News,* vol. 13, no. 7, Oct. 1999, p. 7; *www.holographynews.info.*

33. *Authentication News,* "Counterfeit Drugs."

34. *Authentication News,* "Pharmaceutical Counterfeiting."

35. *Authentication News,* "Counterfeit Drugs."

36. Arthur Best. "Manufacturers' Responsibility for Harms Suffered by Victims of Counterfeits." *Currents in International Trade Law Journal,* vol. VIII, no. 1, Summer 1999, pp. 43, 49.

37. Dr. Nick Firrell. "Case Study: Bitter Medicine for the Counterfeiter—Zantac." *Protecting Medicines & Pharmaceuticals: A Manual of AntiCounterfeiting Solutions,* edited by Magali LeParc, Greenwood Village, CO: Reconnaissance International. See *www.pharma-anticounterfeiting.info.*

38. Ibid.

CHAPTER 5

1. Editorial Staff Report. "Bogus Parts—Detecting the Hidden Threat." *Flight Safety Foundation Flight Safety Digest,* Jan., Feb. 1994, pp. 1–30.

2. "Counterfeit Aviation Parts Ring Busted in Italy." *Authentication News,* vol. 8, no. 1, Feb. 2002, pp. 1, 7; *www.AuthenticationNews.Info.*

3. Mary Schiavo. *Flying Blind, Flying Safe.* New York: Avon, April 1998.

4. Paul Paradise. "Counterfeit Airplane Parts and Unfinished Issue." *Authentication News,* vol. 5, no. 8/9, Nov./Dec. 1999, pp. 10–11.

5. "Bell Fights Helicopter Remanufacturing Backed by Dataplates." *Authentication News,* vol. 6, no. 2, April 2000, p. 3.

6. "NEC Combats Fake Printer Ribbons." *Authentication News,* vol. 2, no. 5, Oct. 1996, p. 10.

7. "NEC Combats Fakes with Holograms, Investigates Other Systems." *Holography News,* vol. 10, no. 4, Sept. 1996, p. 5.

8. Paul Paradise. "Imaging Supplies Coalition Develops." *Authentication News,* vol. 5, no. 8, Nov. 1999, p. 6.

9. "ISC Reports Tripling of 'When in Doubt' Usage." *Authentication News,* vol 6, no. 9, Dec. 2000, p. 6.

10. "GM's Strategic Enforcement to Fight Counterfeiters." *Authentication News,* vol. 2, no. 6, Dec. 1996, pp. 3–4.

11. Comments by John Crux, T&N, Ltd., at *Product Counterfeiting Protection,* June 20, 1996, Copthorne Tara Hotel, London, UK (Contact: Reconnaissance International, *www.Reconnaissance-Intl.com*).

12. Comments by Beate Lauk-Menzel, Daimler Chrysler, at *Authentication: Counterfeiting Protection,* January 31, 2002, Hyatt Renaissance, Atlanta, GA (Contact: Reconnaissance International, *www.Reconnaissance-Intl.com.*).

13. "A Systems Approach to the Counterfeiting Problem, Genuine or Bogus: How Can You Tell?" *Standardization News.* American Society for Testing Materials (ASTM). April 1990, p. 38.

14. Commission of the European Communities. "Followup on the Green Paper on Combatting Counterfeiting and Piracy in the Single Market." Brussels, Nov. 30, 2000, COM (2000) 789 Final.

15. Todd Zuan. "Motorcycle Knockoffs Rumbling Through China." *Pittsburgh Post-Gazette,* July 29, 2001, p. A6.

16. Ibid.

17. Ibid.

18. *Authentication News,* "GM's Strategic Enforcement."

19. Ibid.

20. "Ford Parts Success Story." *Authentication News,* vol. 3, no. 3, May 1997, pp. 4−5.

21. "Auto Industry Alliance to Stop Parts Counterfeiting." *Authentication News,* vol. 7, no. 7, Oct. 2001, pp. 1−2.

22. "Sunoco Tests for Illegal Fuel Additives." *Authentication News,* vol. 8, no. 6, Aug. 2002, p. 10.

23. "Fuels Identification Project Reclaims $100M in Tax Revenue." *Authentication News,* vol. 8, no. 2, April 2002, p. 10.

24. Ibid.

25. "UL & Customs Pull Plug on Counterfeit Electrical Products." *Authentication News,* vol. 5, no. 1, Feb. 1999, p. 1.

26. Ibid.

27. Ibid.

28. Ibid.

29. "Global AntiCounterfeiting Awards Announced." *Authentication News,* vol. 6, no. 1, March 2000, p. 10.

CHAPTER 6

1. "Phonies Galore." *The Economist,* November 8, 2001; *www.classified.economist.com/PrinterFriendly.cfm?Story_ID=853362* (accessed August 9, 2002).

2. Caroline Jenkins. "New Protection Against Online Pirates." *Folio,* September 1, 2000, p. 5.

3. Geoffrey James. "Organized Crime and the Software Biz." *MC Technology Marketing Intelligence,* New York: January 2000, vol. 20, no. 1, pp. 40−44.

4. "Microsoft Moves to Combat Software Piracy in State with the Nation's Highest Piracy Rate." *M2 PressWIRE,* Reuters Business Briefing, February 2, 2000.

5. P.J. Huffstutter, Tini Tran, and David Reyes. "Pirates of the High-Tech Age." *Los Angeles Times,* July 25, 1999, Home Edition, p. 1.

6. James, "Organized Crime."

7. Stephen Baker and Inka Resch. "Piracy!" *Business Week,* July 26, 1999, p. 90.

8. P.J. Huffstutter, Tini Tran, and David Reyes. "Pirates of the High-Tech Age." *Los Angeles Times,* July 25, 1999, Record Edition, p. 1.

9. Jean-Louis Clement and Marina Cohen. "Fake Paintings." *Special Issue: Counterfeiting,* INTERPOL, Lyon, France, International Criminal Police Review, no. 476–477, 1999, pp. 29–33.

10. Philippe Bensimon. "Faked Paintings and the Media." *Special Issue: Counterfeiting,* International Criminal Police Review, INTERPOL, Lyon, France, No. 476–477, 1999, pp. 34–40.

11. Anthony Ramirez. "Manhattan: CD Counterfeiters." *The New York Times* on the Web, Metro Briefing, March 6, 2001; *www.nytimes.qpass.com* (accessed May 22, 2001).

12. Jon Healey and P.J. Huffstutter. "Napster Must Block Songs." *The Denver Post,* March 7, 2001, p. A3.

13. Holman Jenkins, Jr. "How to Survive a Post-Napster Copyright Holocaust." *The Wall Street Journal,* September 6, 2000, Eastern Edition, p. A27.

14. Amy Harmon. "Grudgingly, Music Labels Sell Their Songs Online." *www.nytimes. com,* July 1, 2002.

15. Ibid.

16. Andy Newman. "DVD Counterfeiting Arrests Called Largest Case of Its Kind." *The New York Times* on the Web, January 12, 2002; *www.query.nytimes.com* (accessed June 30, 2002).

17. Ibid.

18. Steve Wilson. "The Pirating Menace." *The Denver Post,* September 6, 1999, p. E7.

19. Elizabeth Rosenthal. "Counterfeiters Turn Magic Into Cash." *The New York Times,* International Section, November 25, 2001, p. A10.

20. Dan Luzadder. "Film Editing Firm Friendly to Families." *The Denver Post,* September 3, 2002, p. C1.

21. "China Shuts Down Large Producer of Pirated VCDs." *AP Worldstream* via COMTEX, August 9, 2000.

22. Kevin Williams. "Lawsuit Targets Scour.com." *Chicago Sun-Times,* August 10, 2000, p. 20.

23. Bob Goodlatte. "Stealing Entertainment." *The Washington Times,* May 27, 2002, p. A21. See also: "Anti-Piracy," The Motion Picture Association; *www.mpaa.org/ anti-piracy/content.htm* (accessed November 11, 2002).

24. "With Beefed Up Budget and Hands-On Approach, AAP Gets Tough on Piracy." *Book Publishing Report,* vol. 26, no. 12, March 19, 2001, p. 1.

25. Matt Forney. "Harry Potter, Meet 'Ha-li Bo-te'." *The Wall Street Journal,* September 21, 2000, Eastern Edition, p. B1.

26. Terry Carter. "The Pen Gains Power." *American Bar Association Journal.* December 2000, vol. 86, pp. 30–31.

27. Ibid.

28. Patti Hartigan. "Fire-Breathing Writer Vows to Fry Net Thieves." *Boston Globe,* August 11, 2000, p. D1.

29. Michael P. Ryan and Justine N. Bednarik. *The U.S.-Korean Dispute Over Intellectual Property Rights.* Case #710, Institute for the Study of Diplomacy, Georgetown University, Washington, D.C., pp. 1–7.

30. Martin Crutsinger. "Bush Administration Threatens Trade Sanctions Against Ukraine." *AP Worldstream* via COMTEX, March 13, 2001.

31. "Digital Millennium Copyright Act Stirs Additional Controversy." *Information Intelligence Online Newsletter.* January 2001, vol. 22, no. 1, p. 6.

32. Andrew Grosso. "The Promise and Problems of the No Electronic Theft Act." Association of Computing Machinery, New York, February 2000, vol. 43, no. 2, pp. 23–26.

33. Harvey Perlman. "Taking the Protection-Access Tradeoff Seriously." *Vanderbilt Law Review,* vol. 53, no. 6, November 2000, pp. 1831–1840.

34. Anna Wilde Matthews and Bruce Orwall. "Industry to Sue People Abetting Net Song Swaps." *The Wall Street Journal,* July 3, 2002, p. B1.

35. Stephen Baker and Inka Resch. "Piracy!" *Business Week,* July 26, 1999, no. 3639, p. 90.

36. Hal Varian. "New Chips Can Keep a Tight Rein on Consumers." *www.nytimes.com,* July 4, 2002.

CHAPTER 7

1. Dexter Roberts, Frederik Balfour, Paul Magnusson, Pete Engardio, and Jennifer Lee. "China's Piracy Plague." *Business Week,* June 5, 2000, p. 44.

2. CACC. "Document Brand Destruction in Case Studies." *Authentication News,* vol. 5, no. 8, December 1999, p. 5.

3. The Business Software Alliance. *The Seventh Annual BSA Global Software Piracy Study.* June 2002; *www.bsa.org.*

4. Bob Goodlatte. "Stealing Entertainment." *The Washington Times,* May 27, 2002, p. A21. See also The Recording Industry Association of America, *www.riaa.org.*

5. International AntiCounterfeiting Coalition. *Get the Facts; www.iacc.org* (accessed January 14, 2003).

6. World Health Organization. "Prevention of Counterfeit Drugs: Working Together for Safe Drugs." Counterfeit Drug Action Sheet, November 14, 2002. See *www.who.int/medicines/organization/gsm/activities/qualityassurance/counterfeit/ counterfeit_info_facts.shtml.*

7. John MacDonald. "Counterfeit Drugs Penetrate Market." *Contra Costa Times,* September 3, 2002; *www.bayarea.com* (accessed October 28, 2002).

8. International Trademark Association. *Estimation of the Impact of Trademark Counterfeiting and Infringement on Worldwide Sales of Apparel and Footwear.* April, 1998.

9. Applied Optical Technologies plc. *OpSec Solutions: Increase Your Royalties.* See *www. appliedopsec.com/opsec/brochures/licensed.htm* (accessed January 14, 2003).

10. Naomi Klein. *No Logo.* New York: Picador, 1999, p. 12.

11. "The 100 Top Brands." *Business Week.* August 5, 2002, p. 95.

12. Arthur Best. "Manufacturers' Responsibility for Harms Suffered by Victims of Counterfeits." *Currents in International Trade Law Journal,* vol. VIII, no. 1, Summer 1999, pp. 43, 49.

13. "Talking Points: Fake Drugs." *The Lancet,* vol. 357, no. 9272, June 16, 2001.

14. Claudio Csillag. "Epidemic of Counterfeit Drugs Causes Concern in Brazil." *The Lancet,* vol. 352, no. 9127, August 15, 1998, p. 553.

15. Bernard Pecoul, Pierre Chirac, Patrice Trouiller, and Jacques Pinel. "Access to Essential Drugs in Poor Countries—A Lost Battle." JAMA, vol. 281, 1999, pp. 361–367.

16. David Ingham. "Fake Auto Parts a Big Problem." The Information and Technology Publishing Company, Ltd., September 3, 2002. See *www.itp.net/news/10310441 0595292.htm.*

17. Philip Willan and Julian Borger. "Used Parts Scam Rocks Airline Industry." The Age Company, Ltd., January 30, 2002. See *www.theage.com.au/news/world/2002/ 01/30/FFXF14EK0XC.html.*

18. The Associated Press. "Plane Parts on Black Market Plague Airline Industry." December 8, 1996; *www.lubbockonline.com/nes/120896/plane.htm* (accessed November 1, 2002).

19. "Counterfeit Alcohol: It Could Cost You More Than a Hangover." Press Release, Issued on behalf of the Anti-Counterfeiting Group by Blueprint Marketing Services Limited, November 19, 1999.

20. J. Dey. "Bad Wine in Old Bottles: Bootleggers Held." *The Indian Express,* April 5, 1998; *www.expressindia.com* (accessed January 31, 2001).

21. International AntiCounterfeiting Coalition. "Hall of Shame." *http.publish.iacc.org/* (accessed January 14, 2003).

22. "Customs Swoop on Tobacco Fraudsters." May 1998; *www.wightonline.co.uk/news/news_ pages/may98/12391.html* (accessed January 18, 2001).

23. The European Commission. "The Commission Adopts a Green Paper on Tackling the Problem of Counterfeiting and Piracy in the Single Market." October 22, 1998; see *www.europa.eu.int/comm/internal_market/en/indprop/piracy/922.htm.*

24. Microsoft. "Piracy—It's Bad Business." See *windowslicensing.msoem.com/english/ 2mod_whatswrong.asp* (accessed October 28, 2002).

25. U.S. Customs. "U.S. Customs Top IPR Seizures." *www.customs.gov/imp-exp2/ipr/ stats.htm* (accessed January 14, 2003).

26. European Union. "Customs Seizures 2001." *www.europa.eu.int/comm/taxation_customs/ customs/counterfeit_piracy/index_en.htm* (accessed January 14, 2003).

27. "China Urged to Get Tougher on Intellectual Property Rights Offenders." AP WorldStream. COMTEX, October 16, 2000.

28. Nasseem Ackbarally. "Fakes for a Fraction of the Price." *Middle East News Online,* December 26, 2000.

29. "China's Pirates." *Business Week,* June 5, 2000, p. 26.

30. "China Criticized Over Fake Goods." *The New York Times* on the Web, November 10, 2000; *www.nytimes.qpass.com/qpass-archives.html* (accessed May 22, 2001).

31. Stryker McGuire, Richard Ernsberger, Jr., and Tony Emerson. "Software Pirates, Beware." *Newsweek,* vol. 138, issue 18, October 29, 2001, p. 68C.

32. Robert Marquand. "China's Pirate Industry Thriving." *Christian Science Monitor.* January 9, 2000, p. 6.

CHAPTER 8

1. The Associated Press. "Feds Track Counterfeit Goods Sales." Oct. 24, 2002. See also Peter Lowe. "Criminal Attacks—Anatomy of Crime." International Chamber of Commerce Counterfeiting Intelligence Bureau; Jesse J. Holland. "U.S. Study Warns of Foreign Crime Cartels." *Chicago Sun-Times,* December 16, 2000, p. 14.

2. Peter Lowe. "Criminal Attacks—Anatomy of Crime." International Chamber of Commerce Counterfeiting Intelligence Bureau.

3. Jesse J. Holland. "U.S. Study Warns of Foreign Crime Cartels." *Chicago Sun-Times,* December 16, 2000, p. 14.

4. Ibid.

5. Roslyn A. Mazer. "USA: From T-Shirts to Terrorism—That Fake Nike Swoosh May Be Helping to Fund Bin Laden's Network." Editorial. *The Washington Post,* September 30, 2001, Outlook section, p. B02.

6. John Mintz and Douglas Farah. "Small Scans Probed for Terror Ties." *The Washington Post,* August 12, 2002, p. A01.

7. Lowe, "Criminal Attacks."

8. Mazer, "USA: From T-Shirts."

9. Ibid.

10. Ibid.

11. Peter Lowe. "Counterfeiters Know No Boundaries But They Import Job Losses." International Chamber of Commerce Counterfeiting Intelligence Bureau.

12. Ibid.

13. Alexei Beltyukov, M. James Kondo, William W. Lewis, Michael M. Obermayer, Vincent Palmade, and Alex Reznikovitch. "Reflections on Russia." *The McKinsey Quarterly,* 2000 Number 1.

14. International Chamber of Commerce Counterfeiting Intelligence Bureau. *Countering Counterfeiting.* Paris, France: ICC Publishing SA, 1997.

15. *The Economic Impact of Counterfeiting.* Organisation for Economic Co-Operation and Development. Paris, France: 1998.

CHAPTER 9

1. Magali LeParc. "Impact on the Company." *Protecting Medicines & Pharmaceuticals, A Manual of Anti-Counterfeiting Solutions.* Greenwood Village, CO: Reconnaissance International, 2002.

2. Ibid; *www.Pharma-anticounterfeiting.info.*

3. Miriam Jordan. "In Wooing Brazil's Teens, Converse Has Big Shoes to Fill: Local Makers of Knockoff Offer Cheap, Jazzy Sneakers; Can the U.S. Original Compete?" *The Wall Street Journal,* July 18, 2002, p. B1.

CHAPTER 10

1. Magali LeParc, ed., *Protecting Medicines & Pharmaceuticals: A Manual of Anti-Counterfeiting Solutions,* p. 76, "The Need for Private Investigation," Greenwood Village, CO: Reconnaissance International, 2002.

2. Stu Drobny, telephone interview, August 2002.

3. Ibid.

4. Ibid.

5. Ibid.

6. Peter Lowe, telephone interview, August 2002.

7. Ibid.

8. Ibid.

9. "Atlanta Olympics Wins Gold Medal for Product Protection." *Authentication News,* vol. 3, no. 1, Feb. 1997, p. 3.

10. Bill Thompson, telephone interview, August 2002.

11. Peter Lowe, telephone interview, August 2002.

12. Stu Drobny, telephone interview, August 2002.

13. California Business and Professions Code Section 7520–7539.

14. Florida Department of State—Division of Licensing Section 493.6203.

15. U.S. Bureau of Labor Statistics. See *www.bls.gov/oco/ocos157.htm.*

16. Ryan Beckwith. "No Faking It: Investigators Track Counterfeiters." *Newsday,* July 15, 2002, p. D01.

17. See the following organizations' websites; ASIS: *www.asisonline.org;* Fraud Exam: *www.cfenet.com;* National Association of Drug Diversion Investigators: *www.naddi.org.*

18. Chris Buckner, telephone interview, August 2002.

19. Dexter Roberts, Frederik Balfour, Paul Magnusson, Pete Engardio, and Jennifer Lee. "China's Pirates."*Business Week International Edition,* June 5, 2000.

20. Richard Behar. "Beijing's Phony War on Fakes." *Fortune,* Monday, October 30, 2000.

21. Pinkerton website. See *www.ci-pinkerton.com/brand/brand.html* (accessed September 2002).

22. Ibid.

23. See *www.bls.gov/oco/ocos157.htm* (accessed September 2002).

24. Robin Fields. "He Gets Paid to Chase Down Product Counterfeiters." *Los Angeles Times,* June 9, 1999, p. C1.

25. Chris Buckner, telephone interview, August 2002.

26. See *www.ifpi.org* (accessed September 2002).

27. "IFPI Enforcement Bulletin," Issue 15, June 2002, p. 5.

28. Counterfeiting Intelligence Bureau. *Countering Counterfeiting—A Guide to Protecting and Enforcing Intellectual Property Rights.* Counterfeiting Intelligence Bureau, April 16, 1997.

29. See *www.tradingstandards.gov.uk* (accessed September 2002).

30. George Abbott and Lee Sporn. *Trademark Counterfeiting.* New York: Aspen Law and Business, pp. 7–25, 26.

31. Richard Behar. "Drug Spies Piracy—The Pharmaceutical Industry's Dirty Little Secret." *Fortune,* June 9, 1999, pp. 230–234.

32. "SIIA Fights Exploding Auction Site Piracy." *Authentication News,* vol. 6, no. 2, April 2000, p. 4.

33. Ibid.

34. Matt Richtel. "Credit Card Theft Thrives Online as Global Market Losses Grow." *New York Times,* May 13, 2002; *www.nytimes.com/2002/05/13/technology/13CARD. html?todaysheadlines.*

35. See *www.cyveillance.com* (accessed September 2002).

36. See *www.genuone.com* (accessed September 2002).

37. See *www.i2.com* (accessed September 2002).

CHAPTER 11

1. *Black's Law Dictionary,* 7th ed. Eagan, MN: West Publishing, 1999.

2. "Terrorist Links to Counterfeiting and Diversion." *Authentication News,* vol. 7, no. 7, Oct. 2001, p. 9.

3. George Abbott and Lee Sporn. *Trademark Counterfeiting.* New York: Aspen Law & Business, 2002.

4. Testimony of John Bliss, President IACC, before the House Judiciary Committee, Hearing on Trademark Counterfeiting, Dec. 7, 1995.

5. U.S. Department of Justice, *Criminal Resource Manual,* Title 9. See *www.usdoj.gov/ usao/eousa/foia_reading_room/usam/title9/crm01700.htm.*

6. Ibid.

7. Abbott and Sporn, "Trademark Counterfeiting," pp. 2–17; 18 U.S.C. § 23RO.

8. 18 U.S.C. § 2318.

9. Ibid.

10. "Diversion: Its Causes, Impacts and Cures." *Authentication News,* vol. 3, no. 8, Dec. 1997, pp. 1, 4; *www.AuthenticationNews.Info.*

11. Jim Vandehei. "Politics and Policy—Bill Meant to Protect Baby Formula Spills All Over Unsavvy Web Stores." *The Wall Street Journal,* April 28, 2000, p. A20.

12. "U.S. Courts Protect Product Codes/Thwart Diversion." *Authentication News,* vol. 7, no. 7, Oct. 2001, p. 12.

13. U.S. Department of Justice, *Criminal Resource Manual,* op. cit.

14. Abbott and Sporn, "Trademark Counterfeiting," chs. 4, 6.

15. Abbott and Sporn, "Trademark Counterfeiting," pp. 4–5.

16. Ibid.

17. Mass. Gen. Laws Chapter 266, Sect. 147.

18. Kentucky Rev. Statutes Sect. 516.110.

19. Abbott and Sporn, "Trademark Counterfeiting," pp. 6–11.

20. FDA Cf Provisions, 21 U.S.C. § 321(g)(2).

21. William K. Hubbard. Senior Associate Commissioner for Policy, Planning and Legislation, Food and Drug Administration speaking before the Special Committee on Aging. United States Senate, July 9, 2002.

22. Public Law 106–181.

23. Ibid. § 505, this part known as the Aircraft Safety Act of 2000.

24. Abbott and Sporn, "Trademark Counterfeiting," ch. 2.

25. Counterfeiting Intelligence Bureau. *Countering Counterfeiting.* Paris, France: ICC Publishing SA (ICC No. 574, April 1997).

26. "New U.K. AntiCounterfeiting Bill Strengthens Enforcement." *Authentication News,* vol. 8, no. 7, Sept. 2002, p. 12.

27. Abbott and Sporn, "Trademark Counterfeiting," pp. 7–26.

28. "Microsoft Measures 5-10x Return on Enforcement." *Authentication News,* vol. 3, no. 3, May 1997, p. 5.

29. "Product Counterfeiting Protection Conference." *Authentication News,* vol. 3, no. 3, May 1995, p. 4.

30. Jenny Hatton, Alfred Dunhill, Ltd. presentation at IACC Annual Conference, April 27, 2000, Denver, CO. "The Criminal Trial for Product Counterfeiting."

31. Ralph Sutton, telephone interview, August 2002.

32. Arthur Best. "Manufacturers' Responsibility for Harms Suffered by Victims of Counterfeits." *Currents in International Trade Law Journal,* vol. VIII, no. 1, Summer 1999, pp. 43, 49.

33. Abbott and Sporn, "Trademark Counterfeiting," pp. 5–98, 113.

34. "Legal Stakes Rise in U.S. Counterfeiting Cases." *Authentication News,* vol. 3, no. 7, Dec. 1997, pp. 3, 4.

35. Abbott and Sporn, "Trademark Counterfeiting," pp. 1–7.

36. Ibid.

37. Lanham Act, 15 U.S.C. §§ 1051–1127.

38. See *www.usdoj.gov/jmd/2003summary* (accessed March 2000).

39. "IACC Urges Tougher Penalties for Counterfeiting, Piracy." *IACC Update,* March 2000, p. 5.

40. Ibid.

41. *1165 Broadway Corp. v. Bayana of NY Sportswear, Inc.,* 633 N.Y.S.2d 724 (N.Y.C. Civ. Ct., Oct. 4, 1995).

42. Abbott and Sporn, "Trademark Counterfeiting."

43. "U.S. Courts Protect Product Codes/Thwart Diversion." *Authentication News,* vol. 7, no. 7, Oct. 2001, p. 10.

44. Tim Trainer. IACC, *International Intellectual Property Enforcement SOP,* IACC, Washington, D.C., 2002.

45. Ibid.

CHAPTER 12

1. "Strategic Plan Defeats Nescafé Counterfeiters." *Authentication News,* vol. 3, no. 1, Feb. 1997, pp. 4–5. See also Chris Williams FIOP, LRSC, M. Inst. Pack. *The Future of Anti-Counterfeiting, Brand Protection and Security Packaging—Strategic Five-Year Forecasts and Company Intelligence Profiles.* United Kingdom: Pira International, 2001.
2. See *www.glaxowellcome.co.uk/world/policies.html* (1996).
3. "Caykur's 14x Return on Authentication Holograms." *Authentication News,* vol. 4, no. 9/10, Dec. 1998, p. 4. See also Chris Williams FIOP, LRSC, M. Inst. Pack. *The Future of Anti-Counterfeiting, Brand Protection and Security Packaging—Strategic Five-Year Forecasts and Company Intelligence Profiles.* United Kingdom: Pira International, 2001.
4. "NEC Stops Counterfeits, Assures Customers." *Authentication News,* vol. 2, no. 5, 1996.
5. Chris Williams FIOP, LRSC, M Inst. Pack. *The Future of Anti-Counterfeiting, Brand Protection and Security Packaging—Strategic Five-Year Forecasts and Company Intelligence Profiles.* United Kingdom: Pira International, 2001, p. 111.
6. "Montagut: Security Labels as Product Enhancement." *Authentication News,* vol. 4, no. 4, May 1998, p. 4.
7. This model was initially proposed by Bill Watson, The Resource Group, and was developed more fully by Lewis Kontnik, "Analyzing the Benefits of Product Protection." *Authentication News,* vol. 4, no. 4, May 1998, p. 3.
8. Peter Lowe. "Criminal Attacks—Anatomy of Crime." International Chamber of Commerce Counterfeiting Intelligence Bureau. See also *www.microsoft.com/press pass/press/1997/NOV97/thompspr.asp.*

CHAPTER 13

1. Charles W. Kegley, Jr. and Eugene R. Wittkopf. *World Politics.* New York: St. Martin's Press, 1981.
2. *World Intellectual Property Organization.* "What Is a Patent?" Publication no. L450PA/E.
3. *World Intellectual Property Organization.* "What Is a Copyright?" Publication no. L450CR/E.
4. Ibid.
5. *World Intellectual Property Organization.* "What Is a Trademark?" Publication no. L450TM/E.
6. *United States v. Torkington,* 812 F.2d 1347 (11th Cir. 1987), appeal after remand, 874 F.2d 1441 (11th Cir. 1989).
7. *Hunting World Inc. v. Reboans Inc.,* 24 U.S.P.Q.2d 1844 (N.D. Cal. 1992).
8. *General Electric Co. v. Speicher,* 877 F.2d 531 (7th Cir. 1989).
9. Tamar Niv. "A Variety of Weapons Against Counterfeits." *Managing Intellectual Property,* no. 92, September 1999, pp. 62–63.

10. *World Intellectual Property Organization.* "What Is a Geographical Indication?" Publication no. L450GI/E.

11. *World Intellectual Property Organization,* "What Is an Industrial Design?" Publication no. L450ID/E.

12. *World Intellectual Property Organization.* "Domain Name Dispute Resolution Service in 2000." Publication no. 457(E), January 2001.

13. Ibid.

14. See *www.iccwbo.org/ccs/menu_cib_bureau.asp.*

15. See 2002 Special 301 Report: *www.ustr.gov/reports/2002/special301.htm.*

16. See *www.customs.ustreas.gov/news/news.htm.*

17. "EU to Hold Anti-Piracy Meeting for ASEAN Delegates." *AP WorldStream,* COMTEX, April 19, 2002.

18. "China's Pirates." *Business Week,* June 5, 2000, p. 26.

19. Katalin Szamosi and Laszlo Berczes. "Actions Against Counterfeiters in Hungary." *Managing Intellectual Property,* no. 92, September 1999, pp. 34–35.

20. Ella Cheong and G. Mirandah. "Catching the Infringers in the Act." *Managing Intellectual Property,* no. 92, September 1999, pp. 55–56.

21. Vladimir Anohin and Agris Bitans. "Counterfeit Products in Latvia: Problems and Prospects." *Managing Intellectual Property,* no. 92, September 1999, pp. 39–40.

22. Augustin Valazques. "Enforcing Rights in Mexico." *Managing Intellectual Property,* no. 92, September 1999, pp. 41–44.

23. "Counterfeiting Protection in Mexico." *Authentication News,* vol. 4, nos. 5 and 6, June/July 1998.

24. Lucian Enecu and Crina Frisch. "Fighting Against Counterfeiting in Romania." *Managing Intellectual Property,* no. 92, September 1999, pp. 49–51.

25. Yoshiya Ishimura and John Kakinuki. "Practical Tips for Combatting Counterfeits." *Managing Intellectual Property,* no. 92, September 1999, pp. 36–38.

26. Esme Du Plessis. "South Africa." *Managing Intellectual Property,* no. 94, November 1999, pp. 39–40.

27. Donald G. McNeil, Jr. "Selling Cheap 'Generic' Drugs, India's Copycats Irk Industry. *The New York Times,* Late Edition, December 1, 2000, p. A1.

Index